No Copies Required – C

Copyright © 2006 by L. Lee
In the United States of America

All rights reserved. No part of this publication may be reproduced or distributed in any form, or by any means, or stored in a database or retrieval system, without the prior written permission of the publisher. For more information contact the author by email: nocopiesrequired@gmail.com

First printing February 2007

Published by L. Lee
Printed in the United States of America

Disclaimer

No Copies Required provides information and activities that are useful to elementary educators throughout the United States of America. No Copies Required does not express or imply inclusion of all areas of subject matter, nor does it express or imply responsibility for errors and/or omissions.

Copyright © 2006 L. Lee

How This Book Works

As a substitute teacher, you have probably experienced the missing lesson plans. You show up to a classroom and there are no lesson plans - what are you to do? Or, maybe the teacher left lesson plans, but they ran out before the day ended - now you have a room full of students with nothing to do. We all know what happens when students have nothing to do!

If you are a well organized person, with some extra cash, you have probably made thousands of copies at your own expense to handout per grade-level and subject; and you probably organized them in a big box that you lugged around - just in case.

What if you could walk into any (elementary) classroom, any grade level, and be prepared without making those costly copies and lugging them around in a big box? What if you could carry around hundreds of standards-based activities for each primary grade level in just one book, and there are ***No Copies Required***?

Finally, a lifesaver for those days we all have experienced and dreaded. This edition of ***No Copies Required*** classroom activities was designed by a substitute teacher with substitute teaching in mind. Substitute teachers face many challenges each day, and trying to figure out what to do in the absence of lesson plans should not be one of them.

This edition of ***No Copies Required*** classroom activities has hundreds of standards-based activities for kindergarten through fifth grade that do not require copies. All of the activities have a specific skill focus that is easy for the teacher to follow; and they are exciting, as well as fun, for the students to learn. Each activity contains step-by-step instructions for the teacher, along with directions and instructions that involve the student from start to finish.

There are four academic focuses in ***No Copies Required*** classroom activities: Vocabulary Development, Elements and Styles of Writing, Grammar, Usage and Mechanics, and Mathematics. We are confident that you and your students will enjoy the activities in this book, and that these activities will add structure, confidence, and stability to the classrooms you visit.

Lesson Format

Each lesson follows the same general format and contains the following information to create ease of use.

1. **Activity Introduction and Explanation** - This explains the topic and focus of the lesson.
2. **Time Frame** - Gives estimated times for each part of the lesson.
3. **Lesson Objective** - Identifies the focus point of the lesson and expected outcomes.
4. **Materials and Resources** - Lists any materials needed to complete the lesson.
5. **Instruction Procedure** - Explains exactly how to deliver the instructions.
6. **Whole Group Activity** - Designed to involve all students and allow whole group practice.
7. **Independent Activity** - Designed to allow students to practice what they have learned on their own.
8. **Challenges** - Designed to extend the lesson for more advanced students.
9. **Lesson Assessments** - Designed to insure student's understanding of the objective.
10. **Reflection** - An opportunity for students to discuss what they have learned and how they can apply these concepts in their lives.

Vocabulary Development

Table of Contents

Clapping Syllables	7
Rhyming Words	11
Names of Objects	15
Color Names	18
Sight Words	21
Short Vowel Patterns	26
Long Vowel Patterns	32
Compound Words	36
Antonyms	45
Synonyms	54
Homographs	63
Homophones	70
Prefixes	79
Suffixes	85

Grammar, Usage & Mechanics

Table of Contents

GRAMMAR

Parts of Speech 92
    Verbs, Nouns, Proper Nouns, Pronouns, Adjectives, Adverbs, Prepositions, Conjunctions, and Interjections.

Sentence Construction 100

Types of Sentences 108

Paragraph Construction 115

USAGE

Abbreviations 121

Capitalization 126

Contractions 135

Verb Tense & Irregular Verbs 139

Subject-Verb Agreement 144

Figurative Language 150
    Hyperboles, Metaphors, Personifications, and Similes.

MECHANICS

Punctuation Marks 157
    End Marks, Commas, Colons, Semi-Colons, Quotations, Underlining, Apostrophes, Question Marks, Exclamation Marks, Dashes, Hyphens, and Parentheses.

The Elements & Styles of Writing

Table of Contents

WRITING PROCESS

The Writing Process 170
  (Brainstorming, Drafting, Proofreading, Editing, and Finalizing)
Graphic Organizers 180
Writing Prompts 186
Story Starters 190
Finishing the Story 198

TYPES OF WRITING

Descriptive Writing 204
Comparison & Contrast 210
Persuasive Writing 217
Lists & Journals 221
Writing Letters (Personal and Business) 226
Directions and Instructions 234
Personal Narrative 239
Fantasy Stories 243

Mathematics Made Fun

Table of Contents

NUMBER SENSE

Count, Read, & Write Whole Numbers ……………………………………………..247

Compare & Order Numbers ……………………………………………………251

Place Value …………………………………………………………………...256

Rounding Numbers …………………………………………………………..…261

Money …………………………………………………………………………...266

Addition & Subtraction ………………………………………………………….278

Multiplication & Division ……………………………………………………….297

Fractions ………………………………………………………………………..311

MEASUREMENTS

Measurements, Tools, Length, Width, and Weight, ………………....…..318

Time, Duration, Concept & Intervals ………………………………………….324

STATISTICS, DATA ANALYSIS, & PROBABILITY

Graphs, Charts, and Tally Marks ………………………………………..337

Mean Average, Mode, Median, Range, & Outliers ……………………...349

Language Arts Word Usage
Lesson Title: <u>Clapping Syllables</u>

The ability to determine the number of syllables in a word is important for building reading and writing skills. Each syllable contains vowels and consonants, which, when put together, make up a word. Clapping syllables is a fun way for young students to learn how to count syllables.

Time Frame: **35 - 65 Minutes**
    5 - 10 Activity introduction and explanation.
    5 - 10 List words.
    5 - 10 Whole group discussion.
    10 - 15 Independent student activity.
    5 - 10 Activity assessment.
    5 - 10 Reflection on the activity.

Lesson Objectives: To increase student knowledge of syllables in words, thereby increasing their reading and spelling skills.

Materials & Resources: Paper and pencil.

Instruction Procedure: Explain the lesson and lesson objective to the students.

Whole Group Activity:

Have the students focus on one list at a time. Start with student names and then move on to other lists. Have the students sit in a circle on the mat (this allows students to work together in a large group and observe each other). Select a student to begin by saying their name aloud, and then have all the students say that student's name while clapping the syllables. (**Example**: Kelly - Kel / ly.) Notice that each syllable has a vowel. As the students say their names, list them on the board. As they say the name and clap the syllable, insert the slash (/) to separate the syllables. Do this with several (or all) of the student's names to make sure that they all understand what to do, and to make sure that they are all involved. Once they understand the activity, move on to the level-appropriate activities on the following pages.

GRADE LEVELS	**INDEPENDENT ACTIVITY – Clapping Syllables**
Kindergarten	Assign a group of words for the students to work with. You may come up with a list of your own or use the list on the following pages.
Assessment Option:	Select a few words (from those they just practiced) to assess what the students have learned. Say the word aloud and have the students come up, one at a time, and clap out the syllables. Make sure that the student also tells you the total number of syllables in the word.

Clapping Syllables Activity Word Chart

Animals	Classroom	Home	Playground	Food
tiger	chalkboard	kitchen	handball	hotdog
dog	eraser	bedroom	kickball	hamburger
cat	chair	sofa	swing	pizza
lion	desk	family	slide	chicken
rabbit	table	house	bars	soup
gorilla	rug	garage	soccer	corn
monkey	door	bathroom	tennis	rice
zebra	closet	table	hopscotch	enchilada
lizard	teacher	chair	playing	bean

Reflection: Clapping Syllables

It is important for students to understand why they are learning this process and how they can apply it to their daily lives. Explain that words are made up of sounds, and together those sounds make words. Knowing the number of syllables in a word will help students improve their reading and spelling skills.

In this reflection, ask the students these questions in an open discussion:

1. What did they learn?
2. How can they use what they learned in their daily activity?
3. Can they teach what they have learned to someone else?
4. What did they like most about the activity?
5. What did they like least about the activity?

Language Arts Word Usage
Lesson Title: <u>Rhyming Words</u>

Rhyming words are fun to play with and they serve a multitude of purposes. This is a great way for young students to learn how to spell new words - and it's fun!

Time Frame: **35 - 65 Minutes**
- 5 - 10 Activity introduction and explanation.
- 5 - 10 List words.
- 5 - 10 Whole group discussion.
- 10 - 15 Independent student activity.
- 5 - 10 Activity assessment.
- 5 - 10 Reflection on the activity.

Lesson Objectives: To increase student knowledge of rhyming words and increase their spelling skills.

Materials & Resources: Paper and pencil.

Instruction Procedure: Explain the lesson and lesson objective to the students.

Whole Group Activity:

Begin by listing a word family on the board. Explain to the students that they can make new words simply by adding a new beginning sound. (**Example**: Using the word family - <u>at</u>, add a '<u>b</u>' to the beginning of the word - <u>b</u> + <u>at</u> = <u>**bat.**</u>) Students can go through the alphabet to select a beginning sound, add it to the word family, say it aloud and produce a new word.

GRADE LEVELS	INDEPENDENT ACTIVITY – Rhyming Words
Kindergarten	1) Have the students write the word family being used. Next, have the students create as many new words as they can with this word family by changing the first letter.

2) List a word family on the board. Allow the students to make up as many new words as they can on their own. |
| **Assessment Option:** | Select a few words (from those they just practiced) to assess what the students have learned. Say the words aloud and have the students write the words on a new sheet of paper. |
| **1st Grade** | 1) Have the students write the word family being used. Next, have the students create as many new words as they can with this word family by changing the first letter.

2) List a selection of word families on the board. Allow the students to make up as many new words as they can on their own. |
| **Assessment Option:** | Select a few words (from those they just practiced) to assess what the students have learned. Say the words aloud and have the students write the words on a new sheet of paper. |

Word Families and Sample Words
Rhyming Words

ad	**ag**	**an**	**ap**	**ar**	**at**	**aw**	**ay**
bad	bag	can	cap	bar	bat	jaw	bay
dad	lag	fan	gap	car	cat	law	day
had	nag	man	lap	far	fat	paw	hay
mad	rag	pan	map	jar	hat	saw	lay

ed	**eg**	**en**	**et**	**ew**	**id**	**ig**	**in**
bed	beg	den	bet	dew	bid	big	bin
fed	leg	hen	get	few	did	fig	fin
led	keg	men	jet	new	hid	jig	pin
red	peg	pen	let	sew *	lid	pig	tin

ip	**it**	**og**	**on**	**op**	**ot**	**ow**	**ox**
dip	bit	dog	don *	cop	dot	bow *	box
hip	fit	hog	son	hop	got	cow	fox
lip	hit	jog	ton	mop	hot	how	lox
rip	pit	log	won	pop	pot	low *	pox

oy	**ub**	**ud**	**ug**	**um**	**un**	**ut**
boy	cub	bud	bug	bum	bun	but
coy	hub	cud	dug	gum	fun	cut
joy	rub	dud	hug	hum	run	hut
toy	tub	mud	lug	sum	sun	nut

These words do not rhyme with the set.

Reflection: Rhyming Words

It is important for students to understand why they are learning this process and how they can apply it to their daily lives. Explain that words are made up of sounds, and together those sounds make words. This is just another step in communication.

In this reflection, ask the students these questions in an open discussion:

1. What did they learn?
2. How can they use what they learned in their daily activity?
3. Can they teach what they have learned to someone else?
4. What did they like most about the activity?
5. What did they like least about the activity?

Language Arts Word Usage
Lesson Title: <u>Names of Objects</u>

Another step in writing is being able to identify the names of objects. Most young students know the names of ordinary objects that they see everyday, but they may not know how to spell them. This is an activity to help students increase their spelling word bank by being able to identify the written words of objects that they are already familiar with.

Time Frame: **40 - 75 Minutes**
    5 - 10 Activity introduction and explanation.
    10 - 20 List the words and review their meaning.
    5 - 10 Whole group discussion.
    10 - 15 Independent student activity.
    5 - 10 Activity assessment.
    5 - 10 Reflection on the activity.

Lesson Objectives: To increase student ability to spell common names of objects and increase their spelling word bank.

Materials & Resources: Paper and pencil.

Instruction Procedure: Explain the lesson and lesson objectives to the students.

Whole Group Activity:

    Begin the lesson by selecting one category. Ask the students what kind of things they would find in that area (**Example**: "Home".) When the students give you a name of an object found in the particular area, ask them what sounds they hear in that word. As they give you the sounds, write the word on the board. Try to stick to simple words that are easy for them to sound out and remember. If they have trouble coming up with names; either make up your own, or use the list on the following pages. Repeat this activity with several words. Say each word as you write it and have the students repeat the word after you. This does two things: 1) helps the student identify the written word with the spoken word, and 2) keeps the students involved while you are doing preparation work for the lesson. After you finish listing the words on the board, take some time to go over each word several times while pointing to each word as you say the word aloud. Select several students to come up to the board to point out and pronounce a few words that they know. After the students have a few minutes to practice, move on to the level-appropriate activities on the following pages.

GRADE LEVELS	INDEPENDENT ACTIVITY – Names of Objects
Kindergarten	Select a few words for the students to focus on. First, have the students say the word aloud, next have them spell the word, finally have them write the word several times for practice. Once this is complete, select another word. Repeat this process with a few words from the list to have students practice. You may want to allow the students to select which words to practice, this will motivate them to participate.
Assessment Option:	Have the students select one word, write it, and draw a picture of the item.

Reflection: Names of Objects

It is important for students to understand why they are learning this process and how they can apply it to their daily lives. Explain that being able to communicate, both verbally and written, is important because this is one way we relate to other people. Let the students know that they are increasing their spelling word bank and this will improve their written communication skills as well as their verbal skills.

In this reflection, ask the students these questions in an open discussion:

1. What did they learn?
2. How can they use what they learned in their daily activity?
3. Can they teach what they have learned to someone else?
4. What did they like most about the activity?
5. What did they like least about the activity?

Names of Objects Word List
Kindergarten

<u>Home</u>	<u>Kitchen</u>	<u>Bathroom</u>	<u>School</u>	<u>Park</u>
door	spoon	tub	classroom	swing
wall	fork	sink	office	slide
floor	pot	shower	playground	sand
sofa	pan	cabinet	cafeteria	grass
chair	kettle	floor	bench	bars
table	plate	towel	desk	trees
window	cup	soap	chalkboard	birds
bed	glass	mirror	mat/rug	pond
pillow	bowl	drawer	closet	ducks
blanket	stove	toilet	paper	bushes

Language Arts Word Usage
Lesson Title: <u>Color Names</u>

Color names are important for identifying specific colors and describing objects. Color names are used in writing or telling stories, or simple things like describing an outfit.

Time Frame: **40 - 75 Minutes**
                                        5 - 10 Activity introduction and explanation.
                                        10 - 20 List the words and give an example.
                                        5 - 10 Whole group discussion.
                                        10 - 15 Independent student activity.
                                        5 - 10 Activity assessment.
                                        5 - 10 Reflection on the activity.

Lesson Objectives: To increase student spelling word bank and learn how to spell color names.

Materials & Resources: Paper and pencil.

Instruction Procedure: Explain the lesson and lesson objectives to the students.

Whole Group Activity:

Begin the lesson by asking the students what their favorite color is. Next, ask the students if they know how to spell the color name. Begin by sounding out the color name and writing each sound until the word is completely spelled out. Be careful, some colors are not written as they sound. (**Example**: blue - it sounds like bloo, but it is spelled blue.) Ask other students to identify other items in the room of the same color. Repeat this activity asking other students their favorite color until you have several colors listed on the board. Next, ask the students to identify something outside of the room that would be a certain color (one that is listed on the board). (**Example**: A bear is brown). After you finish listing the words on the board, take some time to go over each word several times. Point to each word as you say the word aloud and associate the color name with several things that are that color.

GRADE LEVELS	INDEPENDENT ACTIVITY – Color Names
Kindergarten	Have each student decide on a color and draw a picture of something that is the color they selected. Have them write the color name and try to write a simple sentence telling the name of the object and the name of the color. (**Example**: The __object__ is __color__.) Color names should be listed on the board for their reference..
Assessment Option:	Have the students spell the color word (without looking) that they selected to use in their picture. Additionally, have the students verbally use the color word in a complete sentence.

Reflection: Color Names

It is important for students to understand why they are learning this process and how they can apply it to their daily lives. Explain that being able to identify colors helps them to describe things to other people much easier.

In this reflection, ask the students these questions in an open discussion:

1. What did they learn?
2. How can they use what they learned in their daily activity?
3. Can they teach what they have learned to someone else?
4. What did they like most about the activity?
5. What did they like least about the activity?

Color Names Words List
All Grades

Select appropriate words for grade levels

blue	orange	navy blue	charcoal
red	gray	baby blue	midnight
yellow	brown	sea green	teal
green	lime	magenta	gold
pink	peach	fuchsia	bronze
purple	lemon	cranberry	platinum
black	tangerine	canary	silver
white	cherry	smoke	copper

Language Arts Word Usage
Lesson Title: <u>Sight Words</u>

Sight words are words that appear at a high rate of frequency throughout most written text and are used frequently in verbal communication. Some sight words are easy to spell; some are not. Because of these reasons, students should begin recognizing and memorizing these words right away. The ability to recognize and read sight words will increase reading fluency.

Time Frame: **35 - 65 Minutes**
    5 - 10 Activity introduction and explanation.
    5 - 10 List the words and give an example.
    5 - 10 Whole group discussion.
   10 - 15 Independent student activity.
    5 - 10 Activity assessment.
    5 - 10 Reflection on the activity.

Lesson Objective: To increase student use of sight words.

Materials & Resources: Paper and pencil.

Instruction Procedure: Explain the lesson and lesson objective to the students.

Whole Group Activity:

List some of the sight words (make up your own words or use the list on the following pages) on the board. Say each word as you write it and have the students repeat the word after you. This does two things: 1) helps the student identify the written word with the spoken word, and 2) keeps the students involved while you are doing preparation work for the lesson.

After you finish listing the words on the board, take some time to go over each word several times while pointing to each word as you say the word aloud. Select several students to come up to the board to point out and pronounce a few words that they know.

GRADE LEVELS	INDEPENDENT ACTIVITY – Sight Words
Kindergarten	Have the students say the word, next have them spell the word, finally have them write the word several times for practice. Once this is complete, select several other words and repeat the same process with each. You may want to allow the students to select the words to practice. This motivates them to participate.
Assessment Option:	Select a few words (from those they just practiced) to assess what the students have learned. Say the words aloud and have the students write them on a new sheet of paper.
1st Grade	1) Have the students say the words, next have them spell the words, finally have them write the words several times for practice. Once this is complete, select several other words and repeat the same process with each word. 2) Have the students select any book from their classroom library. Have them open the book to any page. Now, have them select any sight word and count how many times they can find their selected sight word on a single page within the book. Have the students select additional sight words and repeat this activity.
Assessment Option:	Select a few words (from those they just practiced) to assess what the students have learned. Say the words aloud and have the students write the words on a new sheet of paper.
2nd Grade	1) Have the students say the words, next have them spell the words, finally have them write the words several times for practice. Once this is complete, select several other words and repeat the same process with each. Have the students write a meaningful sentence using each of the sight words and underline each sight word in the sentence. Make sure each sentence begins with a capital letter and has an end mark.

GRADE LEVELS   **INDEPENDENT ACTIVITY – Sight Words**

Assessment Option: Select a few words (from those they just practiced) to assess what the students have learned. Say the words aloud and have the students write them on a new sheet of paper. The students may also wish to read their sentence.

Reflection: Sight Words

It is important for students to understand why they are learning this process and how they can apply it to their daily lives. Explain that being able to communicate, both verbally and written, is important because it is how people relate to one another. Further, being able to recognize and read sight words from memory will increase their reading fluency.

In this reflection, ask the students these questions in an open discussion:

1. What did they learn?
2. How can they use what they learned in their daily activity?
3. Can they teach what they have learned to someone else?
4. What did they like most about the activity?
5. What did they like least about the activity?

Sight Words List
Kindergarten

a	help	say
after	her	says
all	here	see
am	him	she
an	how	so
and	I	some
are	if	stop
as	in	that
at	is	the
be	it	them
big	just	then
but	less	they
by	like	this
can	likes	three
come	look	to
did	may	too
do	me	two
does	more	up
five	no	was
for	not	we
four	now	what
from	of	when
get	off	where
had	on	who
has	one	will
have	out	yes
he	said	you

Sight Words List
1st & 2nd Grade

a	can	was	most	after
I	cat	who	must	first
am	did	why	name	never
an	dog	yes	near	other
as	for	you	next	right
at	get	also	open	there
be	had	sway	over	these
by	has	both	play	thing
do	her	come	read	think
go	him	dear	said	those
he	how	does	says	three
if	its	each	seem	under
in	may	five	some	until
is	not	four	stop	where
me	now	from	such	which
no	off	have	tell	would
of	one	help	that	write
on	out	here	them	always
so	own	into	then	around
to	red	just	they	before
up	say	kind	this	better
us	see	less	upon	little
we	she	like	very	people
all	sit	look	walk	please
and	the	made	want	pretty
are	too	make	when	should
big	two	many	will	another
but	use	more	your	because

Language Arts Word Usage
Lesson Title: Short Vowel Patterns

There are many words that follow a pattern. These words are easy to spell and sometimes rhyme. Pattern words are made by changing the vowel or consonant cluster in each word to make a new word. There are several common short vowel patterns such as CVC (Consonant-Vowel-Consonant), CCVC, CVCC, and CCVCC. These are the easiest words for young students to learn to read as well as write. Students should practice writing these words to increase their spelling word bank.

Time Frame: 35 - 65 Minutes
    5 - 10 Activity introduction and explanation.
    5 - 10 List the words.
    5 - 10 Whole group discussion.
    10 - 15 Independent student activity.
    5 - 10 Activity assessment.
    5 - 10 Reflection on the activity.
    Allow additional time for multiple activities.

Lesson Objective: To increase student spelling skills.

Materials & Resources: Paper and pencil.

Instruction Procedure: Explain the lesson and lesson objective to the students.

Whole Group Activity:

Select a pattern to focus on and write it on the board. (Example: bad, which uses the CVC pattern.) Next, list a few words that follow this pattern and make sure to point out the pattern in each word for the students. Say each word as you write it and have the students repeat the word after you. This does two things: 1) helps the student identify the written word with the spoken word, and 2) keeps the students involved while you are doing preparation work for the lesson.

After you finish listing the words on the board, take some time to go over each word several times while pointing to each word as you say the word aloud. Select several students to come up to the board to point out and say the word and identify the pattern. Once the students have had a few minutes to practice, move on to the level-appropriate independent activities on the following pages.

GRADE LEVELS Patterns	INDEPENDENT ACTIVITY – Short Vowel
Kindergarten	Using the CVC word list, have the students write the word family being used. Next, have the students create as many new words as they can with this word family by changing the first letter.
Assessment Option:	Select a few words (from those they just practiced) to assess what the students have learned. Say the words aloud and have the students write them on a new sheet of paper.
1st Grade	Using the CCVC, and/or CVCC word list, have the students write the word family being used. Next, have the students create as many new words as they can with this word family by changing the first letter.
Assessment Option:	Select a few words (from those they just practiced) to assess what the students have learned. Say the words aloud and have the students write the words on a new sheet of paper.
2nd Grade	1) Using any of the spelling pattern lists, have the students write the word family being used. Next, have the students create as many new words as they can with this word family by changing the first letter. 2) List any of the patterns on the board and have the students make up words according to the pattern. **Challenge:** Have the students make up as many rhyming words as they can and create a poem.
Assessment Option:	Select a few words (from those they just practiced) to assess what the students have learned. Say the words aloud and have the students write them on a new sheet of paper. If the students elected to do the challenge, they may choose to read their poem aloud.

Reflection: Short Vowel Patterns

It is important for students to understand why they are learning this process and how they can apply it to their daily lives. Explain that words are made up of sounds, and together those sounds make words. This is just another step in communication.

In this reflection, ask the students these questions in an open discussion:

1. What did they learn?
2. How can they use what they learned in their daily activity?
3. Can they teach what they have learned to someone else?
4. What did they like most about the activity?
5. What did they like least about the activity?

CVC Word List – Short Vowel Patterns
Kindergarten

ad	**ag**	**an**	**ap**	**ar**	**at**	**aw**	**ay**
bad	bag	can	cap	bar	bat	jaw	bay
dad	lag	fan	gap	car	cat	law	day
had	nag	man	lap	far	fat	paw	hay
mad	rag	pan	map	jar	hat	saw	lay

ed	**eg**	**en**	**et**	**ew**	**id**	**ig**	**in**
bed	beg	den	bet	dew	bid	big	bin
fed	leg	hen	get	few	did	fig	fin
led	Meg	men	jet	new	hid	jig	pin
red	peg	pen	let	sew *	lid	pig	tin

ip	**it**	**og**	**on**	**op**	**ot**	**ow**	**ox**
dip	bit	dog	don *	cop	dot	bow	box
hip	fit	hog	son	hop	got	cow	fox
lip	hit	jog	ton	mop	hot	how	lox
rip	pit	log	won	pop	pot	low *	

oy	**ub**	**ud**	**ug**	**um**	**un**	**ut**
boy	cub	bud	bug	bum	bun	but
coy	hub	cud	dug	gum	fun	cut
joy	rub	dud	hug	hum	run	hut
toy	tub	mud	lug	sum	sun	nut

*These words do not rhyme with the set.

CCVC/CVCC Word List – Short Vowel Patterns
1st Grade

Beginning Consonant Clusters

bl	cr	gl	pr	sm	sw
br	dr	gr	sc	sn	th
ch	fr	ph	sh	sp	tr
cl	fl	pl	sl	sy	wh

Ending Consonant Clusters

ch	lf	mp	pt	sh	th
ck	mb	nt	rt	st	

Word Families

ad	ar	eg	ig	on	oy	un
ag	at	en	in	op	ub	ut
am	aw	et	ip	ot	ud	
an	ay	ew	it	ow	ug	
ap	ed	id	og	ox	um	

Examples

	-at	**-ew**	**-in**	**-ip**
ch-	chat	chew	chin	chip
fl-	flat	flew		flip
pl-	plat			
sp-	spat	spew	spin	

CCVCC, CCVC, & CVCC Word List – Short Vowel Patterns
2nd Grade

Beginning Consonant Clusters

bl	cr	gl	pr	sm	sw
br	dr	gr	sc	sn	th
ch	fr	ph	sh	sp	tr
cl	fl	pl	sl	sy	wh

Ending Consonant Clusters

ch	lf	mp	pt	sh	th
ck	mb	nt	rt	st	

Word Families

ad	ar	eg	ig	on	oy	un
ag	at	en	in	op	ub	ut
am	aw	et	ip	ot	ud	
an	ay	ew	it	ow	ug	
ap	ed	id	og	ox	um	

Examples of CCVCC Words

black	draft	shirt
brown	frown	smash
chest	flick	stamp
clash	graph	thick
crack	plant	track

Language Arts Word Usage
Lesson Title: <u>Long Vowel Patterns</u>

After creating two and three letter words with the short vowel sounds, the next step is to spell short words using the long vowel sounds. Words that end in "e" are the easiest and therefore the logical next step in learning how to read and write. Most of these words follow a pattern which we will call the long vowel pattern words. Keep in mind that there are other patterns used to make the long vowel sound; however, for this activity, we will only focus on the CVCV (Consonant-Vowel-Consonant-Vowel) pattern.

Time Frame: **35 - 65 Minutes**
  5 - 10 Activity introduction and explanation.
  5 - 10 List the words.
  5 - 10 Whole group discussion.
  10 - 15 Independent student activity.
  5 - 10 Activity assessment.
  5 - 10 Reflection on the activity.
  * Allow additional time for multiple activities.

Lesson Objectives: To increase spelling skills and spelling work bank.

Materials & Resources: Paper and pencil.

Instruction Procedure: Explain the lesson and lesson objectives to the students.

Whole Group Activity:

List one long vowel pattern and a few matching words on the board (make up your own or use the list on the following pages). Be sure to point out the CVCV pattern and how the "e" on the end of the word makes the first vowel say its' name (a long vowel). Say each word as you write it and have the students repeat the word after you. This does two things: 1) helps the student identify the written word with the spoken word, and 2) keeps the students involved while you are doing preparation work for the lesson.

Once you finish listing the first pattern and words on the board, take some time to go over each word several times while pointing to each word as you say the word aloud. After the students have had a few minutes to practice creating new words, move on to the level-appropriate independent activities on the following pages.

GRADE LEVELS	INDEPENDENT ACTIVITY - Long Vowel Patterns
1st Grade	Have the students create at least five new words. Next, have them write a sentence for each new word and underline the new word in each sentence. Make sure each sentence begins with a capital letter and has an end mark.
Assessment Option:	Have each student read (and spell) a few words from their list and select their best sentence to read aloud.
2nd Grade	Have the students create at least seven new words. Next, have them write a sentence for each new word and underline the new word in each sentence. Make sure each sentence begins with a capital letter and has an end mark. **Challenge:** Have the students create a list of rhyming words using the spelling patterns.
Assessment Option:	Have the students select their best work to share with the class.
3rd Grade	Have the students create at least ten new words. Next, have them write a sentence for each new word and underline the new word in each sentence. Make sure each sentence begins with a capital letter and has an end mark. **Challenge 1:** Have the students create a list of rhyming words using the spelling patterns. **Challenge 2:** Have the students make up a poem using their list of rhyming words.
Assessment Option:	Have the students share their story or poem with the class.

Reflection: Long Vowel Patterns

It is important for students to understand why they are learning this process and how they can apply it to their daily lives. Explain that being able to communicate, both verbally and written, is important because it is how people relate to one another. Further explain that knowing spelling patterns can improve their spelling skills - this is also a valuable tool for song writers and poets, because most song lyrics and poetry rhyme.

In this reflection, ask the students these questions in an open discussion:

1. What did they learn?
2. How can they use what they learned in their daily activity?
3. Can they teach what they have learned to someone else?
4. What did they like most about the activity?
5. What did they like least about the activity?

Long Vowel Pattern List
1st, 2nd, & 3rd Grade

C (Consonant)	A a___e	I i___e	O o___e	U u___e
b	bake	bike	bore	
c	cave	cite	core	cure
d	dare	dime	dome	
f	fame	fire	fore	fume
g	game		gone	
h	hare	hike	hose	huge
j	jade	jive	joke	
l	lane	lime	lone	lure
m	male	mine	more	mule
n	name	Nile	Nome	
p	pale	pine	pole	pure
s	same	side	sore	sure
t	tale	time	tone	tune
v	vane	vine		
w	wade	wide	wore	

Language Arts Word Usage
Lesson Title: <u>Compound Words</u>

    A compound word is one word made by combining two other words. The two words alone have their own distinct meaning; but once put together, (as a compound word) it has a different meaning. An example is the word cowboy. As a compound word it means a man who rides a horse; however a cow is an animal and a boy is a young human male - cowboy does not mean a male cow. Most compound words are easy to understand and use, but there are some that are not so easy. Practicing the use of compound words can be fun.

Time Frame: **35 - 65 Minutes**
                                  5 - 10 Activity introduction and explanation.
                                  5 - 10 List the words.
                                  5 - 10 Whole group discussion.
                              10 - 15 Independent student activity.
                                  5 - 10 Activity assessment.
                                  5 - 10 Reflection on the activity.
                                  * Allow additional time for multiple activities.

Lesson Objectives: To increase spelling skills and spelling word bank.

Materials & Resources: Paper and pencil.

Instruction Procedure: Explain the lesson and lesson objective to the students.

Whole Group Activity:

    List a few compound words (for the appropriate grade level) on the board (make up your own words or use the list on the following pages). Say each word as you write it and have the students repeat the word after you, then tell the students what the individual words mean as well as the meaning of the compound word. This does two things: 1) helps the student identify the written word with the spoken word, and 2) keeps the students involved while you are doing preparation work for the lesson.

    Once you have finished listing the words on the board, take some time to go over each word several times while pointing to each word as you say the word aloud. Make up a sentence using a word from the board. Repeat this with a few more words from the board. Next, allow a few students to make up their own sentence using a compound word from the board. After the students have had a few minutes to practice creating new words, move on to the level-appropriate independent activities on the following pages.

GRADE LEVELS	INDEPENDENT ACTIVITY – Compound Words
1st Grade	Have the students select three compound words to work with. Have the students use each in a simple sentence and underline the compound word. Make sure each sentence begins with a capital letter and has an end mark.
Assessment Option:	Have each student select their best work to share with the class.
2nd Grade	Have the students select five compound words to work with. Have the students use each in a meaningful sentence and underline the compound word. Make sure the sentence reveals the correct meaning of the compound word, begins with a capital letter, and has an end mark.
Assessment Option:	Have each student select their best work to share with the class.
3rd Grade	Have the students select seven compound words to work with. Have the students use each in a meaningful sentence and underline the compound word. Make sure the sentence reveals the correct meaning of the compound word, begins with a capital letter, and has an end mark.
Assessment Option:	Have each student select their best work to share with the class.
4th Grade	Have the students select nine compound words to work with. Have the students use each in a meaningful sentence and underline the compound word. Make sure the sentence reveals the correct meaning of the compound word, begins with a capital letter, and has an end mark. **Challenge:** Have the students use the compound word and the two individual words in a single sentence. Repeat this activity with each of the seven compound words they selected.
Assessment Option:	Have each student select their best work to share with the class.

GRADE LEVELS	INDEPENDENT ACTIVITY – Compound Words
5th Grade	Have the students select ten or more compound words to work with. Have the students use each in a meaningful sentence and underline the compound word. Make sure the sentence reveals the correct meaning of the compound word, begins with a capital letter, and has an end mark.
	Challenge 1: Have the students use the compound word and the two individual words in a single sentence. Repeat this activity with each of the seven compound words they selected.
	Challenge 2: Have the students try to mix and rematch the compound words. (**Example:** Using part of firefly and part of baseball, you can create the word fireball.)
Assessment Option:	Have each student select their best work to share with the class.

Reflection: Compound Words

It is important for students to understand why they are learning this process and how they can apply it to their daily lives. Explain that being able to communicate, both verbally and written, is important because it is how people relate to one another.

In this reflection, ask the students these questions in an open discussion:

1. What did they learn?
2. How can they use what they learned in their daily activity?
3. Can they teach what they have learned to someone else?
4. What did they like most about the activity?
5. What did they like least about the activity?

Compound Word List
1st Grade

anyhow	into	shortbread	upon
anyone	itself	showoff	uppercase
anyway	lifeboat	sidewalk	upset
earring	lowercase	showdown	upstairs
eyeball	moonlight	snowball	walkway
eyelid	nobody	softball	wallpaper
firefly	notebook	somebody	washboard
fishbowl	nowhere	someday	washcloth
forehead	pancake	somehow	washroom
forever	playhouse	someone	washtub
forget	ponytail	someplace	wastebasket
forgot	popcorn	something	watercolor
forgive	railroad	sometime	watermelon
goodnight	raincoat	stoplight	weekday
gumball	sailboat	Sunday	weekend
haircut	schoolbook	sunflower	weeknight
hamburger	schoolhouse	teapot	whatever
handbook	schoolwork	today	wheelchair
however	shoelace	toenail	within
inside	shoemaker	toolbox	without

Compound Word List
2nd Grade

airport	wheelchair	waterproof	fruitcake
armchair	weekend	waterfall	blackbird
backbone	lifesaver	spaceship	doorbell
backstop	teaspoon	spaceman	doorknob
bankbook	thunderstorm	toothache	scarecrow
baseball	tiptoe	summertime	newsstand
beehive	rosebud	surfboard	nighttime
blackboard	quicksand	supermarket	homework
campfire	snowman	shoestring	houseboat
chalkboard	raincoat	skateboard	goldfish
classmate	roundup	moonlight	nightmare
cupcake	horseback	oversleep	teacup
daydream	hilltop	ponytail	grasshopper
daylight	keyhole	railroad	lunchbox
doghouse	indoor	lawnmower	shoelace
fingernail	downstairs	sandbox	toothpaste
flagpole	cowboy	sailboat	toothbrush
godmother	breakfast	rosebud	mailbox
hairbrush	birthday	snowstorm	mailman
bathroom	birdhouse	bluebird	haircut

Compound Word List
3rd Grade

airmen	mountaintop	baseball	gentleman
backyard	bandstand	handball	fireplace
ballplayer	eyelid	blackboard	flashlight
brainstorm	lampshade	driveway	countryside
carefree	campfire	classmate	daydream
headlight	footprint	countdown	nightmare
fireman	crossword	farmyard	eyeglass
flowerpot	football	cardboard	fishpond
beefsteak	downstream	footstool	policeman
billboard	courtroom	highway	grasshopper
breadbox	nearby	birthday	quicksand
candlestick	pitchfork	playground	handbag
pinwheel	bricklayer	reindeer	bookkeeper
bookworm	caretaker	hilltop	snowflake
salesman	teenage	sunflower	songwriter
skyline	basketball	outfield	upstairs
backstroke	sunlight	infield	apart
raincoat	fairground	inward	oatmeal
sailboat	steamship	wastebasket	waterfall
dustpan	wallpaper	storybook	fisherman

Compound Word List
4th Grade

tabletop	beside	bathroom	godmother
dressmaker	upstairs	bookworm	godfather
courtroom	bellbottoms	watercolor	wheelchair
suitcase	downstairs	fieldtrip	handball
sunburn	backtrack	shoemaker	highchair
supermarket	boardwalk	touchdown	cupcake
scarecrow	pickup	handwriting	bookstore
countryside	birthday	evergreen	underground
starfish	playground	billfold	dustpan
fishpond	birthplace	skateboard	lifeboat
fisherman	paperback	bedrock	doghouse
farsighted	apart	nearby	snowflake
nearsighted	lamppost	cowpoke	popcorn
snowman	fingerprint	overhead	schoolhouse
footstool	footprint	summertime	skyline
downpour	weeknight	hilltop	teenage
fruitcake	hairbrush	storehouse	townhouse
grandmother	backward	blackbird	flashlight
grandfather	ballplayer	birdhouse	eyeball
roadmap	storybook	sunbeam	bookkeeper

Compound Word List
5th Grade

upstage	landmark	railroad	ballroom
typewriter	hometown	masterpiece	uproot
trademark	lifetime	toadstool	teenage
letdown	seaport	wristwatch	breakfast
waterproof	outcast	nutcracker	textbook
hairline	toothbrush	snowplow	backwoods
sandpaper	summertime	horserace	waistband
racehorse	overload	quarterback	sugarcane
toothpaste	homemade	cartwheel	bygone
sunlight	sawmill	wheelchair	sunburn
stoplight	stepladder	caretaker	suntan
topcoat	mushroom	scoreboard	wallpaper
sparerib	mountaintop	riverboat	warehouse
henhouse	hallway	songbird	halftime
salesman	mainland	songwriter	smokestack
fairground	skateboard	handbag	heavyweight
downpour	upstream	goalkeeper	farmyard
overcoat	countdown	bellbottom	firefly
steamship	streetcar	horseshoe	campfire
superglue	racecar	touchdown	backyard

Language Arts Word Usage
Lesson Title: <u>Antonyms</u>

An antonym is a word that has an opposite meaning. (**Example:** "<u>hot</u>" - "<u>cold</u>".) Antonyms are important for making comparisons or explaining a degree of difference.

Time Frame: **35 - 65 Minutes**
              5 - 10 Activity introduction and explanation.
              5 - 10 List the words.
              5 - 10 Whole group discussion.
             10 - 15 Independent student activity.
              5 - 10 Activity assessment.
              5 - 10 Reflection on the activity.
              * Allow additional time for multiple activities.

Lesson Objectives: To increase vocabulary and knowledge of antonyms.

Materials & Resources: Paper and pencil.

Instruction Procedure: Explain the lesson and lesson objective to the students.

Whole Group Activity:

   List a few antonym sets (for the appropriate grade level) on the board (make up your own words or use the list on the following pages). Say each word as you write it and have the students repeat the word after you. This does two things: 1) helps the student identify the written word with the spoken word, and 2) keeps the students involved while you are doing preparation work for the lesson.

   Once you have finished listing the word sets on the board, take some time to go over each word giving a brief definition of each and pointing to each word as you say the word aloud. Make up a sentence using an antonym set from the board. Repeat this with a few more sets from the board. Next, allow a few students to make up their own sentence using an antonym set from the board. After the students have had a few minutes to practice creating using the sets, move on to the level-appropriate independent activities on the following pages.

GRADE LEVELS	INDEPENDENT ACTIVITY - Antonyms
1st Grade	Have the students select three antonym sets from the board and use each individual word in a simple sentence. Have the students underline the antonym in each sentence. Make sure each sentence begins with a capital letter and has an end mark. **Challenge:** Have the students use a complete antonym set in a single sentence.
Assessment Option:	Have each student select their best work to share with the class.
2nd Grade	Have the students select five antonym sets from the board and use each set in a single meaningful sentence. Have the students underline the antonyms in each sentence. Make sure each sentence begins with a capital letter and has an end mark. **Challenge:** List three more antonym sets on the board, this time unmatched. Have the students match the antonyms.
Assessment Option:	Have each student select their best work to share with the class.
3rd Grade	Have the students select seven antonym sets from the board and use each set in a single meaningful sentence. Have the students underline the antonyms in each sentence. Make sure each sentence begins with a capital letter and has an end mark. **Challenge 1:** List five more antonym sets on the board, this time unmatched. Have the students match the antonyms. **Challenge 2:** List five additional antonym sets on the board this time without their match. Have the students come up with their own antonym to match the words listed on the board.
Assessment Option:	Have each student select their best work to share with the class.

GRADE LEVELS	INDEPENDENT ACTIVITY - Antonyms
4th Grade	Have the students select nine antonym sets from the board and use each set in a single meaningful sentence. Have the students underline the antonyms in each sentence. Make sure each sentence begins with a capital letter and has an end mark.

Challenge 1: List seven additional antonym sets on the board this time without their match. Have the students come up with their own antonym to match the words listed on the board.

Challenge 2: Have students add a third word to each antonym set they have used. |
| **Assessment Option:** | Have each student select their best work to share with the class. |
| 5th Grade | Have the students select ten or more antonyms sets from the board and use each set in a single meaningful sentence. Have the students underline the antonyms in each sentence. Make sure each sentence begins with a capital letter and has an end mark.

Challenge 1: List nine additional antonym sets on the board this time without their match. Have the students come up with their own antonym to match the words listed on the board.

Challenge 2: Separate the class into groups of three. Each set will have player A, player B, and a judge. Begin by having both players make a private list of ten antonyms. Once the lists are complete, have the two players sit facing each other with the judge sitting next to player A (in order to view the list). Player A will begin the game. With player A and the judge able to view the list of antonyms, have player A read each word on the list allowing three seconds for Player B to reply with an antonym. (The judge quietly counts to three for each word and keeps score of the number correct for each player). When player A completes the list, |

GRADE LEVELS   **INDEPENDENT ACTIVITY - Antonyms**

the judge sits next to player B (in order to view the list) and it is player B's turn. The student who gives the most correct responses in the shortest time is the winner. Have the students work in groups. Each group will participate as in pairs. One student is needed to be the judge.

Assessment Option: Have each student select their best work to share with the class.

Reflection: Antonyms

It is important for students to understand why they are learning this process and how they can apply it to their daily lives. Explain that being able to communicate, both verbally and written, is important because it is how people relate to one another. Further, explain that the use of antonyms makes their communication more interesting.

In this reflection, ask the students these questions in an open discussion:

1. What did they learn?
2. How can they use what they learned in their daily activity?
3. Can they teach what they have learned to someone else?
4. What did they like most about the activity?
5. What did they like least about the activity?

Antonym List
1st Grade

high - low	wet - dry	large - small
top - bottom	sharp - dull	tall - short
black - white	true - false	hot - cold
deep - shallow	love - hate	happy - sad
give - receive	start - stop	begin - end
dirty - clean	loud - silent	fast - slow
day - night	yes - no	stay - go
rich - poor	good - bad	sweet - sour
long - short	fresh - stale	up - down
asleep - awake	wild - tame	brave - coward
straight - crooked	different - same	add - subtract
soft - hard	far - near	low - high
early - late	spend - save	lost - found
always - never	AM - PM	inside - outside
behind - ahead	forward - backward	push - pull
over - under	boy - girl	neat - messy
whisper - scream	ignore - attentive	win - lose

Antonym List
2nd Grade

high - low	wet - dry	large - small
top - bottom	sharp - dull	tall - short
black - white	true - false	hot - cold
deep - shallow	love - hate	happy - sad
give - receive	start - stop	begin - end
dirty - clean	loud - silent	fast - slow
day - night	yes - no	stay - go
rich - poor	good - bad	sweet - sour
long - short	fresh - stale	up - down
asleep - awake	wild - tame	brave - coward
straight - crooked	different - same	add - subtract
soft - hard	far - near	low - high
early - late	spend - save	lost - found
always - never	AM - PM	inside - outside
behind - front	forward - backward	push - pull
over - under	boy - girl	neat - messy
whisper - yell	ignore - attentive	win - loose
enormous - tiny	move - still	few - many
hide - seek	enter - exit	rude - kind
lie - truth	dawn - dusk	sharp - dull
true - false	float - sink	more - less

Antonym List
3rd Grade

broad - narrow	beautiful - ugly	common - unique
begin - finish	clever - foolish	man - woman
men - women	death - life	left - right
free - imprison	old - young	faulty - perfect
fail - pass	freeze - thaw	dangerous - safe
decrease - increase	whisper - yell	maximum - minimum
tender - tough	inward - outward	summer - winter
inside - outside	enter - exit	inbound - outbound
cry - laugh	indoors - outdoors	difficult - easy
prefix - suffix	day - night	above - below
imaginary - real	appear - vanish	heavy - light
clap - boo	on - off	arrive - depart
mix - sort	asleep - awake	fancy - plain
ashamed - proud	fat - skinny	back - front
far - near	over - under	bring - take
many - few	more - less	hide - seek
sink - float	left - right	right - wrong
true - false	morning - evening	midnight - noon
sharp - dull	light - dark	good - bad
yes - no	win - lose	tight - loose

Antonym List
4th Grade

accidental - intentional	bitter - sweet	arrogant - humble
attack - defend	broad - narrow	borrow - lend
cautious - reckless	blame - forgive	chaos - order
live - die	clumsy - graceful	capture - escape
complex - simple	calm - nervous	contract - expand
ceiling - floor	decrease - increase	bring - take
defense - offense	bottom - top	inflate - deflate
cheap - expensive	shrink - grow	careful - careless
miniature - gigantic	private - public	hero - villain
daughter - son	hollow - solid	mother - father
major - minor	different - same	movable - stationary
dull - sharp	nourish - starve	dumb - smart
occupied - vacant	east - west	often - seldom
everybody - nobody	north - south	AM - PM
midnight - noon	inbound - outbound	arrive - depart
always - never	more - less	full - empty
spend - save	give - take	enter - exit
used - new	divide - multiply	add - subtract
sum - difference	rarely - often	early - late
fancy - plain	none - all	indoor - outdoor

Antonym List
5th Grade

abundance - scarce	discord - harmony	agony - ecstasy
cease - commence	authentic - imitation	buy - sell
broad - narrow	brave - coward	civilian - military
approximate - exact	concur - protest	approve - reject
condemn - condone	applaud - boo	contract - expand
prior - subsequent	cruel - merciful	negative - positive
defeat - triumph	narrow - wide	despair - hope
limp - stiff	divest - invest	guilty - innocent
exclude - include	illegal - lawful	dwarf - giant
ignorance - knowledge	emerge - submerge	poverty - wealth
inhale - exhale	optimist - pessimist	exotic - ordinary
ordinary - rare	shrink - expand	permanent - temporary
import - export	loose - tight	exterior - interior
friend - foe	raw - cooked	liquid - solid
macro - micro	major - minor	dead - alive
borrow - lend	straight - crooked	chaos - order
frugal - wasteful	impeccable - flawed	massive - minute
past - future	occupied - vacant	antonym - synonym
excel - fail	deplete - increase	gain - lose
damage - repair	deflate - inflate	sturdy - frail

Language Arts Word Usage
Lesson Title: <u>Synonyms</u>

Synonyms are words that have the same or similar meanings. (**Example:** "<u>large</u>" and "<u>big</u>".) Synonyms can be interchanged to increase interest and limit repetition. The use of synonyms can also increase your vocabulary and make your stories and conversations more interesting.

Time Frame: **35 - 65 Minutes**
                                       5 - 10 Activity introduction and explanation.
                                       5 - 10 List the words.
                                       5 - 10 Whole group discussion.
                                      10 - 15 Independent student activity.
                                       5 - 10 Activity assessment.
                                       5 - 10 Reflection on the activity.
                                     * Allow additional time for multiple activities.

Lesson Objectives: To increase vocabulary and knowledge of synonyms.

Materials & Resources: Paper and pencil.

Instruction Procedure: Explain the lesson and lesson objectives to the students.

Whole Group Activity:

List a few synonym sets (for the appropriate grade level) on the board (make up your own sets or use the list on the following pages). Read each set as you write it on the board and have the students repeat the set after you. This does two things: 1) helps the student identify the written word with the spoken word, and 2) keeps the students involved while you are doing preparation work for the lesson.

Once you have finished listing the word sets on the board, take some time to go over each word giving a brief definition of each and pointing to each set as you say the word aloud. Make up a sentence using a synonym set from the board. Repeat this with a few more sets from the board. Next, allow a few students to make up their own sentence using a synonym set from the board. After the students have had a few minutes to practice, move on to the level-appropriate independent activities on the following pages.

GRADE LEVELS	INDEPENDENT ACTIVITY – Synonyms
1st Grade	Have the students select three synonym sets from the board and use each individual word in a simple sentence. Have the students underline the synonym in each sentence. Make sure each sentence begins with a capital letter and has an end mark. **Challenge:** Have the students use a complete synonym set in a single sentence using one or all three sets.
Assessment Option:	Have each student select their best work to share with the class.
2nd Grade	Have the students select five synonym sets from the board and use each set in a single meaningful sentence. Have the students underline the synonyms in each sentence. Make sure each sentence begins with a capital letter and has an end mark. **Challenge:** List three more synonym sets on the board, this time unmatched. Have the students match the synonyms.
Assessment Option:	Have each student select their best work to share with the class.
3rd Grade	Have the students select seven synonym sets from the board and use each set in a single meaningful sentence. Have the students underline the synonyms in each sentence. Make sure each sentence begins with a capital letter and has an end mark. **Challenge 1:** List five more synonym sets on the board, this time unmatched. Have the students match the synonyms. **Challenge 2:** List five additional synonym sets on the board this time without their match. Have the students come up with their own synonyms to match the words listed on the board.
Assessment Option:	Have each student select their best work to share with the class.

GRADE LEVELS	INDEPENDENT ACTIVITY – Synonyms
4th Grade	Have the students select nine synonym sets from the board and use each set in a single meaningful sentence. Have the students underline the synonyms in each sentence. Make sure each sentence begins with a capital letter and has an end mark.

Challenge 1: List seven additional synonym sets on the board this time without their match. Have the students come up with their own synonym to match the words listed on the board.

Challenge 2: Have students add a third word to each synonym set they have used. |
| **Assessment Option:** | Have each student select their best work to share with the class. |
| **5th Grade** | Have the students select ten or more synonym sets from the board and use each set in a single meaningful sentence. Have the students underline the synonyms in each sentence. Make sure each sentence begins with a capital letter and has an end mark.

Challenge 1: List nine additional synonym sets on the board this time without their match. Have the students come up with their own synonym to match the words listed on the board.

Challenge 2: Separate the class into groups of three. Each set will have player A, player B, and a judge. Begin by having both players make a private list of ten synonyms. Once the lists are complete, have the two players sit facing each other with the judge sitting next to player A (in order to view the list). Player A will begin the game. With player A and the judge able to view the list of synonyms, have player A read each word on the list allowing three seconds for Player B to reply with a synonym. (The judge quietly counts to three for each word and keeps score of the number correct for each player.) When player A completes the list, the judge |
| **GRADE LEVELS** | **INDEPENDENT ACTIVITY – Synonyms** |

sits next to player B (in order to view the list) and it is player B's turn. The student who gives the most correct responses in the shortest time is the winner. Have the students work in groups. Each group will participate as in pairs. One student is needed to be the judge.

Assessment Option: Have each student select their best work to share with the class.

Reflection: Synonyms

It is important for students to understand why they are learning this process and how they can apply it to their daily lives. Explain that being able to communicate, both verbally and written, is important because it is how people relate to one another. Further, explain that the use of synonyms makes their communication more interesting. The knowledge and use of synonyms is a great way to increase your vocabulary bank.

In this reflection, ask the students these questions in an open discussion:

1. What did they learn?
2. How can they use what they learned in their daily activity?
3. Can they teach what they have learned to someone else?
4. What did they like most about the activity?
5. What did they like least about the activity?

Synonym List
1st Grade

tell - say	large - big	small - little
smile - grin	leap - jump	neat - tidy
above - over	end - complete	near - close
shout - scream	start - begin	trash - garbage
fast - quick	woman - lady	gift - present
enormous - gigantic	tiny - small	easy - simple
mean - evil	glad - happy	pretty - cute
push - shove	walk - stroll	breeze - wind
talk - speak	pair - match	fix - repair
throw - toss	chore - work	stone - rock
angry - mad	happy - jolly	look - stare
hope - wish	enjoy - like	smart - wise
difficult - hard	reply - answer	finish - complete
nap - sleep	stay - remain	right - correct
rush - hurry	under - beneath	dirty - filthy
messy - sloppy	ugly - unattractive	tight - snug
baggy - loose	scream - yell	hear - listen
touch - feel	see - view	sniff - smell
rest - relax	show - display	flick - fling
fast - quick	angry - upset	painful - hurtful

Synonym List
2nd Grade

rude - mean	little - tiny	friend - pal
some - part	tidy - neat	girl - gal
all - whole	cute - pretty	boy - guy
reduce - decrease	sloppy - messy	chore - work
add - increase	show - reveal	start - begin
under - below	nap - sleep	end - finish
stay - remain	answer - reply	big - large
grip - hold	begin - start	like - enjoy
store - stash	shy - bashful	hear - listen
forgive - excuse	close - near	smell - sniff
prank - joke	allow - let	garbage - trash
lie - fib	jump - hop	relax - rest
tiny - small	silent - quiet	scream - yell
more - plus	smile - grin	avoid - dodge
subtract - less	sad - gloomy	skinny - thin
gift - present	happy - jolly	terrific - great
giggle - laugh	tell - say	nice - good
lead - guide	throw - toss	leave - go
stay - remain	above - over	ill - sick
follow - trail	painful - hurtful	chubby - fat

Synonym List
3rd Grade

above - over - top	easy - simple	absent - missing
hateful - mean	love - adore	glad - happy
allow - let	jump - hop	upset - mad
sick - ill	bad - terrible	little - small
baggy - loose	silent - quiet	barefoot - shoeless
fast - quick	shy - bashful	nap - sleep
begin - start	part - some	large - big
rock - stone	friend - buddy	speak - talk
money - cash	say - tell	work - chore
shove - push	giggle - laugh	tug - pull
close - near	close - seal	end - finish
rush - hurry	pretty - cute	thin - skinny
fib - lie	fat - chunky	gift - present
painful - hurtful	allow - let	capture - catch
excuse - forgive	go - leave	acquire - attain
guide - lead	dodge - avoid	increase - add
go - leave	guide - lead	pointed - sharp
excellent - great	remain - stay	trace - copy
gloomy - sad	ground - earth	scamper - dash
shout - scream	follow - trail	turn - rotate

Synonym List
4th Grade

stroll - walk	dirty - soiled	answer - reply
cash - money	smart - wise	criticize - blame
scream - shout	babble - chatter	messy - sloppy
avoid - dodge	slender - thin	alter - change
snooze - sleep	admire - adore	safe - secure
naughty - misbehave	neat - tidy	bashful - shy
nap - sleep	beneath - below	kind - friendly
cautious - watchful	leap - jump	celebration - party
here - present	chuckle - giggle	grin - smile
continue - proceed	lady - woman	halt - stop
final - complete	easy - simple	dirt - soil
man - male	hard - difficult	youngster - child
correct - right	enormous - gigantic	content - satisfied
achieve - accomplish	level - even	pretend - fake
veracity - accuracy	invent - create	stretch - extend
drift - flow	fling - toss	play - frolic
center - middle	drool - slobber	risk - gamble
original - first	mob - crowd	ownership - possession
fasten - attach	accord - agree	modest - humble
grumble - complain	grip - hold	clear - transparent

Synonym List
5th Grade

stride - step	stroll - walk	grasp - seize
clutch - hold	respond - reply	currency - money
intelligent - wise	condemn - criticize	bellow - shout
ramble - babble	clutter - messy	shun - avoid
lean - slender	modify - alter	doze - snooze
regard - admire	protect - defend	secure - safe
awful - bad	orderly - neat	timid - bashful
teach - educate	underneath - beneath	cordial - kind
vigilance - watchful	spring - leap	festivity - celebration
in attendance - present	cackle - chuckle	beam - smile
ensue - continue	female - gal	discontinue - halt
conclude - complete	effortless - easy	filthy - dirty
guy - male	complex - difficult	youth - child
accurate - correct	massive - enormous	content - satisfied
achieve - accomplish	circle - revolve	parched - dry
fake - pretend	inner - inside	defunct - extinct
risk - gamble	prolong - extend	drool - slobber
push - thrust	suppress - crush	elude - evade
devise - design	even - level	invisible - transparent
precision - accuracy	fasten - attach	invent - create

Language Arts Word Usage
Lesson Title: <u>Homographs</u>

A homograph is a word that has different meanings, although it is spelled the same and sometimes pronounced the same. (**Example:** "Fly" - this can be an insect or the act of moving through the air.)

Time Frame: **35 - 65 Minutes**
        5 - 10 Activity introduction and explanation.
        5 - 10 List the words and the multiple meanings.
        5 - 10 Whole group discussion.
      10 - 15 Independent student activity.
        5 - 10 Activity assessment.
        5 - 10 Reflection on the activity.
       * *Allow additional time for multiple activities.*

Lesson Objectives: To increase vocabulary and knowledge of word meanings.

Materials & Resources: Paper and pencil.

Instruction Procedure: Explain the lesson and lesson objective to the students.

Whole Group Activity:

List a few homographs on the board. You may make up your own or use the following list. according to the grade level. Say each word as you write it giving both definitions. Have the students repeat the words after you. This does two things: 1) helps the student identify the written word with the spoken word, and 2) keeps the students involved while you are doing preparation work for the lesson.

After you finish listing the words on the board, take some time to go over each word several times while pointing to each word as you say the word aloud and repeat both definitions. For more practice and better understanding, make up sentences to demonstrate the multiple uses of the homographs. Repeat this activity with a few of the homographs listed on the board. Next, allow a few students to practice using the homographs in a sentence of their own. Once the students have had a few minutes to practice using homographs, move on to the level-appropriate independent activities on the following pages.

GRADE LEVELS	INDEPENDENT ACTIVITY - Homographs
1st Grade	Have the students select three homographs to work with. Next, have them write individual simple sentences using each homograph listed on the board. They should underline the homograph, begin the sentence with a capital letter, and use an end mark.

Challenge: Have the students select one additional homograph and determine its multiple meanings. |
| Assessment Option: | Have each student share their work with the class. |
| 2nd Grade | Have the students select five homographs to work with. Next, have them write a meaningful sentence using each homograph they have selected. They should underline the homograph, begin the sentence with a capital letter, and include an end mark.

Challenge: Have the students select one homograph and write one sentence containing both meanings. (**Example:** The fly broke his wing and couldn't fly away.) |
| Assessment Option: | Have each student share their work with the class. |
| 3rd Grade | Have the students select seven homographs to work with. Next, have them write a meaningful sentence using each homograph they have selected. They should underline the homograph, begin the sentence with a capital letter, and include an end mark.

Challenge: Have the students select three homographs and write one sentence containing both meanings for each. (**Example:** The fly broke his wing and couldn't fly away.) |
| Assessment Option: | Have each student share their work with the class. |

GRADE LEVELS	INDEPENDENT ACTIVITY - Homographs
4th Grade	Have the students select nine homographs to work with. Next, have them write a meaningful sentence using each homograph they have selected. They should underline the homograph, begin the sentence with a capital letter, and include an end mark.

Challenge: Have the students select five homographs and write one sentence for each word selected containing both meanings for each. (**Example:** The fly broke his wing and couldn't fly away.) |
| **Assessment Option:** | Have each student share their work with the class. |
| **5th Grade** | Have the students select ten or more homographs to work with. Next, have them write a meaningful sentence using each homograph they have selected. They should underline the homograph, begin the sentence with a capital letter, and use an end mark.

Challenge: Have the students select seven homographs and write one sentence for each word selected containing both meanings for each. (**Example:** The fly broke his wing and couldn't fly away.) |
| **Assessment Option:** | Have each student share their work with the class. |

Reflection: Homographs

It is important for students to understand why they are learning this process and how they can apply it to their daily lives. Explain that being able to communicate, both verbally and written, is important because it is how people relate to one another. Further explain that the use and understanding of homographs is very important, especially for clear written communication.

In this reflection, ask the students these questions in an open discussion:

1. What did they learn?
2. How can they use what they learned in their daily activity?
3. Can they teach what they have learned to someone else?
4. What did they like most about the activity?
5. What did they like least about the activity?

Homograph List
2nd Grade

back	A.	In reverse direction.	B.	The rear part of a body.
bark	A.	The outer part of a tree.	B.	A sound a dog makes.
bat	A.	A club or stick.	B.	A flying mammal.
block	A.	A solid square object.	B.	A street section.
bow	A.	A looped knot.	B.	To bend the head or body forward.
can	A.	Able to.	B.	A metal container.
file	A.	Storage for papers.	B.	A tool used to smooth a surface.
hide	A.	Keep secret.	B.	Animal skin.
kind	A.	Compassionate.	B.	A group of individual objects that share features.
lap	A.	The top of one's thighs when they are sitting.	B.	One circuit of a tract.
lie	A.	To lay horizontally.	B.	To tell an untruth.
light	A.	Energy producing brightness.	B.	Not heavy.
rock	A.	A stone or boulder.	B.	To sway back and forth.
sheet	A.	A cloth used on a bed.	B.	A flat baking pan.
skip	A.	A bouncy step or walk.	B.	To omit or pass over.
soil	A.	Top layer of land.	B.	To make dirty.
tip	A.	To knock over.	B.	The end of a thing.
top	A.	The highest part of something.	B.	A spinning toy.
wave	A.	Move the hand repeatedly.	B.	A moving ripple on a liquid surface (ocean).
well	A.	A hole made to draw up fluid.	B.	Pleasingly or desirably. Healthy.

Homograph List
3rd Grade

act	A.	Something done.	B.	Part of a play.
base	A.	A mat in baseball.	B.	A military location.
calf	A.	The back part of the leg below the knee.	B.	A baby cow.
crow	A.	A large black bird.	B.	A rooster's cry.
dull	A.	Boring.	B.	Blunt.
float	A.	To rest on a liquid surface.	B.	A vehicle in a parade.
fly	A.	An insect.	B.	The act of moving through the air.
jam	A.	Fruit spread.	B.	To clog something up.
last	A.	Most recent.	B.	To endure longer.
letter	A.	Message sent by mail.	B.	A unit of the alphabet.
like	A.	Resembling.	B.	Enjoy.
loaf	A.	Spend time lazily.	B.	A quantity of bread.
mold	A.	A tool for making a shape.	B.	A fungus.
note	A.	A jotted record or summary.	B.	A symbol in music.
pool	A.	A form of billiards.	B.	A hole with water.
pound	A.	To beat something.	B.	A unit of measure.
right	A.	Correct.	B.	A direction. Opposite of left.
roll	A.	Turn over and over.	B.	Dinner bread.
rose	A.	A flower.	B.	Past tense of rise.
sink	A.	To fall beneath a liquid surface.	B.	A basin.
speaker	A.	Someone who makes speeches.	B.	A box that emits sound.
spoke	A.	A supporting rod of a wheel rim.	B.	Past tense of speak.
spring	A.	To move forward or upward.	B.	A season of the year.
watch	A.	A small personal clock.	B.	Observe.

Homograph List
4th Grade

bear	A.	A large furry animal.	B.	Tolerate.
bed	A.	Patch of soil.	B.	Furniture used for sleeping.
box	A.	A container.	B.	Fight using the fists.
brand	A.	A particular type of product.	B.	To mark, or label.
dart	A.	A small arrow with a point.	B.	A fast movement.
deck	A.	A part of a ship.	B.	A collections of playing cards.
down	A.	Feathers of a baby goose.	B.	A direction.
ear	A.	Plant part containing grain.	B.	An organ used for hearing.
head	A.	Most forward section.	B.	Top part of the body.
left	A.	A direction. (West when facing north).	B.	Departed.
log	A.	A piece from a tree.	B.	A record or journal.
match	A.	Contest.	B.	A stick for producing fire.
nail	A.	A short pointed metal pin.	B.	The hard area on a finger or toe.
park	A.	An area for public recreation.	B.	To stop and leave a vehicle.
part	A.	A portion or division.	B.	To divide.
perch	A.	A place for a bird to sit.	B.	A type of fish.
ruler	A.	A leader of many.	B.	A tool used to measure.
scales	A.	Weighing tools.	B.	The bony plates on fish.
shed	A.	To lose hair.	B.	An outside storage bin or container.
squash	A.	A vegetable of the gourd family.	B.	To flatten using pressure.
stick	A.	A thin branch.	B.	To fasten with adhesive.

Homograph List
5th Grade

ball	A.	A fancy dance.	B.	A sphere shaped toy.
bluff	A.	To pretend.	B.	A steep and broad embankment..
buck	A.	Male animal.	B.	Throw a rider.
cast	A.	Participants in a play or show.	B.	To throw or toss.
check	A.	Examine something.	B.	Paper money substitute.
duck	A.	A common water bird.	B.	To bend quickly.
faint	A.	Dim.	B.	Dizzy.
fall	A.	A season between summer and winter.	B.	To drop down.
felt	A.	A type of material.	B.	Past tense of feel.
fit	A.	Sudden outburst.	B.	The right size.
iron	A.	Metallic element.	B.	A heated tool.
mean	A.	Intend to do something.	B.	Unkind.
miss	A.	A young woman.	B.	To not hit the target.
pet	A.	To stroke or comfort.	B.	A loved animal kept at home.
pitcher	A.	A large single-handled jug.	B.	The player who throws the ball to the batter in baseball.
play	A.	To take part in a game.	B.	To perform on a musical instrument.
pupil	A.	A student.	B.	A part of the eye.
race	A.	A contest of speed.	B.	A group of humans.
range	A.	A category defined by limits.	B.	An open area of land used for grazing farm animals.
rare	A.	Partially cooked.	B.	Not happening or found often.
seal	A.	Fish eating marine mammal.	B.	To close tightly.
swallow	A.	A small songbird.	B.	To take in food from the mouth to the body.

Language Arts Word Usage
Lesson Title: <u>Homophones</u>

Homophones are words that sound alike but are spelled different and have different meanings. (**Example:** "**buy**", **bye**", and "**by**".)

Time Frame: **35 - 65 Minutes**
    5 - 10 Activity introduction and explanation.
    5 - 10 List the words and the individual meanings.
    5 - 10 Whole group discussion.
    10 - 15 Independent student activity.
    5 - 10 Activity assessment.
    5 - 10 Reflection on the activity.
    * Allow additional time for multiple activities.

Lesson Objectives: To increase vocabulary and knowledge of homophones.

Materials & Resources: Paper and pencil.

Instruction Procedure: Explain the lesson and lesson objective to the students.

Whole Group Activity:

List one word from a homophone set, and a few other (according to grade level) homophone sets along with their meanings on the board (make up your own or use the list on the following pages). Have the students repeat each word and their meaning while you are listing them. This does two things: 1) helps the student identify the written word with the spoken word, and 2) keeps the students involved while you are doing preparation work for the lesson.

After you finish listing the words on the board, take some time to go over each word several times while pointing to each word as you say the word aloud and give the definitions. For more practice and better understanding, make up a sentence to demonstrate the multiple uses of the homophones. Repeat this activity with a few of the homophones listed on the board. Next, allow a few students to practice using the homophones in sentences of their own. Once the students have had a few minutes to practice using the sets, move on to the level-appropriate independent activities on the following pages.

GRADE LEVELS	INDEPENDENT ACTIVITY - Homophones
1st Grade	Have the students select three homophone sets to work with. Next, have them write one simple sentence for each set. They should underline the homophone, begin the sentence with a capital letter, and include an end mark.

Challenge: Using the additional single word from a different homophone set, have the student determine the other words in the set and their meanings (**Example:** You list the word "by", this means nearby or close. The other two are "bye", which is a closing for departing, and "buy", which means to purchase something.) |
| **Assessment Option:** | Have each student select their best work to share with the class. |
| 2nd Grade | Have the students select five homophone sets to work with. Next, have them write one meaningful sentence for each set. They should underline the homophone, begin the sentence with a capital letter, and include an end mark.

Challenge: Using the additional single word from a different homophone set, have the student determine the other words in the set and their meanings (**Example:** You list the word "by", this means nearby or close. The other two are "bye", which is a closing for departing, and "buy", which means to purchase something.) |
| **Assessment Option:** | Have each student select their best work to share with the class. |
| 3rd Grade | Have the students select seven homophone sets to work with. Next, have them write one meaningful sentence for each set. The sentence must demonstrates an understanding of each word using each homophone. They should underline the homophone, begin the sentence with a capital letter, and include an end mark. |

GRADE LEVELS	INDEPENDENT ACTIVITY - Homophones
	Challenge: Using three additional single words from a different homophone set, have the student determine the other words in the set and their meanings (**Example:** You list the word "by", this means nearby or close. The other two are "bye", which is a closing for departing, and "buy", which means to purchase something.)
Assessment Option:	Have each student select their best work to share with the class.
4th Grade	Have the students select nine homophone sets to work with. Next, have them write one meaningful sentence for each set. The sentences must demonstrates an understanding of each word using each homophone. They should underline the homophone, begin the sentence with a capital letter, and include an end mark.
	Challenge: Using five additional single words from a different homophone set, have the student determine the other words in the set and their meanings (**Example:** You list the word "by", this means nearby or close. The other two are "bye", which is a closing for departing, and "buy", which means to purchase something.)
Assessment Option:	Have each student select their best work to share with the class.
5th Grade	Have the students select ten or more homophone sets to work with. Next, have them write one meaningful sentence for each set. The sentence must demonstrates an understanding of each word using each homophone. They should underline the homophone, begin the sentence with a capital letter, and include an end mark.

GRADE LEVELS **INDEPENDENT ACTIVITY - Homophones**

Challenge: Using seven additional single words from different homophone sets, have the student determine the other words in the sets and their meanings (**Example:** You list the word "by", this means nearby or close. The other two are "bye", which is a closing for departing, and "buy", which means to purchase something.)

Assessment Option: Have each student select their best work to share with the class.

Reflection: Homophones

It is important for students to understand why they are learning this process and how they can apply it to their daily lives. Explain that being able to communicate, both verbally and written, is important because it is how people relate to one another. Further explain that the use and understanding of homophones in written communication is crucial for proper understanding of the written word.

In this reflection, ask the students these questions in an open discussion:

1. What did they learn?
2. How can they use what they learned in their daily activity?
3. Can they teach what they have learned to someone else?
4. What did they like most about the activity?
5. What did they like least about the activity?

Homophone List
1st Grade

ate - eight	hear - here
be - bee	hole - whole
beat - beet	made - maid
buy - by - bye	know - no
blew - blue	pear - pair
brake - break	lone - loan
bread - bred	meat - meet
cell - sell	right - write
cent - scent - sent	tail - tale
days - daze	red - read
dear - deer	wood - would
due - do - dew	sea - see
fair - fare	stake - steak
find - fined	tied - tide
flue - flu	week - weak
fir - fur	male - mail
hair - hare	passed - past
hour - our	hear - here
site - sight - cite	pore - pour - poor
die - dye	role - roll

Homophone List
2nd Grade

bare - bear	knows - nose
boar - bore	made - maid
carrot - karat	meat - meet - mete
chews - choose	pail - pale
close - clothes	pain - pane
genes - jeans	peak - peek
grade - grayed	peal - peel
grate - great	pear - pair
graze - grays	sail - sell - sale
groan - grown	sea - see
hair - hare	sew - so
Harry - hairy	shoe - shoo
hay - hey	shone - shown
hear - here	son - sun
heard - herd	sonny - sunny
hour - our	tea - tee
knew - new	where - ware - wear
knight - night	who's - whose
knot - not	wood - would
know - no	you're - your

Homophone List
3rd Grade

bald - bawled	sail - sale - cell - sell
base - bass	sealing - ceiling
be - bee	seam - seem
beat - beet	serial - cereal
been - bin	shear - sheer
bite - byte	sore - soar
billed - build	sold - soled
blew - blue	some - sum
bolder - boulder	tail - tale
break - brake	tear - tier
Cain - cane	threw - through
heal - heel - he'll	throne - thrown
Maine - main - mane	tooter - tutor
Mary - merry	tow - toe
paste - paced	towed - toad
plain - plane	two - too - to
weight - way	principal - principle
capitol - capital	rain - reign - rein
which - witch	weather - whether
brews - bruise	crews - cruise

Homophone List
4th Grade

ax - acts	sole - soul
bail - bale	steal - steel
bait - bate	sword - soared
bolder - boulder	tacked - tact
bred - bread	team - teem
brewed - brood	tear - tier
brews - bruise	tense - tents
cite - sight - site	tide - tied
coat - cote	tie - Thai
ducked - duct	very - vary
hoard - horde	waist - waste
hole - whole	wait - weight
in - inn	warn - worn
lade - laid	world - whirled
style - stile	yew - you
per - purr	straight - strait
stationary - stationery	whether - weather
need - kneed	wax - whacks
fax - facts	colonel - kernel
their - there	bird - burred

Homophone List
5th Grade

air - heir	ode - owed
awn - on	per - purr
balm - bomb	pi - pie
berry - bury	profit - prophet
berth - birth	saver - savor
bird - burred	sensor - censor
bold - bowled	sight - cite - site
braid - brayed	stationary - stationery
breach - breech	step - steppe
cast - caste	stile - style
Chile - chili - chilly	straight - strait
colonel - kernel	suite - sweet
crews - cruise	thyme - time
currant - current	tracked - tract
cymbal - symbol	vale - veil
facts - fax	wail - wale - whale
graft - graphed	waive - wave
heard - herd	waste - waist
him - hymn	wax - whacks
loot - lute	you'll - Yule

Language Arts Word Usage
Lesson Title: <u>Prefixes</u>

Prefixes are letters that are added before a word to change the word's meaning. (**Example:** re = to do again, back, or backward. Regain = to gain again, or gain back.)

Time Frame: **35 - 65 Minutes**
          5 - 10 Activity introduction and explanation.
          5 - 10 List prefixes with their meanings and words.
          5 - 10 Whole group discussion.
         10 - 15 Independent student activity.
          5 - 10 Activity assessment.
          5 - 10 Reflection on the activity.
          Allow additional time for multiple activities.

Lesson Objectives: To increase vocabulary and knowledge of how to manipulate words with prefixes to change their meaning.

Materials & Resources: Paper and pencil.

Instruction Procedure: Explain the lesson and lesson objective to the students.

Whole Group Activity:

 List a few prefixes (you may make up your own or use the list on the following pages) on the board (according to the grade level). Say each prefix as you write it and give the meaning of it. Have the students repeat the prefix after you as you write them. This does two things: 1) helps the student identify the written word with the spoken word, and 2) keeps the students involved while you are doing preparation work for the lesson.

 After you finish listing the prefixes on the board, take some time to go over each one several times while pointing to each prefix and the meaning as you say it aloud. Next, allow a few students to practice using prefixes with some of the words you have listed in a sentence of their own. Once the students have had a few minutes to practice creating new word meanings by adding prefixes, move on to the level-appropriate independent activities on the following pages.

GRADE LEVELS	INDEPENDENT ACTIVITY - Prefixes
1st Grade	Have the students select three words to add a prefix to and write a simple sentence for each new word. Underline the prefixed word in each sentence. Each sentence must begin with a capital letter and have an end mark. **Challenge:** Have the students select one word and use the word with and without the prefix in the same sentence.
Assessment Option:	Have each student select their best work to share with the class.
2nd Grade	Have the students select two words to add a prefix to and write a meaningful sentence for each new word that reveal the correct understanding of the word with the prefix. Underline the prefixed word in each sentence. Each sentence must begin with a capital letter and have an end mark. **Challenge:** Have the students select three words and use the word with and without the prefix in the same sentence.
Assessment Option:	Have each student select their best work to share with the class.
3rd Grade	Have the students select seven words to add a prefix to and write a meaningful sentence for each new word that reveal the correct understanding of the word with the prefix. Underline the prefixed word in each sentence. Each sentence must begin with a capital letter and have an end mark. **Challenge:** Have the students select three words and use the word with and without the prefix in the same sentence.
Assessment Option:	Have each student select their best work to share with the class.

GRADE LEVELS	INDEPENDENT ACTIVITY - Prefixes
4th Grade	Have the students select nine words to add a prefix to and write a meaningful sentence for each new word that reveal the correct understanding of the word with the prefix. Underline the prefixed word in each sentence. Each sentence must begin with a capital letter and have an end mark. **Challenge:** Have the students select four words and use the word with and without the prefix in the same sentence.
Assessment Option:	Have each student select their best work to share with the class.
5th Grade	Have the students select ten or more words to add a prefix to and write a meaningful sentence for each new word that reveal the correct understanding of the word with the prefix. Underline the prefixed word in each sentence. Each sentence must begin with a capital letter and have an end mark. **Challenge:** Have the students select five words and use the word with and without the prefix in the same sentence.
Assessment Option:	Have each student select their best work to share with the class.

Reflection: Prefixes

It is important for students to understand why they are learning this process and how they can apply it to their daily lives. Explain that being able to communicate, both verbally and written, is important because it is how people relate to one another. Further explain that being able to manipulate words by simply adding a prefix will increase their vocabulary.

In this reflection, ask the students these questions in an open discussion:

1. What did they learn?
2. How can they use what they learned in their daily activity?
3. Can they teach what they have learned to someone else?
4. What did they like most about the activity?
5. What did they like least about the activity?

Prefix List

1st Grade

1	dis-	Undo, opposite, or not.
2	pre-	Before, earlier, or in advance.
3	re-	Again, back, or backward.
4	un-	Not, lack of, opposite, or reverse.

2nd Grade List

5	de-	Reverse, remove, or reduce.
6	en-	Into, to cause, or within.
7	ex-	Outside, away, former, not, or without.
8	mis-	Badly, wrong, opposite, lack of, or failure.

3rd Grade List

9	in-	Not, toward, within, in, or into.
10	ob-	Inverse or against.
11	para-	Beside, near, or beyond.
12	trans-	Across, beyond, change, transfer, or through.

4th Grade List

13	photo-	Light or radiant energy.
14	poly-	Many, more than one, or more than normal.
15	tele-	At a distance.
16	tri-	Three or third.

Prefix List

5th Grade List

17	auto-	Self.
18	bi-	Two, twice, or both.
19	bio-	Life.
20	com-	With or together.
21	inter-	Between, among, or mutual.
22	macro-	Large or inclusive.
23	micro-	Small or minute.
24	pro-	For, forward, or before.
25	sub-	Under, below, or beneath.

Language Arts Word Usage
Lesson Title: <u>Suffixes</u>

Suffixes are letters that are added to the end of a word to change the words meaning. (**Example:** -less = without, therefore the word thought with the suffix of -less is thoughtless, which means without sufficient thought.)

Time Frame: **35 - 65 Minutes**
                      5 - 10 Activity introduction and explanation.
                      5 - 10 List suffixes with their meanings and a few words.
                      5 - 10 Whole group discussion.
                    10 - 15 Independent student activity.
                      5 - 10 Activity assessment.
                      5 - 10 Reflection on the activity.
                      * Allow additional time for multiple activities.

Lesson Objectives: To increase student vocabulary and knowledge of suffixes and how to manipulate words to change their meaning.

Materials & Resources: Paper and pencil.

Instruction Procedure: Explain the lesson and lesson objectives to the students.

Whole Group Activity:

List a few suffixes (you may make up your own or use the list on the following pages) on the board (according to the grade level). Say each suffix and its meaning as you write them. Have the students repeat the suffixes and their meanings after you as you write them. This does two things: 1) helps the student identify the written word with the spoken word, and 2) keeps the students involved while you are doing preparation work for the lesson.

After you finish listing the suffixes and words on the board, take some time to go over each several times while pointing to each as you say them aloud. For more practice and better understanding, make up a sentence to demonstrate the uses of the suffix when added to a word. Next, allow a few students to practice adding a suffix to a word and using the new word in a sentence of their own. Once the students have had a few minutes to practice, move on to the level-appropriate independent activities on the following pages.

GRADE LEVELS	INDEPENDENT ACTIVITY – Suffixes
1st Grade	Have the students select three words to add a suffix to and write a simple sentence for each new word. Each sentence must begin with a capital letter and have an end mark. Underline the suffixed words in each sentence.

Challenge: Have the students select one word and use the word with and without the suffix in the same sentence. |
| Assessment Option: | Have each student select their best work to share with the class. |
| 2nd Grade | Have the students select two words to add a suffix to and write a meaningful sentence for each new word that reveals the correct understanding of the word with the suffix. Each sentence must begin with a capital letter and have an end mark. Underline the suffixed words in each sentence.

Challenge: Have the students select three words and use each word with and without the suffix in the same sentence. |
| Assessment Option: | Have each student select their best work to share with the class. |
| 3rd Grade | Have the students select seven words to add a suffix to and write a meaningful sentence for each new word that reveals the correct understanding of the word with the suffix. Each sentence must begin with a capital letter and have an end mark. Underline the suffixed words in each sentence.

Challenge: Have the students select three words and use the word with and without the suffix in the same sentence. |
| Assessment Option: | Have each student select their best work to share with the class. |
| **GRADE LEVELS** | **INDEPENDENT ACTIVITY – Suffixes** |

4th Grade　　　　　　　　　　Have the students select nine words to add a suffix to and write a meaningful sentence for each new word that reveals the correct understanding of the word with the suffix . Each sentence must begin with a capital letter and have an end mark. Underline the suffixed words in each sentence.

Challenge: Have the students select four words and use the word with and without the suffix in the same sentence.

Assessment Option:　　　Have each student select their best work to share with the class.

5th Grade　　　　　　　　　　Have the students select ten or more words to add a suffix to and write a meaningful sentence for each new word that reveals the correct understanding of the word with the suffix. Each sentence must begin with a capital letter and have an end mark. Underline the suffixed words in each sentence.

Challenge: Have the students select five words and use the words with and without the suffix in the same sentence.

Assessment Option:　　　Have each student select their best work to share with the class.

Reflection: Suffixes

It is important for students to understand why they are learning this process and how they can apply it to their daily lives. Explain that being able to communicate, both verbally and written, is important because it is how people relate to one another. Further explain that being able to manipulate words by simply adding a suffix will increase their vocabulary.

In this reflection, ask the students these questions in an open discussion:

1. What did they learn?
2. How can they use what they learned in their daily activity?
3. Can they teach what they have learned to someone else?
4. What did they like most about the activity?
5. What did they like least about the activity?

Suffix List

1st Grade

1	-ed	Past.
2	-er/-or	Agent, or one who. Indicates person or thing performing the action of.
3	-en	Made of, or to make.
4	-est	Highest comparison.
5	-ful/-full	Full of or tending to.
6	-ing	Action of.
7	-less	Without.
8	-s	Plural or more than one.

2nd Grade

9	-ed	Past.
10	-er -or	Agent, or one who. Indicates person or thing performing the action of.
11	-en	Made of, or to make.
12	-est	Highest comparison.
13	-ful/-full	Full of or tending to.
14	-ing	Action of.
15	-less	Without.
16	-s	Plural or more than one.
17	-ly	Like. Somewhat.
18	-ment	Act of doing, state or quality of.
19	-ness	State of.
20	-ous	Full of.
21	-tion	Action or state of being.
22	-y	Like, or full of action.

Suffix List

3rd Grade

23	-able/-ible	Capable of or worthy of.
24	-age	Process.
25	-ant	Quality of or one who.
26	-dom	State or condition of.
27	-ent	Having the quality of.
28	-ery	A place to practice, or the condition of.
29	-ion	Action or process.
30	-ish	Like.
31	-ist	One who does.
32	-ize	To make.

4th Grade

33	-ance/ence	Act or fact of doing, or the state of.
34	-hood	State of being.
35	-ible/-ile/-il	Capable of being.
36	-ier/-ior	One who.
37	-ship	Quality of, or state of or rank.
38	-some	Like.
39	-ty	Quality or state of.
40	-ward	Directional.

Suffix List

5th Grade

41	-ify	To make.
42	-ism	Fact of being.
42	-ive	Having the nature of.
43	-let	Small.
44	-ology	Study of.
45	-scope	Instrument for seeing or outlook.

Grammar, Usage, and Mechanics
Lesson Title: Parts of Speech

There are many classifications to identify the various parts of speech. However, for this book we will stick to the basics and most frequently used. The parts of speech activities will focus on the use, knowledge and identification of the following nine parts of speech:

1. **Verb** - A word used to indicate an action.
2. **Noun** - A word used to identify a person, place, or thing.
3. **Proper Noun** - The particular name of someone, someplace, or something.
4. **Pronoun** - A word that replaces a noun or a noun phrase.
5. **Adjective** - A word that describes a noun or a pronoun.
6. **Adverb** - A word that modifies a verb.
7. **Preposition** - A word used to show relationship, time, place, or order of a noun.
8. **Conjunction** - A word used to combine two parts, thoughts, or ideas.
9. **Interjection** - A word used to express strong emotion, or sound.

Time Frame: **30 - 60 Minutes (per activity)**
                                        5 - 10   Activity introduction and explanation.
                                        5 - 10   Write the sentence on the board.
                                        5 - 10   Whole group discussion.
                                        5 - 10   Independent student activity.
                                        5 - 10   Activity assessment.
                                        5 - 10   Reflection on the activity.

Lesson Objective: To increase student knowledge of the basic parts of speech.

Materials & Resources: Paper, pencil, and crayons.

Instruction Procedure: Explain the lesson and lesson objective to the students.

Whole Group Activity:

Select one of the sample sentences from the following pages (or make up one of your own). Write the sentence on the board and read the sentence aloud for the students. Next, select a part of speech to focus on and give the definition of the part of speech. Ask the students to help identify that particular part of speech in the sentence listed on the board. Repeat this process with each part of speech until all parts of speech have been covered and the students feel comfortable with identifying all parts of speech.

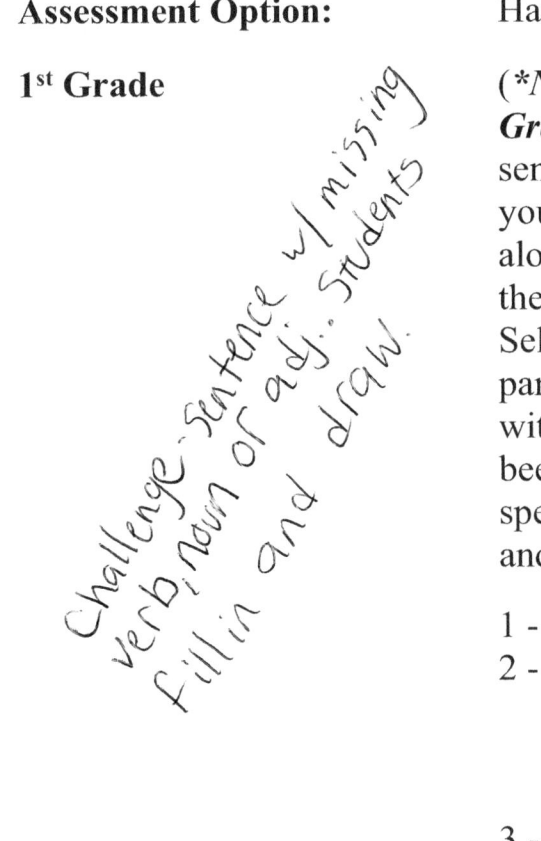

GRADE LEVELS	**INDEPENDENT ACTIVITY – Parts of Speech**
Kindergarten	(*Note: Focus on parts of speech 1 through 3 for Kindergarten.)

Select a sentence from the list of sample sentences on the following pages (or make up one of your own) and write it on the board. Read the sentence aloud. Select a part of speech to focus on and review the definition of that part of speech for the students. Select a few students to tell you the definition of the part of speech in their own words. Repeat this process with the other parts of speech until all three parts have been covered. Have the students complete the following activities:

1 - Copy the sentence in their best writing.
2 - Have the students circle the verb, draw a square around the noun, and underline the adjective.
3 - Draw a picture to go along with the sentence that emphasizes one or all three of the parts of speech.

Assessment Option: Have the students share their best work with the class.

1st Grade (*Note: Focus on parts of speech 1 through 6 for 1st Grade.) Select two sentences from the list of sample sentences on the following pages (or make up two of your own). Write them on the board and read them aloud. Select a part of speech to focus on and review the definition of that part of speech for the students. Select a few students to tell you the definition of the part of speech in their own words. Repeat this process with the other parts of speech until all five parts have been covered. Have the students identify the parts of speech in the second sentence without any assistance and complete the following activities:

1 - Copy the sentence in their best writing.
2 - Using different color crayons or pencils, have the students underline the verbs in blue, the nouns in green, the adjectives in red, the adverbs in yellow, and the prepositions in brown.
3 - Draw a picture to go along with the sentence that emphasizes one or all five of the parts of speech.

[Handwritten note in margin: Challenge - sentence w/ missing verb, noun, or adj. Students fill in and draw.]

GRADE LEVELS	INDEPENDENT ACTIVITY – Parts of Speech
Assessment Option:	Have the students share their best work with the class.
2nd Grade	(***Note: Focus on parts of speech 1 through 6 for 2nd Grade.***) Select three sentences from the list of sample sentences on the following pages (or make up three of your own) and write them on the board. Read the sentences aloud. Select a part of speech to focus on and review the definition of that part of speech for the students. Select a few students to tell you the definition of the part of speech in their own words. Repeat this process with the other parts of speech until all parts have been covered. Have the students identify the parts of speech in the second and third sentence without any assistance and complete the following activities for each sentence:

1 - Copy the sentence in their best writing.
2 - Using different color crayons or pencils, underline the verbs in blue, the nouns in green, the adjectives in red, the adverbs in yellow, and the prepositions in brown.
3 - Draw a picture to go along with the sentence that emphasizes one or all parts of speech.

Assessment Option:	Have the students share their best work with the class.
3rd Grade	(***Note: Focus on parts of speech 1 through 8 for 3rd Grade.***) Select three sentences from the list of sample sentences on the following pages (or make up three of your own) and write them on the board. Read the sentences aloud. Select a part of speech to focus on and review the definition of that part of speech for the students. Select a few students to tell you the definition of the part of speech in their own words. Repeat this process with the other parts of speech until all parts have been covered. Have the students identify the parts of speech in the second and third sentence without any assistance, and complete the following activities for each sentence:

GRADE LEVELS	INDEPENDENT ACTIVITY – Parts of Speech
	1 - Copy the sentences in their best writing. 2 - Using different color crayons or pencils, underline the verbs in blue, the nouns in green, the adjectives in red, the adverbs in yellow, and the prepositions in brown. 3 - Draw a picture to go along with the sentence that emphasizes one or all parts of speech. 4 - Have the students write an alternate word for each part of speech in their third sentence.
Assessment Option:	Have the students share their best work with the class.
4th Grade	(***Note: Focus on all parts of speech.***) Select three sentences from the list of sample sentences on the following pages (or make up three of your own) and write them on the board as you read the sentences aloud. Select a part of speech to focus on and review the definition of that part of speech for the students. Select a few students to tell you the definition of the part of speech in their own words. Repeat this process with the other parts of speech until all parts have been covered. Have the students identify the parts of speech in the second and third sentence without any assistance, and complete the following activities for each sentence: 1 - Copy the sentences in their best writing. 2 - Using different color crayons or pencils, underline the verbs in blue, the nouns in green, the adjectives in red, the adverbs in yellow, and the prepositions in brown. 3 - Draw a picture to go along with the sentence that emphasizes one or all parts of speech. 4 - Have the students write an alternate word for each part of speech in their third sentence.
Assessment Option:	Have the students share their best work with the class.

GRADE LEVELS	**INDEPENDENT ACTIVITY – Parts of Speech**
5th Grade	(*Note: Focus on all parts of speech.*) Select four sentences from the list of sample sentences on the following pages (or make up four of your own) and write them on the board as you read the sentences aloud. Select a part of speech to focus on and review the definition of that part of
	speech for the students. Select a few students to tell you the definition of the part of speech in their own words. Repeat this process with the other parts of speech until all parts have been covered. Have the students identify the parts of speech in their additional sentences without any assistance, and complete the following activities for each sentence:

1 - Copy the sentences in their best writing.
2 - Using different color crayons or pencils, underline the verbs in blue, the nouns in green and the adjectives in red, the adverbs in yellow, and the prepositions in brown.
3 - Draw a picture to go along with the sentence that emphasizes one or all parts of speech.
4 - Have the students write an alternate word for each part of speech in their third sentence.

Assessment Option: Have the students share their best work with the class.

Reflection: Parts of Speech

It is important for students to understand why they are learning this process and how they can apply it to their daily lives. Explain that knowing the parts of speech is important in all communication especially writing.

In this reflection, ask the students these questions in an open discussion:

1. What did they learn?
2. How can they use what they learned in their daily activity?
3. Can they teach what they have learned to someone else?
4. What did they like most about the activity?
5. What did they like least about the activity?

Parts of Speech Sample Sentences
Kindergarten

Key: v = verb, n = noun

1	I quickly <u>ran</u> across the <u>playground</u>. *v* *n*
2	I <u>watched</u> the big brown <u>dog</u> <u>move</u> through the <u>park</u> very slowly. *v* *n* *v* *n*
3	She <u>runs</u> really fast in <u>her</u> new <u>shoes</u>. *v* *p* *n*
4	My <u>friend</u> and I are <u>going</u> to the <u>store</u> today. n v n
5	He <u>kicked</u> the <u>ball</u> really far. v n
6	I <u>spilled</u> the <u>milk</u> on the <u>floor</u>. v n n
7	We <u>played</u> hide and seek in the <u>forest</u> behind the <u>trees</u>. v n n
8	My <u>mom</u> <u>drove</u> my <u>friend</u> and me to <u>school</u> <u>today</u>. n v n n n
9	She <u>turned</u> <u>five</u> on her <u>birthday</u> <u>yesterday</u>. v n n n
10	They all <u>wanted</u> to <u>play</u> <u>basketball</u> in the <u>park</u>. v v n n

Parts of Speech Sample Sentences
1st & 2nd Grade

Key: v = verb, n = noun, pn = proper noun, p = pronoun, adv = adverb, adj = adjective, * = has several functions and varies depending on how it is used.

1	My <u>friend</u> <u>Charles</u> and <u>I</u> <u>rapidly</u> <u>ran</u> to the <u>ice cream</u> <u>truck</u> for a <u>snack</u>. n pn p adv v n n n
2	The <u>thunderstorm</u> <u>rattled</u> the <u>windows</u> and <u>scared</u> <u>all</u> the <u>children</u>. n v n adj * n
3	The <u>floor</u> <u>creaked</u> as <u>we</u> <u>slowly</u> <u>walked</u> across the <u>room</u>. n v p adv v n
4	<u>She</u> <u>snores</u> so <u>loud</u> that <u>I</u> have a <u>hard</u> <u>time</u> <u>trying</u> to <u>sleep</u>. p v adj p adj n v v
5	The <u>frisky</u> <u>puppy</u> likes to <u>play</u> <u>chase</u> with <u>me</u> and <u>my</u> <u>friend</u>. adj n v v/n p adj n
6	The <u>cranky</u> <u>old</u> <u>man</u> <u>angrily</u> <u>yelled</u> at <u>me</u> to "<u>stay</u> out of <u>his</u> <u>yard</u>". adj adj n adv v p v p n
7	<u>My</u> <u>teacher</u> <u>thinks</u> that <u>I</u> am <u>doing</u> a <u>great</u> <u>job</u> on <u>my</u> <u>project</u>. p n v p v adj n p n
8	<u>My</u> <u>goldfish</u> <u>seems</u> <u>perfectly</u> <u>happy</u> to <u>swim</u> in <u>his</u> <u>tank</u> all <u>day</u> and <u>night</u>. p n v adv adj v p n n n
9	<u>I</u> <u>fell</u> down during <u>track</u> <u>practice</u> and <u>hurt</u> <u>my</u> <u>leg</u>. p v n v v p n
10	The whole <u>class</u> <u>began</u> <u>dancing</u> when the <u>teacher</u> <u>played</u> the <u>music</u> on the <u>radio</u>. n v v n v n n

Parts of Speech Sample Sentences
3rd, 4th, & 5th Grade

Key: a = article, v = verb, n = noun, pn = proper noun, p = pronoun, adj = adjective, adv = adverb, pp = preposition, c = conjunction, I = interjection, * = multiple uses

1	The pigs oinked and snorted as they rolled in the mud. a n I c v c n v pp a n
2	"Eek" said the monkey as he played in the tree and swung upside-down. I v a n c p v pp a n c v adj
3	The lightning crackled and the thunder roared during the storm. a n I c a n I pp a n
4	The wind blew through the trees and made a spooky crackling sound. a n v pp a n c v a adj adj n
5	The frosty milk shake was so cool and good that I slurped it down fast. a adj n n v c adj c adj * p v p pp adj
6	Hurrah! I studied hard and passed the class with the best grade possible. I p v adj c v a n c a adj n adj
7	Oops! Harvey did not mean to drop the glass and break it. I pn v adv v * v a n c v p
8	Oh no, we forgot to turn the water off and now the bathroom is flooded. I p v * v a n pp c adv a n * adj
9	I was jogging and slammed right into a tree. Ouch! p v v c v * pp a n I
10	Wow! that dog can jump really high and catch the stick. I * n v v adj adj c v a n

99

Grammar, Usage, and Mechanics
Lesson Title: <u>Sentence Construction</u>

A sentence generally contains a subject and a predicate. The subject is who or what the sentence is about and the predicate gives information about the subject. This is the basic way in which we first learn to speak and therefore the first steps in writing. Students must first learn to write simple basic sentences and grow from there. Once students learn to construct simple sentences, the next step is to combine one or more sentences to construct a compound sentence. This activity focuses on the construction of both the simple and compound sentences.

Time Frame: **40 - 70 Minutes (per activity)**
    5 - 10   Activity introduction and explanation.
    5 - 10   Write the topic choices on the board.
    10 - 15 Whole group discussion.
    10 - 15 Independent student activity.
    5 - 10   Activity assessment.
    5 - 10   Reflection on the activity.

Lesson Objectives: To increase student knowledge and allow practice of sentences construction.

Materials & Resources: Paper, pencil, and crayons.

Instruction Procedure: Explain the lesson and lesson objective to the students.

Whole Group Activity:

    Make a T-Chart on the board to list and separate the information for this activity. Select a few words from both the subject and the predicate list on the following pages (or make up some of your own) and list them on the board next to the T-Chart (do not list the words on the chart at this time). Beginning with the first of the words you have selected to chart, say the word aloud and ask the students to tell you which side of the T-Chart it should be listed on and list the words on the T-Chart. Once you have finished listing all of the selected words on the T-Chart with the student's input, verify that the words are listed correctly (all of the subjects on one side and all of the predicates on the other side). Select a few words from the chart and ask the students why a word listed on the chart is either a subject or a predicate. (Possible answer: subjects are usually nouns, and predicates are usually verbs.)

    Create a sentence using a subject and a predicate listed on the chart. Next, allow a few students to make up their own sentence using a subject and predicate from the board. After the students have had a few minutes to practice, move on to the level-appropriate independent activities on the following pages.

GRADE LEVELS	INDEPENDENT ACTIVITY – Sentence Construction
Kindergarten	List three subjects and three predicates on the board. Write one sample sentence underlining the subject and the predicate as a model for the students. Say each subject and predicate aloud and have the students repeat them after you. Do the same with the sample sentence. Next, point to each focus word and have the students say the words aloud (this will insure that the students know what the words are and how to complete the independent activities on their own). Now, have the students complete the following activities: 1 - Copy the sample sentence in their best writing. 2 - Create their own sentences using one subject and one predicate for each. 3 - Create one sentence for each set. Make sure to underline the subject and predicate in each sentence. Begin each sentence with a capital letter and use the end mark. 4 - Draw a corresponding picture to go along with each sentence.
Assessment Option:	Have the students share their best work with the class.
1st Grade	List four subjects and three predicates on the board. Write one sample sentence underlining the subject and the predicate as a model for the students. Say each subject and predicate aloud and have the students repeat them after you. Do the same with the sample sentence. Next, point to each focus word and have the students say the words aloud (this will insure that the students know what the words are and how to complete the independent activities on their own). Now, have the students complete the following activities: 1 - Copy the sample sentence in their best writing. 2 - Create their own sentences using one subject and one predicate for each.

GRADE LEVELS	INDEPENDENT ACTIVITY – Sentence Construction
	3 - Create one sentence for each set. Make sure to underline the subject and predicate in each sentence. Begin each sentence with a capital letter and use the end mark. 4 - Draw a corresponding picture to go along with each sentence.
Assessment Option:	Have the students share their best work with the class.
2nd Grade	List five subjects and three predicates on the board. Write one sample sentence underlining the subject and the predicate as a model for the students. Say each subject and predicate aloud and have the students repeat them after you. Next, point to each focus word and have the students say the words aloud (this will insure that the students know what the words are and how to complete the independent activities on their own). Now, have the students complete the following activities: 1 - Copy the sample sentence in their best writing. 2 - Create their own sentences using one subject and one predicate for each. 3 - Create one sentence for each set. Make sure to underline the subject and predicate in each sentence. Begin each sentence with a capital letter and use the end mark. 4 - Draw a corresponding picture to go along with each sentence.
Assessment Option:	Have the students share their best work with the class.
3rd Grade	List seven subjects and three predicates on the board. Write one sample sentence underlining the subject and the predicate as a model for the students. Say each subject and predicate aloud and have the students repeat them after you. Next, point to each focus word and have the students say the words aloud (this will insure that

GRADE LEVELS	INDEPENDENT ACTIVITY – Sentence Construction
	the students know what the words are and how to complete the independent activities on their own). Now, have the students complete the following activities:

1 - Copy the sample sentence in their best writing.
2 - Create their own sentences using one subject and one predicate for each.
3 - Create one sentence for each set. Make sure to underline the subject and predicate in each sentence. Begin each sentence with a capital letter and use the end mark.
4 - Draw a corresponding picture for each sentence. |
| **Assessment Option:** | Have the students share their best work with the class. |
| **4th Grade** | List nine subjects and three predicates on the board. Write one sample sentence underlining the subject and the predicate as a model for the students. Say each subject and predicate aloud and have the students repeat them after you. Next, point to each focus word and have the students say the words aloud (this will insure that the students know what the words are and how to complete the independent activities on their own). Now, have the students complete the following activities:

1 - Copy the sample sentence in their best writing.
2 - Create their own sentences using one subject and one predicate for each.
3 - Create one sentence for each set. Make sure to underline the subject and predicate in each sentence. Begin each sentence with a capital letter and use the end mark.
4 - Draw a corresponding picture to go along with each sentence. |

GRADE LEVELS	**INDEPENDENT ACTIVITY – Sentence Construction**
Assessment Option:	Have the students share their best work with the class.
5th Grade	List ten or more subjects and three predicates on the board. Write one sample sentence underlining the subject and the predicate as a model for the students. Say each subject and predicate aloud and have the students repeat them after you. Next, point to each focus word and have the students say the words aloud (this will insure that the students know what the words are and how to complete the independent activities on their own). Now, have the students complete the following activities: 1 - Copy the sample sentence in their best writing. 2 - Create their own sentences using one subject and one predicate for each. 3 - Create one sentence for each set. Make sure to underline the subject and predicate in each sentence. Begin each sentence with a capital letter and use the end mark. 4 - Draw a corresponding picture for each sentence.
Construction	
Assessment Option:	Have the students share their best work with the class.

Reflection: Sentence Construction

It is important for students to understand why they are learning this process and how they can apply it to their daily lives. Explain that knowing the parts of a sentence and how to use them is important for both verbal and written communications.

In this reflection, ask the students these questions in an open discussion:

1. What did they learn?
2. How can they use what they learned in their daily activity?
3. Can they teach what they have learned to someone else?
4. What did they like most about the activity?
5. What did they like least about the activity?

Sentence Construction
Kindergarten

Subject	Predicate
boy	is nine years old
girl	has long hair
teacher	is very nice
bus	carries people
car	is red
water	is warm
house	is green
dog	runs fast
cat	climbs trees
toys	are fun

1st Grade

Subject	Predicate
children	play nicely together
coat	keeps you warm
rain	don't get wet
snow	icy frost
pool	fun to play in
chair	soft to the touch
light	makes everything bright
telephone	rings really loud
food	tastes good
traffic	is very noisy

Sentence Construction
2nd Grade

Subject	Predicate
ball	bounce
sand	white
monkey	swings
dog	barks
rain	pours
I	read
you	hear
we	listen
they	play
she	cries

3rd Grade

Subject	Predicate
someone	called
everyone	danced
children	sang
cars	raced
money	spent
pictures	developed
horse	raced
homework	completed
bell	rang
food	prepared

Sentence Construction
4th Grade

Subject	Predicate
friends	party
pool	nice
mountains	cold
desert	hot
waves	choppy
ocean	deep
music	loud
whisper	soft
book	read
telephone	rang

5th Grade

Subject	Predicate
family	games
vacation	fun
rocket	soar
race	win
turtle	slow
movie	great
bicycle	race
snowman	round
fire	smoky
cat	fuzzy

Grammar, Usage, and Mechanics
Lesson Title: <u>Types of Sentences</u>

There are four basic types of sentences that will be covered in this activity.
1. **Declarative** - makes a statement and ends with a period. (**Example:** I like to play baseball.)
2. **Imperative** - Makes a request or gives an order and ends with a period or exclamation mark. (**Example:** Close the door behind yourself.)
3. **Interrogative** - Asks a question and ends with a questions mark. (**Example:** May I go to the store with you?)
4. **Exclamatory** - Shows excitement or strong feeling and ends with an exclamation mark. (**Example:** I'm having a wonderful time!)

Time Frame:	**30 - 60 Minutes (per activity)**
	5 - 10 Activity introduction and explanation.
	5 - 10 Write the sentences and end marks on the board.
	5 - 10 Whole group discussion.
	5 - 10 Independent student activity.
	5 - 10 Activity assessment.
	5 - 10 Reflection on the activity.
Lesson Objective:	To increase student knowledge of the different types of sentences.
Materials & Resources:	Paper, pencil, and crayons.
Instruction Procedure:	Explain the lesson and lesson objective to the students.

Whole Group Activity:

Write one of each type of sentence on the board using the end marks (select from sentences on the following pages or make up your own). Read each sentence aloud as you write them on the board and have the students repeat the sentences after you. Next, explain each type of sentence and tell the students what makes it that type of sentence. Now, without any assistance from you, have the students read each remaining sentence, identify the type of sentence, and tell you what makes it that type of sentence. After the students have had a few minutes to practice, move on to the level-appropriate independent activities on the following pages.

GRADE LEVELS	INDEPENDENT ACTIVITY – Types of Sentences
Kindergarten	Select four sentences to use in this activity (use the sentences on the following pages or make up sentences of your own). Write the sentences on the board without the end marks. Have the students complete the following activities: 1 - Copy the sentences in their best writing and add appropriate end marks. 2 - Identify the type of each sentence. (At this grade level the students may not be able to identify the sentence using the proper name; therefore, have them describe the kind of sentence it is by its characteristics.) Possible answers are: the sentence gives direction, gives an order, asks a question, shows strong feeling, or relates a fact. 3 - Draw one picture for each sentence.
Assessment Option:	Have the students share their best work with the class.
1st Grade	Select five new sentences to use in this activity (select from sentences on the following pages or make up sentences of your own). Write the sentences on the board without the end marks. Have the students complete the following activities: 1 - Copy the sentences in their best writing and add appropriate end marks. 2 - Identify the type of each sentence. (At this grade level the students may not be able to identify the sentence using the proper name; therefore, have them describe the kind of sentence it is by its characteristics.) Possible answers are: the sentence gives direction, gives an order, asks a question, shows strong feeling, or relates a fact. 3 - Draw one picture for each sentence.
Assessment Option:	Have the students share their best work with the class.

GRADE LEVELS	INDEPENDENT ACTIVITY – Types of Sentences
2nd Grade	Select six sentences to use in this activity (use the sentences on the following pages or make up sentences of your own). Write the sentences on the board without the end marks. Have the students complete the following activities: 1 - Copy the sentences in their best writing and add the appropriate end marks. 2 - Identify the type of each sentence. 3 - Draw one picture for each sentence.
Assessment Option:	Have the students share their best work with the class.
3rd Grade	Select seven sentences to use in this activity (use the sentences on the following pages or make up sentences of your own). Write the sentences on the board without the end marks. Have the students complete the following activities: 1 - Copy the sentences in their best writing and add the appropriate end marks. 2 - Identify the type of each sentence. 3 - Write one additional sentence on their own and identify the sentence type. The students may elect to draw a picture to go along with this sentence.
Assessment Option:	Have the students share their best work with the class.
4th Grade	Select eight sentences to use in this activity (use the sentences on the following pages or make up sentences of your own). Write the sentences on the board without the end marks. Have the students complete the following activities: 1 - Copy the sentences in their best writing and add the appropriate end marks. 2 - Identify the type of each sentence. 3 - Write two additional sentences on their own and identify the sentence type.
Assessment Option:	Have the students share their best work with the class.

GRADE LEVELS	**INDEPENDENT ACTIVITY – Types of Sentences**
5th Grade	Select nine sentences to use in this activity (use the sentences on the following pages or make up sentences of your own). Write the sentences on the board without the end marks. Have the students complete the following activities: 1 - Copy the sentences in their best writing and add the appropriate end marks. 2 - Identify the type of each sentence. 3 - Write three additional sentences on their own and identify the sentence type.
Assessment Option:	Have the students share their best work with the class.

Reflection: Types of Sentences

It is important for students to understand why they are learning this process and how they can apply it to their daily lives. Explain that knowing sentence types is an important part of communication.

In this reflection, ask the students these questions in an open discussion:

1. What did they learn?
2. How can they use what they learned in their daily activity?
3. Can they teach what they have learned to someone else?
4. What did they like most about the activity?
5. What did they like least about the activity?

Types of Sentences
Kindergarten

The ball is big and round.	**declarative**
Please close the door.	**imperative**
Do you like ice cream?	**interrogative**
Wow! That was fun.	**exclamatory**
The cat can jump.	**declarative**
Take the dog outside.	**imperative**
How old are you?	**interrogative**
Oops! I fell down.	**exclamatory**
The cat is white.	**declarative**
Please sit down.	**imperative**

1st Grade

There are more boys than girls in my class.	**declarative**
Raise your hand before speaking.	**imperative**
Do you have your homework today?	**interrogative**
Hey! Let's play another game of ball.	**exclamatory**
Joseph is a good friend.	**declarative**
Clean up behind yourself when you finish.	**imperative**
Have you finished your dinner yet?	**interrogative**
Stop! The light is red.	**exclamatory**
The movie will be over soon.	**declarative**
Put on your coat before going outside.	**imperative**

Types of Sentences
2nd Grade

The full moon scares me.	**declarative**
Make sure to turn off all of the lights when you leave.	**imperative**
Are you staying after school today?	**interrogative**
Hurray! We finally won a game.	**exclamatory**
The printing machines make a lot of noise.	**declarative**
Turn the music up louder.	**imperative**
Will you go to the park with me this weekend?	**interrogative**
Ouch! The bee sting really hurts.	**exclamatory**
Today is a nice sunny day, but it isn't too hot.	**declarative**
Make sure you take the trash out tonight.	**imperative**

3rd Grade

The store closes before it gets dark.	**declarative**
Stay out of the deep end of the swimming pool.	**imperative**
Do you want to play a game?	**interrogative**
Oh! I almost forgot to tell you something.	**exclamatory**
My new bicycle is the nicest one of all.	**declarative**
Do not feed the animals.	**imperative**
Can we be friends?	**interrogative**
Wow! Your birthday party is really fun.	**exclamatory**
The computer games are neat.	**declarative**
Keep off of the grass.	**imperative**

Types of Sentences
4th Grade

My mom picks me up from school everyday.	**declarative**
Hold my hand when we cross the street.	**imperative**
Do you like to eat pizza?	**interrogative**
Stop! My foot is stuck.	**exclamatory**
I like the rain because it cleans the air.	**declarative**
Do not talk to strangers.	**imperative**
What size shoe do you wear?	**interrogative**
Wait for me! I don't want to stay here alone.	**exclamatory**
I like dogs because they are such friendly animals.	**declarative**
Only cross the street when the light is green.	**imperative**

5th Grade

I go to church every Sunday.	**declarative**
Please speak with an inside voice when inside of the classroom.	**imperative**
How many pets do you have?	**interrogative**
Eek! I saw a rat.	**exclamatory**
My father is a police officer.	**declarative**
Look both ways before crossing the street.	**imperative**
When is the last day of school?	**interrogative**
Hurray! Today is the last day of school.	**exclamatory**
When I grow up, I want to be a judge.	**declarative**
Cover your mouth when you cough.	**imperative**

Grammar, Usage, and Mechanics
Lesson Title: <u>Paragraph Construction</u>

The basic paragraph generally contains a topic sentence and supporting details. The topic sentence is usually stated first, although it is not required. For general practice and beginning learners, placing the topic sentence first is the best method. For the previously stated reason, this lesson will focus on placing the topic sentence first and supporting details later.
(For more writing topics, prompts, story starters and graphic organizers, see the writing section.)

Time Frame:	**55-100 Minutes (per activity)**
	5 - 10 Activity introduction and explanation.
	10 - 20 Draw the graphic organizer (use the web),
write the paragraph on the	paragraph components and sample
	board.
	15 - 20 Whole group discussion.
	10 - 20 Independent student activity.
	10 - 20 Activity assessment.
	5 - 10 Reflection on the activity.
Lesson Objectives:	To increase student knowledge of the basic parts and construction of a paragraph.
Materials & Resources:	Paper and pencil.
Instruction Procedure:	Explain the lesson and lesson objectives to the students.

Whole Group Activity:

Select a graphic organizer to work with. Draw it on the board and explain that it is used to organize your thoughts before you begin writing. Use the sample web organizer on the following pages. Draw the organizer and select a topic from the list on the following pages (or make up your own topic). Ask the students for information that can be used as supporting details about the topic and fill in the web organizer using their suggestions. (The sample organizers and topics are listed for your assistance in the event the students have trouble coming up with information or stray from the focus.) Once the web organizer is complete, write a complete sentence for each item beginning with the topic (in the center of the web). Add a conclusion sentence and read the whole paragraph aloud. Make any changes necessary until the paragraph is complete, flows in thought, and is error free; then, re-read the paragraph. This is a great time to point out the steps in the writing process. Explain, identify, and label each step that you went through to reach the final product. (See the example on the following pages.) **Do not erase the complete web organizer, information or paragraph - allow it to remain**

Lesson Title: Paragraph Construction

throughout the balance of the activities as an example. Once this process is complete, the students should be ready to practice on their own using the level-appropriate independent activities on the following pages.

GRADE LEVELS	**INDEPENDENT ACTIVITY – Paragraph Construction**
1st Grade	Draw an additional blank web organizer on the board, and a topic to write about. As a group, generate supporting details, a topic sentence, and a conclusion sentence. Have the students complete the following activities: *(You may want to list the following on the board for the students to follow.)* 1 - Create a sentence for each supporting detail. 2 - Work in pairs to proofread and edit each others work. 3 - Prepare a final, clean, publishable copy of the paragraph. 4 - Label the parts of the writing process.
Assessment Option:	Have the students share their best work with the class.
2nd Grade	Draw a blank web organizer on the board. Insert a topic to write about. As a group, generate supporting details and a topic sentence. Have the students complete the following activities: *(You may want to list the following on the board for the students to follow.)* 1 - Create a sentence for each supporting detail. 2 - Create a sentence for the conclusion of the paragraph. 3 - Work in pairs to proofread and edit each others work. 4 - Prepare a final, clean, publishable copy of the paragraph. 5 - Label the parts of the writing process.
Assessment Option:	Have the students share their best work with the class.
3rd Grade	Draw a blank web organizer on the board, and a topic to write about. As a group, generate supporting details to complete the web. Have the students complete the following activities:

GRADE LEVELS	INDEPENDENT ACTIVITY – Paragraph Construction
	(You may want to list the following on the board for the students to follow.) 1 - Create a topic sentence for the paragraph. 2 - Create a sentence for each supporting detail. 3 - Create a sentence for the conclusion of the paragraph. 4 - Work in pairs to proofread and edit each others work.
Construction	
	5 - Prepare a final, clean, publishable copy of the paragraph. 6 - Label the parts of the writing process.
Assessment Option:	Have the students share their best work with the class.
4th Grade	Draw a blank web organizer on the board and list a few topic choices using the list on the following pages (or you may make up your own). Have the students select a topic from the list on the board and complete the following activities:
	(You may want to list the following on the board for the students to follow.) 1 - Complete the web organizer with the necessary information. 2 - Create a topic sentence for the paragraph. 3 - Create a compound sentence for each supporting detail. 4 - Create a sentence for the conclusion of the paragraph. 5 - Work in pairs to proofread and edit each others work. 6 - Prepare a final, clean, publishable copy of the paragraph. 7 - Label the parts of the writing process.
Assessment Option:	Have the students share their best work with the class.

GRADE LEVELS	INDEPENDENT ACTIVITY – Paragraph Construction
5th Grade	Draw a blank web organizer on the board and list a few topic choices using the list on the following pages (or you may make up your own). Have the students select a topic from the list on the board and complete the following activities:

(You may want to list the following on the board for the students to follow.)

1 - Complete the web organizer with the necessary information.
2 - Create a topic sentence for the paragraph.
3 - Create a compound sentence for each supporting detail.
4 - Create a sentence for the conclusion of the paragraph.
5 - Work in pairs to proofread and edit each others work.
6 - Prepare a final, clean, publishable copy of the paragraph.
7 - Label the parts of the writing process.

Assessment Option: Have the students share their best work with the class.

Reflection: Paragraph Construction

It is important for students to understand why they are learning this process and how they can apply it to their daily lives. Explain that knowing how to construct a paragraph is an essential part of writing.

In this reflection, ask the students these questions in an open discussion:

1. What did they learn?
2. How can they use what they learned in their daily activity?
3. Can they teach what they have learned to someone else?
4. What did they like most about the activity?
5. What did they like least about the activity?

Paragraph Construction
Web Organizer
All Grades
Compare and Contrast

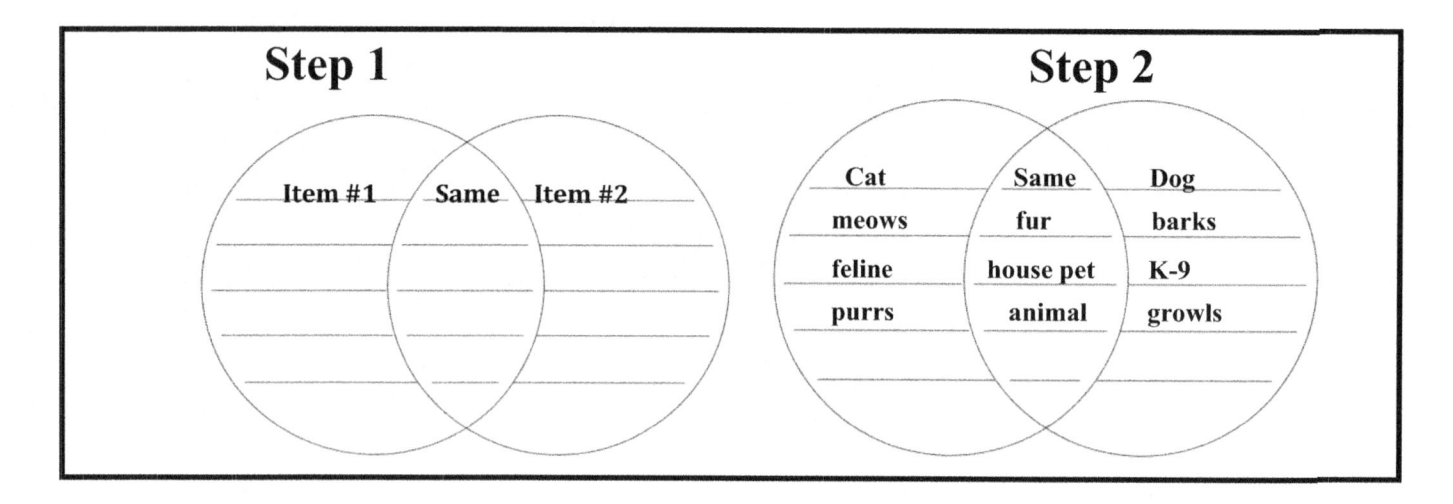

Step 1

Item #1 — Same — Item #2

Step 2

Cat: meows, feline, purrs
Same: fur, house pet, animal
Dog: barks, K-9, growls

Paragraph Topics

1. cats and dogs	11. country and city
2. boys and girls	12. moon and sun
3. children and adults	13. still picture and motion picture
4. summer and winter	14. fruit juice and water
5. spring and fall	15. junk food and vegetables
6. rain and snow	16. any two planets
7. lake and ocean	17. two movies
8. river and stream	18. two tv shows
9. mountain and valley	19. two people
10. house and apartment	20. two cars

For more writing topics, prompt, story starters and graphic organizers, see the writing sections of this book.

Grammar, Usage, and Mechanics
Lesson Title: <u>Abbreviations</u>

An abbreviation, simply put, is a shortened version of a word or words. There are four types of abbreviations: Shortened words, contractions, idealisms, and acronyms. For the activities in this book we will focus on shortened words, and contractions. **Shortened words** generally contain the first few letters of the word with a period (cent. = century). Some shortened words are altered to make a new word (bicycle = bike). **Contractions** are abbreviated words which contains the first letter of the word and one or two others from the word using an apostrophe to represent all omitted letters (cannot = can't).

Although most abbreviations are standard, there is no real standard formula for abbreviations: therefore, they must be memorized.

Time Frame: **30 - 60 Minutes (per activity)**
- 5 - 10   Activity introduction and explanation.
- 5 - 10   Write the words and abbreviations on the board.
- 5 - 10   Whole group discussion.
- 5 - 10   Independent student activity.
- 5 - 10   Activity assessment.
- 5 - 10   Reflection on the activity.

Lesson Objective: To increase student knowledge of abbreviation.

Materials & Resources: Paper, pencil, and crayons.

Instruction Procedure: Explain the lesson and lesson objective to the students.

Whole Group Activity:

Select a set of abbreviations to work with (according to the grade levels listed on the following pages). Write each complete word and its abbreviation on the board. Go over each word and abbreviation with the students, pointing out which letters from the actual word were used to make up the abbreviation. Erase the complete words, leaving only the abbreviations on the board for the independent level-appropriate activities on the following pages.

GRADE LEVELS	INDEPENDENT ACTIVITY - Abbreviations
1st Grade	Have the students complete the following activities: 1 - Circle the letters in the whole word that make up the abbreviation. 2 - Match the whole words with the correct abbreviations from the board on their own paper. 3 - Select at least two word from the list on the board. Write the word, the abbreviation, and draw a picture to go along with it.
Assessment Option:	Have the students share their best work with the class.
2nd Grade	Have the students complete the following activities: 1 - Circle the letters in the whole word that make up the abbreviation. 2 - Match the whole words with the correct abbreviations from the board on their own paper. 3 - Select at least three words from the list on the board. Write the word, the abbreviation, and draw a picture to go along with it.
Assessment Option:	Have the students share their best work with the class.
3rd Grade	Have the students complete the following activities: 1 - Match the whole words with the correct abbreviations from the board on their own paper. 2 - Select at least three words from the list on the board. Write the word, the abbreviation, and draw a picture to go along with it. 3 - Play a game of Hang Man. Use the abbreviations as clues and the students must fill in the blank using the whole words.
Assessment Option:	Have the students share their best work with the class.

GRADE LEVELS	INDEPENDENT ACTIVITY - Abbreviations
4th Grade	Have the students complete the following activities:

1 - Match the whole words with the correct abbreviations from the board on their own paper.
2 - Select at least three words from the list on the board. Write the word, the abbreviation, and tell when the abbreviated word might be used.
3 - Play a game of Hang Man. Use the abbreviations as clues and the students must fill in the blank using the whole word.

Assessment Option: Have the students share their best work with the class.

5th Grade Have the students complete the following activities:

1 - Match the whole words with the correct abbreviations from the board on their own paper.
2 - Select at least five words from the list on the board. Write the word, the abbreviation, and tell when the abbreviated word might be used.
3 - Play a game of Hang Man. Use the abbreviations as clues and the students must fill in the blank using the whole word.

Assessment Option: Have the students share their best work with the class.

Reflection: Abbreviations

It is important for students to understand why they are learning this process and how they can apply it to their daily lives. Explain that knowing the abbreviated form of words is important in both reading and writing.

In this reflection, ask the students these questions in an open discussion:

1. What did they learn?
2. How can they use what they learned in their daily activity?
3. Can they teach what they have learned to someone else?
4. What did they like most about the activity?
5. What did they like least about the activity?

List of Abbreviations
Level I (1st, 2nd, & 3rd)

Abbr.	Abbreviation(s), abbreviated	lb.	Pound
AM	Ante meridian (before noon).	Pop.	Population
PM	Post meridian (after noon)	tbsp.	Table spoon
Ave.	Avenue	tsp.	Tea Spoon
St.	Street	RR	Railroad
Pl.	Place	wt.	Weight
Rd.	Road	N.	North
Blvd.	Boulevard	S.	South
Doz.	Dozen	E.	East
Hr.	Hour	W.	West
Min.	Minute	Yr.	Year
Sec.	Second	Mo.	Month
In.	Inch	Jan.	January
Yd.	Yard	Feb.	February
Mi.	Mile	Mar.	March
Jr.	Junior	Apr.	April
Sr.	Senior	Jun.	June
Ms.	Miss	Jul.	July
Mr.	Mister	Aug.	August
Mrs.	Mistress	Sept.	September
Dr.	Doctor.	Oct.	October
No.	Number	Nov.	November
P.	Page	Dec.	December

List of Abbreviations
Level II (4th & 5th)

abbr.	Abbreviation(s) abbreviated	Temp.	Temperature
A.D	After Death	Kt.	Carat
B.C.	Before Christ	wt.	Weight
b.p.	Boiling Point/birth place	ht.	Height
Bldg.	Building	kg	Kilogram(s)
Cent.	Century	km	Kilometer(s)
cm	Centimeter(s)	l	Liter
Co.	County/Company	lat.	Latitude
Cont.	Continued	long.	Longitude
Cu.	Cubic	m	Meter(s)
D.C.	District of Columbia	M.D.	Medical Doctor
Dist.	District	mg	Milligram(s)
Div.	Division	mm	Millimeter(s)
Dup.	Duplicate	Mt.	Mountain
ed.	Edited, edition, editor(s)/education	Mts.	Mountains
elev.	Elevation	NE	Northeast
enc.	Enclosed	NW	Northwest
F	Fahrenheit	SE	Southeast
ft.	Foot, Feet	SW	Southwest
Fig.	Figure	pt	Pint
gal.	Gallon(s)	qt	Quart
Gov.	Government	Misc.	Miscellaneous
Grad.	Graduate	sq.	Square
Zn.	Zinc	vs.	Versus (against)

Grammar, Usage, and Mechanics
Lesson Title: <u>Capitalization</u>

There are several rules that apply to the use of capital letters. For the purpose of this book we will focus on the basic ten.

1. The first word of a sentence.
2. A person's title and initials.
3. Specific names of people, places and things.
4. Cities, counties, states, and countries.
5. Titles (books, magazines, news papers, songs, poems, and documents).
6. Holidays, months, and days.
7. Quoted words.
8. The greeting and closing of a letter.
9. The letter I when used as a noun.
10. Capitalize titles showing family relationships.

Time Frame: **30 - 60 Minutes (per activity)**
    5 - 10   Activity introduction and explanation.
    5 - 10   Write words/sentences on the board.
    5 - 10   Whole group discussion.
    5 - 10   Independent student activity.
    5 - 10   Activity assessment.
    5 - 10   Reflection on the activity.

Lesson Objective: To increase student knowledge of capitalized words.

Materials & Resources: Paper, pencil, and crayons.

Instruction Procedure: Explain the lesson and lesson objective to the students.

Whole Group Activity:

Select the focus area(s) and a few words/sentences from the sample chart on the following pages to list on the board. Explain the rule of capitalization being addressed in the activity and then read each word/sentence aloud. Go over the words/sentences again, this time identifying and explaining each capital letter. Once you have corrected all the words/sentences, go over the words/sentences a third time. This time, have the students explain the use of the capital letters. Once the students have had some time to practice using capital letters, move on to the level-appropriate independent activities on the following pages.

GRADE LEVELS	INDEPENDENT ACTIVITY - Capitalization
Kindergarten	Kindergarteners should focus on the very basics of capitalization. Each activity should focus on one key aspect of capitalization at a time. Each of the following activities can be repeated with a different focus. Select a few words or sentences from the list on the following pages and write them on the board.

Focus Areas: proper nouns, titles, and the beginning of a sentence.

Have the students complete the following:

1 - Copy the words/sentences from the board and circle all of the lowercase letters that should be capital letters.
2 - Copy the words/sentences from the board placing capital letters in the correct places.
3 - Select a word/sentence from the board, copy it in your best writing, and draw a picture to go along with it. Make sure each sentence begins with a capital letter and has an end mark. |
| **Assessment Option:** | Have the students share their work with the class. |
| **1st Grade** | First graders should focus on the very basics of capitalization. Each activity should focus on one or two key aspects of capitalization at a time. Each of the following activities can be repeated with a different focus. Select a few words or sentences from the list on the following pages and write them on the board.

Focus Areas: proper nouns, titles, the beginning of a sentence, holidays, months, and days.

Have the students complete the following:
1 - Copy the words/sentences from the board and circle all of the lowercase letters that should be capital letters.
2 - Rewrite the words/sentences replacing the circled letters with capital letters.
3 - Select a sentence from the board, copy it in your best writing, and draw a picture to go along with it. Make sure each sentence begins with a capital letter and has an end mark. |

GRADE LEVELS	INDEPENDENT ACTIVITY - Capitalization
Assessment Option:	Have the students share their work with the class.
2nd Grade	Each activity should focus on one or two key aspects of capitalization at a time. Each of the following activities can be repeated with a different focus. Select a few words or sentences from the list on the following pages and write them on the board.

Focus Areas: proper nouns, titles, holidays, months, days, and the first word of a sentence.

1 - Copy the words/sentences from the board and circle all of the lowercase letters that should be capital letters.
2 - Rewrite the words/sentences replacing the circled letters with capital letters.
3 - Select a sentence from the board, copy it in your best writing, and draw a picture to go along with it. Make sure each sentence begins with a capital letter and has an end mark.

Assessment Option:	Have the students share their work with the class.
3rd Grade	Students should be able to concentrate on all of the focus areas of capitalization within the same activity. Select a few words and sentences from the list on the following pages and write them on the board. (You may want to list the focus areas on the board for the students to check their work.)

Focus Areas: proper nouns, titles, holidays, months, days, the first word of a sentence, a persons title and name, greetings and closings of a letter, and city, state, and country.

1 - Copy the words/sentences from the board and circle all of the lowercase letters that should be capital letters.
2 - Rewrite the words/sentences replacing the circled letters with capital letters.
3 - Copy the letter's opening and closing from the board making the needed corrections to the capital letters.

GRADE LEVELS	INDEPENDENT ACTIVITY - Capitalization
	Challenge: Students may include a body for their letter. Make sure the letter contains the proper capitalizations. (Although this is not a grammar lesson, you may also want to check for other errors, but keep in mind that the focus of this activity is capitalization.)
Assessment Option:	Have the students share their work with the class.
4th Grade	Students should be able to concentration on all of the focus areas of capitalization within the same activity. Select a few words and sentences from the list on the following pages and write them on the board. (You may want to list the focus areas on the board for the students to check their work.)
	Focus Areas: proper nouns, titles, holidays, months, days, the first word of a sentence, a persons title, name and initials, greetings and closings of a letter, city, state, and country, capitalization to show family relationships, and quoted words.

1 - Copy the words/sentences from the board and circle all of the lowercase letters that should be capital letters.
2 - Rewrite the words/sentences replacing the circled letters with capital letters.
3 - Copy the letter opening and closing from the board making the needed corrections to the capital letters.

Challenge: Students may include a body for their letter. Make sure the letter contains the proper capitalizations. (Although this is not a grammar lesson, you may also want to check for other errors, but keep in mind that the focus of this activity is capitalization.)

Assessment Option:	Have the students share their work with the class.
5th Grade	Students should be able to concentration on all of the focus areas of capitalization within the same activity. Select a few words and sentences from the list on the following pages and write them on the board. (You may want to list the focus areas on the board for the students to check their work.)

GRADE LEVELS	INDEPENDENT ACTIVITY - Capitalization
	Focus Areas: proper nouns, titles, holidays, months, days, the first word of a sentence, a persons title, name and initials, greetings and closings of a letter, city, state, and country, capitalization to show family relationships, and quoted words.

1 - Copy the words/sentences from the board and circle all of the lowercase letters that should be capital letters.
2 - Rewrite the words/sentences replacing the circled letters with capital letters.
3 - Copy the letter opening and closing from the board making the needed corrections to the capital letters.

Challenge: Students may include a body for their letter. Make sure the letter contains the proper capitalizations. (Although this is not a grammar lesson, you may also want to check for other errors, but keep in mind that the focus of this activity is capitalization.)

Assessment Option:	Have the students share their work with the class.

Reflection: Capitalization

It is important for students to understand why they are learning this process and how they can apply it to their daily lives. Explain that knowing which words to capitalize is especially important in written communication.

In this reflection, ask the students these questions in an open discussion:

1. What did they learn?
2. How can they use what they learned in their daily activity?
3. Can they teach what they have learned to someone else?
4. What did they like the most about the activity?
5. What did they like the least about the activity?

Capitalization
Kindergarten

Note: All of the words and sentences are properly capitalized. List all of them on the board in lowercase letters to start.

Which words should be capitalized?

I	Mary
_____ Elementary School	Kim
List some student names	teacher
Tom	cartoon
Kevin	Hello Kitty

Which words in the sentence should be capitalized?

1	Today is Monday.
2	My name is Tina.
3	My dogs name is Rover.
4	My cats name is Paws.
5	My school name is _____ (list their school name).
6	Red is my favorite color.
7	Today I have two snacks.
8	Tomorrow I will be five years old.
9	Every Saturday I play in the park.
10	Yesterday I went to the zoo.

Capitalization
1st Grade

Note: All of the words and sentences are properly capitalized. List all of them on the board in lowercase letters to start.

Which words should be capitalized?

Christmas	Easter	___ Elementary School
Saturday	January	March
Harry Potter	Time For Kids	Los Angeles, CA
California	United States of America	
Las Vegas	Mother's Day	California

Which words in the sentence should be capitalized?

1	This year I plan to spend Easter with my family.
2	Last week on Tuesday I went to the Los Angeles Zoo.
3	Next Saturday I am going to Texas to see my friend Kevin.
4	Have you read the Harry Potter book?
5	My favorite poem is Roses are Red, Violets are Blue.
6	My friend Ronald likes to read the Time for Kids magazine and I don't like to read magazines.
7	My favorite month of the year is April because there are so many holidays, but I like December too.
8	My cousin's birthday is in May and it sometimes falls on Mother's Day, but my birthday is in January and it doesn't fall on any holiday.
9	I always go to Redondo Park on Saturday morning to walk my dog Alex and play with my friends.
10	I plan to invite Racquel, Keisha, Ronald and some other friends to my birthday party this summer.

Capitalization
2nd Grade

Note: All of the words and sentences are properly capitalized. List all of them on the board in lowercase letters to start.

Which words should be capitalized?

Los Angeles, CA	California	United States of America
September	Friday	St. Patrick's Day
Harry Potter	Karen	Marvin
People Magazine	(Student's School Name) _____ Elementary School	Payless Store
Aunt Rebecca	Uncle Ted	Mom

Which words in the sentence should be capitalized?

1	My Cousin Kelly moved to North Carolina with my aunt and uncle in January of last year.
2	On Tuesday I attended the Down Town Music School and had lunch at the Uptown Sandwich Shop with my friend Sandra.
3	Billy Bear and Marvin Monkey are my favorite cartoon characters on the Saturday Morning Cartoon Club.
4	I flew on the airplane from Los Angeles to Texas with my Aunt Sally and Uncle Joe.
5	My favorite basketball player was Michael Jordan when he played for the Chicago Bulls.
6	This summer I am going camping at Camp Winter Lake with the Children's Club and I know it will be great fun.
7	Principal Campbell is a very nice lady and so is my new teacher.
8	My neighbor Vicky and her son are going to the new movie theater with me and my Mom on Wednesday.
9	Dear Uncle Sam, Best wishes, **closing.** *Letter greeting and
10	Dear Mr. Robertson, Sincerely yours, **and closing.** *Letter greeting

Capitalization
3rd, 4th & 5th Grade

Note: All of the words and sentences are properly capitalized. List all of them on the board in lowercase letters to start.

Which words should be capitalized?

Grandma Jordan	United States Air Force	The New York Times/news paper
Aunt Mary /aunt	Los Angeles, Ca/city, state	February
Sir Isaac Newton/name	California	Christmas
Principal Thomas/principal	United States of America	Tuesday
Roses are Red, Violets are Blue/poem	(Student's School Name) Elementary School/school	People Magazine/magazine

Which words in the sentence should be capitalized?

1	I have a meeting this Tuesday with Principal T.C. Martin and the director from Selma Middle School.
2	I traveled to St. Martinique by airplane for my vacation last fall with my Aunt Sally and Uncle George along with my cousins.
3	I met the authors of Left Behind while I was in Los Angeles and they gave me a free book.
4	Last Tuesday the New York Times said "The real estate market is booming..." so I decided to sell my Fairview Estate this week.
5	I have to take math, science, and Creative English 101 when I get to high school.
6	I live in a big house with my dog Rover, my fish Tiger, and my cat.
7	I don't have a favorite movie, but my favorite television shows are cartoons, Friends, and America's Funniest Video's.
8	I went to the Academy Awards Show in my new Calvin Klein jeans, Tommy Hilfiger jacket, Elizabeth Taylor blouse, and some very nice high heel shoes.
9	Dear Dean Henry, Kindest regards, **closing.** ***Letter greeting &**
10	Dear Dr. Roberts, Sincerely yours, **closing.** ***Letter greeting &**

Grammar, Usage, and Mechanics
Lesson Title: <u>Contractions</u>

The word 'contraction' is a derivative of the word contract which means to make smaller or reduce. In the case of grammar, a contraction means to make a word, or a group of words, shorter. Therefore, a contraction in grammar takes two words, shortens them by eliminating some letters, and putting them into one word using an apostrophe to take the place of one or more missing letter(s). (**Example:** can not = can't. The letters 'n' and 'o' were eliminated and replaced with an apostrophe.)

Time Frame:	**30 - 60 Minutes (per activity)**
	5 - 10 Activity introduction and explanation.
	5 - 10 Write word sets on the board and one example.
	5 - 10 Whole group discussion.
	5 - 10 Independent student activity.
	5 - 10 Activity assessment.
	5 - 10 Reflection on the activity.
Lesson Objectives:	To increase student knowledge of how to read, spell and use contractions.
Materials & Resources:	Paper and pencil.
Instruction Procedure:	Explain the lesson and lesson objectives to the students.

Whole Group Activity:

List a few word-sets on the board from the list on the following pages (or use your own) and one example of how that word-set is changed into a contraction. Have the students notice which letters are omitted and replaced by an apostrophe. Although there is not a set patterns for contractions, some are similar. (**Example:** have not = haven't, would not = wouldn't. Notice that when the second word in the word-set is 'not', the ending for the contraction is usually <u>n't.</u> Also when the word-set ends with 'will', the contraction ending is <u>'ll</u> - she will = she'll, they will = they'll.) Help the students find other such similarities. This will help them when writing contractions. Using the word-sets you have listed on the board, have the students assist you in formulating the contractions.

GRADE LEVELS	INDEPENDENT ACTIVITY - Contractions
2nd Grade	List five word-sets on the board and the contractions for two of them, but do not match them. Have the students complete the following activities: 1 - Match the word-sets with the contractions listed on the board. 2 - Complete the list by adding the missing contractions. 3 - Using parenthesis, list the letters that are omitted to make the contraction. **Example:** can not = can't (n and o).
Assessment Option:	Have the students verbally share their work.
3rd Grade	List seven word sets on the board and the contractions for three of them, but do not match them. Have the students complete the following activities: 1 - Match the word-sets with the contractions listed on the board. 2 - Complete the list by adding the missing contractions. 3 - Using parenthesis, list the letters that are omitted to make the contraction. **Example:** can not = can't (n and o).
Assessment Option:	Have the students verbally share their work.
4th Grade	List nine word-sets on the board and the contractions for four of them, but do not match them. Have the students complete the following activities: 1 - Match the word-sets with the contractions listed on the board. 2 - Complete the list by adding the missing contractions. 3 - Using parenthesis, list the letters that are omitted to make the contraction. **Example:** can not = can't (n and o).
Assessment Option:	Have the students verbally share their work.

GRADE LEVELS	**INDEPENDENT ACTIVITY - Contractions**
5th Grade	List ten or more word-sets on the board and the contractions for five of them, but do not match them. Have the students complete the following activities: 1 - Match the word-sets with the contractions listed on the board. 2 - Complete the list by adding the missing contractions. 3 - Using parenthesis, list the letters that are omitted to make the contraction. **Example:** can not = can't (n and o).
Assessment Option:	Have the students verbally share their work.

Reflection: Contractions

It is important for students to understand why they are learning this process and how they can apply it to their daily lives. Explain that knowing how to construct and read contractions is important in all communications, especially writing.

In this reflection, ask the students these questions in an open discussion:

1. What did they learn?
2. How can they use what they learned in their daily activity?
3. Can they teach what they have learned to someone else?
4. What did they like most about the activity?
5. What did they like least about the activity?

Contractions
All Grades

	Word Set	Contraction		Word Set	Contraction
1	I am	I'm	20	she would	she'd
2	I have	I've	21	it is	it's
3	I will	I'll	22	it will	it'll
4	you are	you're	23	that will	that'll
5	you have	you've	24	must have	must've
6	you will	you'll	25	could have	could've
7	we are	we're	26	would have	would've
8	we have	we've	27	should have	should've
9	we will	we'll	28	does not	doesn't
10	we would	we'd	29	do not	don't
11	they are	they're	30	can not	can't
12	they have	they've	31	will not	*won't
13	they will	they'll	32	is not	isn't
14	they would	they'd	33	did not	didn't
15	he is	he's	34	could not	couldn't
16	he will	he'll	35	should not	shouldn't
17	he would	he'd	36	would not	wouldn't
18	she is	she's	37	must not	mustn't
19	she will	she'll	38	have not	haven't

***Notice that the vowel spelling changes from i to o.**

Grammar, Usage, and Mechanics
Lesson Title: <u>Verb Tense & Irregular Verbs</u>

A verb can be stated in different forms to express the different times that something takes place. These verb forms are referred to as verb-tense. The verb-tense tells if it already happened, is currently happening, or may happen in the future. The tense of the verb can be changed from present to past by adding the suffix **-ed**. (**Example:** She skipp**ed** = past tense, she skip**s** = present, she will skip = future.) In some cases the spelling of the verb changes completely, these are known as irregular verbs. (**Example:** He **came** to the door = past tense. He will **come** to the door = present and future tense.)

Time Frame: **40 - 75 Minutes (per activity)**
          5 - 10   Activity introduction and explanation.
          5 - 10   Set up the chart on the board
         15 - 25 Whole group Activity.
          5 - 10   Independent student activity.
          5 - 10   Activity assessment.
          5 - 10   Reflection on the activity.

Lesson Objectives: To increase student knowledge of verb tense, irregular verbs, and how to use them.

Materials & Resources: Paper and pencil.

Instruction Procedure: Explain the lesson and lesson objectives to the students.

Whole Group Activity:

Copy the Regular Verb Chart from the next page on the board and explain the lesson and lesson objective to the students. Explain your examples and have the students assist you in completing the chart. Extend the chart using verbs from the students. As you fill in the chart with the correct verb form, review the rule with the students. Select a student to make up a sentence using a regular present tense verb; a second student to change the sentence to accommodate the same verb in the past tense; and a third student to change the sentence to accommodate the same verb in the future tense. Document each change to the sentence to enable the students to visualize the change in the sentence wording and structure.

Once the students are comfortable with altering regular verbs to change the tense, switch to irregular verbs and repeat the activity. After the students have had some time to practice, move on to the level-appropriate independent activities on the following pages.

Verb Tense
All Grades

(Use the italicized words to set up your charts)
will is a helping verb

Present Tense	Past Tense	Future Tense
sip	*sipped*	*will sip*
jump	jumped	will jump
laugh	laughed	will laugh
happen	happened	will happen
sail	sailed	will sail
camp	camped	will camp
vacation	vacationed	will vacation
walk	walked	will walk

Irregular Verbs
(Use the italicized words to set up your charts)

A participle is a verb that is used to form complex tenses "was helpful" and " has helped."

Base Form	Past Tense	Past Participle	Present Participle
break	*broke*	*broken*	*breaking*
begin	began	begun	beginning
draw	drew	drawn	drawing
ride	rode	ridden	riding
rise	rose	risen	rising
sing	sang	sung	singing
ring	rang	rung	ringing
see	saw	seen	seeing

GRADE LEVELS	INDEPENDENT ACTIVITY – Verb Tense & Irregular Verbs
1st Grade	Once the chart is completed from the whole group activity, have the students select two regular base verbs to work with and complete the following activities: 1 - Write one sentence for each verb selected using its base form. 2 - Rewrite the same sentence for each verb, this time in its past tense form. 3 - Rewrite the same sentence again, this time in its future tense form. 4 - Repeat activities 1 - 3 using two irregular verbs.
Assessment Option:	Have the students share their best work with the class.
2nd Grade	Once the chart is completed from the whole group activity, have the students select three regular base verbs to work with and complete the following activities: 1 - Write one sentence for each verb selected using its base form. 2 - Rewrite the same sentence for each verb, this time in its past tense form. 3 - Rewrite the same sentence again, this time in its future tense form. 4 - Repeat activities 1 - 3 using three irregular verbs.
Assessment Option:	Have the students share their best work with the class.
3rd Grade	Once the chart is completed from the whole group activity, have the students select four regular base verbs to work with and complete the following activities: 1 - Write one sentence for each verb selected using its base form. 2 - Rewrite the same sentence for each verb, this time in its past tense form. 3 - Rewrite the same sentence again, this time in its future tense form. 4 - Repeat activities 1 - 3 using four irregular verbs.

GRADE LEVELS	INDEPENDENT ACTIVITY – Verb Tense & Irregular Verbs
Assessment Option:	Have the students share their best work with the class.
4th Grade	Once the chart is completed from the whole group activity, have the students select four regular base verbs to work with and complete the following activities: 1 - Write one sentence for each verb selected using its base form. 2 - Rewrite the same sentence for each verb, this time in its past tense form. 3 - Rewrite the same sentence again, this time in its future tense form. 4 - Repeat activities 1 - 3 using four irregular verbs. **Challenge:** Write a single meaningful sentence that contains two forms of one verb. Make sure each sentence has correct punctuation and grammar.
Assessment Option:	Have the students share their best work with the class.
5th Grade	Once the chart is completed from the whole group activity, have the students select four regular base verbs to work with and complete the following activities: 1 - Write one sentence for each verb selected using its base form. 2 - Rewrite the same sentence for each verb, this time in its past tense form. 3 - Rewrite the same sentence again, this time in its future tense form. 4 - Repeat activities 1 - 3 using four irregular verbs. 5 - Write a single meaningful sentence that contains two forms of one verb. Make sure each sentence has correct punctuation and grammar.
Assessment Option:	Have the students select their best work to share with the class.

Reflection: Verb Tense & Irregular Verbs

It is important for students to understand why they are learning this process and how they can apply it to their daily lives. Explain that knowing verb tenses and how to use them, both in written and spoken communication, is important.

In this reflection, ask the students these questions in an open discussion:

1. What did they learn?
2. How can they use what they learned in their daily activity?
3. Can they teach what they have learned to someone else?
4. What did they like most about the activity?
5. What did they like least about the activity?

Grammar, Usage, and Mechanics
Lesson Title: <u>Subject-Verb Agreement</u>

Whenever speaking or writing, the subject (who or what) must agree with the verb or verb form (the action). When the subject is singular (only one) you must add an **-s or -es** to the end of the verb for it to agree. (**Example:** Mary dance**s** fast.) When the subject is plural (more than one) use the base form of the verb. (**Example:** They dance fast.) The subject-verb agreement rule for irregular verbs is different. The verb changes completely for singular and plural irregular verb forms. (See the chart on the following page.)

Time Frame: 30 - 60 Minutes (per activity)
                         5 - 10   Activity introduction and explanation.
                         5 - 10   Copy the chart and examples on the following page.

                         5 - 10   Whole group discussion.
                         5 - 10   Independent student activity.
                         5 - 10   Activity assessment.
                         5 - 10   Reflection on the activity.

Lesson Objective: To increase student knowledge of subject verb agreement.

Materials & Resources: Paper and pencil.

Instruction Procedure: Explain the lesson and lesson objective to the students.

Whole Group Activity:

Copy the Regular Subject-Verb Agreement chart from the following page on the board. Explain your examples and have the students assist you in completing the chart. Extend the chart using subject-verb agreements from the students. As you fill in the chart with the correct subject-verb agreements, review the rules for each with the students. Using one chart at a time, select a student to make up a sentence using a singular subject with agreeing verb and another student to repeat the sentence using the plural form and agreeing verb. Write the sentence on the board and document each change, allowing the students to visualize the change in the sentence wording and structure. Repeat this activity a few times using each chart.

After the students have had some time to practice, move on to the level-appropriate independent activities on the following pages.

Subject-Verb Agreement of Regular Verbs
(Use the italicized words to set up your charts)

Singular

Subject	Verb
Kevin	reads
ball	bounces
dog	barks
branch	falls
fox	hides

Plural

Subject	Verb
students	read
balls	bounce
dogs	bark
branches	fall
foxes	hide

(**Example**: Kevin read**s**. Kevin read).

Subject-Verb Agreement of Irregular Verbs
(Use the italicized words to set up your charts)

Verb forms of:	*Singular*	*Plural*
be	am, is, was	are, were
do	does	do
have	has	have

(**Example:** The chair **is** broken. The chairs **are** broken).

Subject-Verb Agreement of Pronoun as the Subject
(Use the italicized words to set up your charts)

*(Do not add **-s** or **-es** when the subject is **I** or **you**)

	Subject	*Verb*
***Singular Pronoun** (**I, You**)	*I, you*	*talk*
Singular	*he, she*	*talks*
Plural	*we, you, they*	*talk*

(**Example:** I talk. You talk. She talks.)

GRADE LEVELS **INDEPENDENT ACTIVITY – Subject-Verb Agreement**

The verb form of 'to be' is the most irregular verb in the English language. This form usually links the actual verb to the subject. This verb form changes depending on the time being referred to.

infinitive - the base form of the verb.	to be
present -	am, is, are
past	was, were
present participle - suggest a continuous or active sense and ends with -*ing*.	being
past participle - suggests a past or completed.	been
present subjective - suggest an action at the current time.	be
past subjunctive - suggest an action that has been completed	were (Example: We were very sad.)
imperative	be

GRADE LEVELS	INDEPENDENT ACTIVITY – Subject-Verb Agreement
1st Grade	Once the chart is completed from the whole group activity, have the students select one subject from each chart and complete the following activities: 1 - Using the regular subject-verb agreement, write one sentence that contains a singular subject and one sentence that contains a plural subject. 2 - Using the irregular subject-verb agreement, write one sentence that contains a singular subject and one sentence that contains a plural subject. 3 - Using the pronoun as a subject, write one sentence that contains a singular pronoun and one sentence that contains a plural pronoun. ***Each sentence should be grade level appropriate and have proper grammar and punctuation.***
Assessment Option:	Have the students share their best work with the class.
2nd Grade	Once the chart is completed from the whole group activity, have the students select two subjects from each chart and complete the following activities: 1 - Using the regular subject-verb agreement, write one sentence that contains a singular subject and one sentence that contains a plural subject. 2 - Using the irregular subject-verb agreement, write one sentence that contains a singular subject and one sentence that contains a plural subject. 3 - Using the pronoun as a subject, write one sentence that contains a singular pronoun and one sentence that contains a plural pronoun. ***Each sentence should be grade level appropriate and have proper grammar and punctuation.***
Assessment Option:	Have the students share their best work with the class.

GRADE LEVELS	INDEPENDENT ACTIVITY – Subject-Verb Agreement
3rd Grade	Once the chart is completed from the whole group activity, have the students select three subjects from each chart and complete the following activities: 1 - Using the regular subject-verb agreement, write one sentence that contains a singular subject and one sentence that contains a plural subject. 2 - Using the irregular subject-verb agreement, write one sentence that contains a singular subject and one sentence that contains a plural subject. 3 - Using the pronoun as a subject, write one sentence that contains a singular pronoun and one sentence that contains a plural pronoun. ***Each sentence should be grade level appropriate and have proper grammar and punctuation.***
Assessment Option:	Have the students share their best work with the class.
4th Grade	Once the chart is completed from the whole group activity, have the students select three subjects from each chart and complete the following activities: 1 - Using the regular subject-verb agreement, write one sentence that contains a singular subject and one sentence that contains a plural subject. 2 - Using the irregular subject-verb agreement, write one sentence that contains a singular subject and one sentence that contains a plural subject. 3 - Using the pronoun as a subject, write one sentence that contains a singular pronoun and one sentence that contains a plural pronoun. ***Each sentence should be grade level appropriate and have proper grammar and punctuation.***
Assessment Option:	Have the students share their best work with the class.

GRADE LEVELS	**INDEPENDENT ACTIVITY – Subject-Verb Agreement**
5th Grade	Once the chart is completed from the whole group activity, have the students select four subjects from each chart and complete the following activities:

1 - Using the regular subject-verb agreement, write one sentence that contains a singular subject and one sentence that contains a plural subject.
2 - Using the irregular subject-verb agreement, write one sentence that contains a singular subject and one sentence that contains a plural subject.
3 - Using the pronoun as a subject, write one sentence that contains a singular pronoun and one sentence that contains a plural pronoun.

Each sentence should be grade level appropriate and have proper grammar and punctuation.

Assessment Option: Have the students share their best work with the class.

Reflection: Subject-Verb Agreement

It is important for students to understand why they are learning this process and how they can apply it to their daily lives. Explain that understanding subject-verb agreements and how to use them, both in written and spoken communication, is important.

In this reflection, ask the students these questions in an open discussion:

1. What did they learn?
2. How can they use what they learned in their daily activity?
3. Can they teach what they have learned to someone else?
4. What did they like most about the activity?
5. What did they like least about the activity?

Grammar, Usage, and Mechanics
Lesson Title: <u>Figurative Language</u>

Figurative language conveys information in a colorful way. This does not mean that it is written in color, it simply means that the writing is exciting or dull and boring. There are several types of figurative language; however, for this activity we will focus on the hyperboles, metaphors, personifications, and similes. Definitions are listed with each chart on the following pages.

Time Frame: **30 - 60 Minutes (per activity)**
  5 - 10   Activity introduction and explanation.
  5 - 10   Write types and definitions along with examples..
  5 - 10   Whole group discussion.
  5 - 10   Independent student activity.
  5 - 10   Activity assessment.
  5 - 10   Reflection on the activity.

Lesson Objectives: To increase student knowledge and use of figurative language.

Materials & Resources: Paper, pencil, and crayons.

Instruction Procedure: Explain the lesson and lesson objectives to the students.

Whole Group Activity:

Unless the students are already familiar with these forms of figurative language, focus on one type at a time. If the students are familiar with all four types of figurative language, select two or more forms to practice and expand their knowledge.

Draw a T chart on the board and select one example to begin with. Write it on the board. In your example, include both the plain and figurative form of the same sentence. This will allow the students to visually see how the figurative form adds a little spice to their writing. Next, list another plain sentence on the board and have the students help you change the wording (not the meaning) by using figurative language. Repeat this activity a few more times, allowing the students to do most of the work.

After the students have had some time to practice, move on to the level-appropriate independent activities on the following pages.

Figurative Language

Hyperboles - An extreme exaggeration usually expressed in a humorous manner.

Plain Sentence	Hyperbole
I'm very tired.	I'm so tired that I could sleep for a year.
She's very angry.	She was so angry, she spat fire.
It's raining very hard.	It's raining cats and dogs.
Don't be so angry with me.	Don't bite my head off.

Metaphors - A comparison of two different things without using the words *as* or *like*.

I am so rich I have a mountain of money.	I have a lot of money.
The leaves danced in the wind.	The leaves blew in the wind.
My heart pours out to you.	I have sympathy for you.
I've bent over backwards to help you.	I've done everything possible to help you.

Figurative Language

Personifications - Giving human quality to something that is not human.

The monkeys smiled with joy as they played in the trees.	The monkeys were happily playing in the trees.
The bright stars in the night sky winked at me to say goodnight.	The stars twinkled in the night.
The wind danced with the clouds as they both moved through the sky.	The wind blew the clouds through the sky.
The sunflower stretched and reached out for the warmth of the sun.	The sunflower grow toward the sun.

Similes - Comparing two unlike things that are usually introduced with *like* or *as*.

Her teeth were as white as the snow in the photograph.	Her teeth were very white in the photograph.
My mouth is as dry as the desert.	My mouth is very dry.
He is as hairy as a bear.	He is very hairy
She is as blind as a bat without her glasses.	She can not see very well without glasses.

GRADE LEVELS	INDEPENDENT ACTIVITY – Figurative Language
1st Grade	Focus on one type of figurative language at a time. Select one set to work with. Explain and practice with the students as in the whole group activity. Select an additional sentence in the figurative form for the students to work with and have them complete the following activities:

1 - Copy the figurative language sentence in their best writing and write the sentence again in its plain form.
2 - Make up your own figurate language sentence.
3 - Draw a picture to go along with the figurative sentence you created. Make sure each sentence is grade level appropriate and contains the proper punctuation and grammar.

Game - Select a few students to share their figurative sentences (without the picture) with the class and see if the other students can translate it into a plain sentence.

Repeat this activity with each of the four types of figurative language.

Assessment Option:	Have the students share their best work with the class.
2nd Grade	Focus on one type of figurative language at a time. Select one set to work with. Explain and practice with the students as in the whole group activity. Select two additional sentences in the figurative form for the students to work with and have them complete the following activities:

1 - Copy the figurative language sentences in their best writing and write each sentence again in its plain form.
2 - Make up two figurate language sentences.
3 - Draw a picture to go along with each figurative sentence you created. Make sure each sentence is grade level appropriate and contains the proper punctuation and grammar.

Game - Select a few students to share their figurative sentences (without the picture) with the class and see if the other students can translate it into a plain sentence.

GRADE LEVELS	INDEPENDENT ACTIVITY – Figurative Language
	Repeat this activity with each of the four types of figurative language.
Assessment Option:	Have the students share their best work with the class.
3rd Grade	Focus on one type of figurative language at a time. Select one set to work with. Explain and practice with the students as in the whole group activity. Select three additional sentences in the figurative form for the students to work with and have them complete the following activities: 1 - Copy the figurative language sentences in their best writing and write each sentence again in its plain form. 2 - Make up three figurate language sentences. 3 - Draw a picture to go along with each figurative sentence you created. Make sure each sentence is grade level appropriate and contains the proper punctuation and grammar. **Game** - Select a few students to share their figurative sentences (without the picture) with the class and see if the other students can translate it into a plain sentence. ***Repeat this activity with each of the four types of figurative language.***
Assessment Option:	Have the students share their best work with the class.
4th Grade	Select one sentence from each category of the figurative language charts, including the definitions of each. Explain and practice with the students as in the whole group activity. Select four additional sentences (one from each category) for the students to work with and have them complete the following activities: 1 - Copy the figurative language sentences in their best writing and write each sentence again in its plain form.

GRADE LEVELS	INDEPENDENT ACTIVITY – Figurative Language
	2 - Make up one figurate language sentences for each type.
3 - Select one sentence and draw a picture that reveals its meaning. Make sure each sentence is grade level appropriate and contains the proper punctuation and grammar.

Game - Select a few students to share their figurative sentences (without the picture) with the class and see if the other students can translate it into a plain sentence. |
| **Assessment Option:** | Have the students share their best work with the class. |
| **5th Grade** | Select one sentence from each category of the figurative language charts including the definitions of each. Explain and practice with the students as in the whole group activity. Select four additional sentences (one from each category) for the students to work with and have them complete the following activities:

1 - Copy the figurative language sentences in their best writing and write each sentence again in its plain form.
2 - Make up one figurate language sentences for each type.
3 - Select one sentence and draw a picture that reveals its meaning.

Challenge: Select one additional sentence from any category, write it on the board and have the students translate it into a plain sentence and identify the type.

Make sure each sentence is grade level appropriate and contains the proper punctuation and grammar.

Game - Select a few students to share their figurative language sentences (without the picture) with the class and see if the other students can translate them into a plain sentence. |
| **Assessment Option:** | Have the students share their best work with the class. |

Reflection: Figurative Language

It is important for students to understand why they are learning this process and how they can apply it to their daily lives. Explain that knowing how to use figurative language makes their conversations and writings more stimulating and interesting. Further explain that people in entertainment and marketing use these techniques to get our attention and it works!

In this reflection, ask the students these questions in an open discussion:

1. What did they learn?
2. How can they use what they learned in their daily activity?
3. Can they teach what they have learned to someone else?
4. What did they like most about the activity?
5. What did they like least about the activity?

Grammar, Usage, and Mechanics
Lesson Title: **Punctuation Marks**

Punctuation marks are alphabetic symbols used to separate, end, or give additional meaning to the written words. Each mark has a distinct meaning and serves a distinct purpose. There are thirteen punctuation marks that we will focus on in this book. However, these punctuation marks are introduced at different grade levels; therefore, not all punctuation marks will be used in each lesson. (See the list of punctuation marks, definitions, examples, and grade level introduction on the following page.)

Time Frame: **30 - 60 Minutes (per activity)**
                    5 - 10   Activity introduction and explanation.
                    5 - 10   Write the sentence on the board.
                    5 - 10   Whole group discussion.
                    5 - 10   Independent student activity.
                    5 - 10   Activity assessment.
                    5 - 10   Reflection on the activity.

Lesson Objectives: To increase student knowledge of punctuation marks and their usage.

Materials & Resources: Paper, pencil, and crayons.

Instruction Procedure: Explain the lesson and lesson objectives to the students.

Whole Group Activity:

Select a few sentences from the list of practice sentences on the following page (or make up your own). Write them on the board as you read each aloud. Next, list the symbols for the grade level being covered. Review the meaning of each symbol with the students by either telling them what each one means or asking the students to tell you. During this part of the whole group instruction, it is important to indicate the reason(s) why a certain symbol belongs in a certain place. Using the practice sentences you have listed on the board, have the students verbally indicate where each mark should be placed and why. (**Example:** The milk spilled on the floor. The end mark used is a "period" because it ends a statement.) After the students have had a few minutes to practice, move on to the level-appropriate independent activities on the following pages.

Punctuation Marks and Definitions

1. **Period** - The most common way to end a sentence that is a statement. **(Example: .)**

2. **Exclamation Mark** - Used to end a sentence with strong emotion, emergency, or excitement. **(Example: !)**

3. **Question Mark** - Used to end a sentence that asks a question or requires a response. If the sentence contains a question word, that's a good indication that the end mark should be a question mark. **(Example: ?)**

4. **Comma** - Used in several ways: **(Example: ,)**
   I. Before a coordinating conjunction that joins independent clauses.
   II. After an introductory phrase.
   III. To separate items in a series.

5. **Colon** - Used to focus the readers attention on what is to come next: introduce a list, summary, or complete your introduction, but only after an independent clause. The colon is also used to separate the numbers in time (see our book on mathematics) **(Example: :)**

6. **Semi-Colon** - Used to link closely related independent clauses that are not joined together by a coordinating conjunction. **(Example: ;)**

7. **Quotation** - Used before and after a direct quote and words of dialogue. **(Example: " ")**

8. **Underline** - Used to stress the importance of a certain word or phrase. **(Example: _____).**

9. **Apostrophe** - Used to form a possessive noun or to take the place of the missing letter in a contraction. **(Example: ')**

10. **Hyphen** - There are several uses for the hyphen in writing, however; for this book we will only focus on the following uses:. **(Example: -)**
    I. At the end of a line to break a word at the syllable and continue it on the next line.
    II. In some compound nouns and titles.
    III. With written numbers (see our book on mathematics).

11. **Parenthesis** - Used to provide additional or instructional information, or otherwise separate comment within a sentence. **(Example: ( ))**

12. **Dash** – Used to create emphasis on a particular sentence.
13. **Ellipsis** - To indicate that something has been omitted. **(Example: ...)**

14. **Italics** – To add emphasis to a particular word or group of words.

Punctuation Marks by Grade

Punctuation Mark	K	1st	2nd	3rd	4th	5th
Period	✓	✓	✓	✓	✓	✓
Exclamation Mark	✓	✓	✓	✓	✓	✓
Question Mark	✓	✓	✓	✓	✓	✓
Comma		✓	✓	✓	✓	✓
Colon			✓	✓	✓	✓
Semi Colon			✓	✓	✓	✓
Quotation Marks			✓	✓	✓	✓
Underlining			✓	✓	✓	✓
Apostrophe			✓	✓	✓	✓
Hyphen				✓	✓	✓
Parentheses				✓	✓	✓
Dash					✓	✓
Ellipsis						✓
Italics						✓

GRADE LEVELS	INDEPENDENT ACTIVITY – Punctuation Marks
Kindergarten	(**Note: see the chart on the pages following this lesson for items to cover.*)

Select three sentences from the list of practice sentences on the following pages (or make up your own). Write them on the board as you read each sentence aloud. Next, list the three punctuation marks. Review the meaning of each mark with the students by either telling them what each one means or asking the students to tell you. Make sure to indicate the reason(s) why a certain mark belongs in a certain place. Have the students complete the following activities:

1 - Copy the sentences in their best writing, placing the punctuation marks in the correct place.
2 - Complete a picture to go along with one or all three of their sentences.
3 - Individually make up their own sentence and correctly place the punctuation mark. They may also elect to complete a drawing to go along with this sentence. Make sure their sentence begins with a capital letter and has the correct end mark.

Assessment Option: Have the students share their best work with the class.

1st Grade (*Note: see the chart on the pages following this lesson for items to cover.*)

Select a few sentences from the list of practice sentences on the following pages (or make up your own). Write them on the board as you read each sentence aloud. Next, list the punctuation marks being covered (you decide which to select, one or all). Review the meaning of each mark with the students by either telling them what each one means or asking the students to tell you. Make sure to explain the reason(s) why a certain mark belongs in a certain place. Have the students complete the following activities:

1 - Copy the sentences in their best writing, placing the punctuation marks in the correct places.

GRADE LEVELS	INDEPENDENT ACTIVITY – Punctuation Marks
	2 - Complete a picture to go along with each of their sentences.
3 - Individually make up two sentences of their own and place the punctuation marks in the correct places. They may also elect to complete a drawing to go along with these sentences. Make sure each sentence begins with a capital letter and has the marks correctly placed.
Assessment Option:	Have the students share their best work with the class.
2nd Grade	(*Note: see the chart on the pages following this lesson for items to cover.)

Select several sentences from the list of practice sentences on the following pages (or make up your own). Write them on the board as you read each sentence aloud. Next, list the punctuation marks being covered (you decide which to select, one or all). Review the meaning of each mark with the students by either telling them what each one means or asking the students to tell you. Make sure to indicate the reason(s) why a certain mark belongs in a certain place. Have the students complete the following activities:

1 - Copy the sentences in their best writing, placing the punctuation marks in the correct places.
2 - Complete a picture to go along with one or all of their sentences.
3 - Make up two sentences of their own and place the punctuation marks in the correct places. They may also elect to complete a drawing to go along with these sentences.

Make sure each sentence begins with a capital letter and has all marks correctly placed. |
| Assessment Option: | Have the students share their best work with the class. |

GRADE LEVELS	INDEPENDENT ACTIVITY – Punctuation Marks
3rd Grade	(*Note: see the chart on the pages following this lesson for items to cover.)

Select several sentences from the list of practice sentences on the following pages (or make up your own). Write them on the board as you read each sentence aloud. Next, list the punctuation marks being covered (you decide which to select, one or all). Review the meaning of each mark with the students by either telling them what each one means or asking the students to tell you. Make sure to indicate the reason(s) why a certain mark belongs in a certain place. Have the students complete the following activities:

1 - Copy the sentences in their best writing, placing the punctuation marks in the correct places.
2 - Complete a picture to go along with one or all of their sentences.
3 - Make up one sentence of their own and include two or more punctuation marks in the same sentence.

Make sure each sentence begins with a capital letter and has the marks correctly placed.

Assessment Option: Have the students share their best work with the class.

4th Grade (*Note: see the chart on the pages following this lesson for items to cover.)

Select several sentences from the list of practice sentences on the following pages (or make up your own). Write them on the board as you read each sentence aloud. Next, list the punctuation marks being covered (you decide which to select, one or all). Review the meaning of each mark with the students by either telling them what each one means or asking the students to tell you. Make sure to indicate the reason(s) why a certain mark belongs in a certain place. Have the students complete the following activities:

GRADE LEVELS	**INDEPENDENT ACTIVITY – Punctuation Marks**
	1 - Copy the sentences in their best writing, placing the punctuation marks in the correct places.
	2 - Make up one sentence of their own and include three or more punctuation marks in the same sentence.
	Make sure each sentence begins with a capital letter and is correctly punctuated.
Assessment Option:	Have the students share their best work with the class.
5th Grade	(*Note: see the chart on the pages following this lesson for items to cover.)*
	Select several sentences from the list of practice sentences on the following pages (or make up your own). Write them on the board as you read each sentence aloud. Next, list the punctuation marks being covered (you decide which to select, one or all). Review the meaning of each mark with the students by either telling them what each one means or asking the students to tell you. Make sure to indicate the reason(s) why a certain mark belongs in a certain place. Have the students complete the following activities:
	1 - Copy the sentences in their best writing, placing the punctuation marks in the correct places.
	2 - Make up one sentence of their own and include three or more punctuation marks in the same sentence.
	Make sure each sentence begins with a capital letter and has the marks correctly placed.
Assessment Option:	Have the students share their best work with the class.

Reflection: Punctuation Marks

It is important for students to understand why they are learning this process and how they can apply it to their daily lives. Explain that how and why punctuation marks are used makes their writings clear and easy to read.

In this reflection, ask the students these questions in an open discussion:

1. What did they learn?
2. How can they use what they learned in their daily activity?
3. Can they teach what they have learned to someone else?
4. What did they like most about the activity?
5. What did they like least about the activity?

Sample Sentences for Punctuation Marks
Kindergarten

Period (.), Question Mark (?), or Exclamation Mark (!)

1	Where is my hat?
2	How old are you?
3	Are you my friend?
4	Can we go play?
5	Is it time for lunch?
6	Today is Monday.
7	My dog is brown.
8	His name is Ron.
9	My coat is red.
10	She is the teacher.
11	We won the game!

Sample Sentences for Punctuation Marks
1st Grade

Period (.) Exclamation (!) Question Mark (?) comma (,)

1	My name is (insert your name) .
2	Today is (insert the day of the week).
3	I have a dog named Rover.
4	The store is not far from here.
5	I found a dollar!
6	I won the race!
7	Stay out of the street!
8	Your birthday party was great!
9	How old are you going to be on your next birthday?
10	Why are you wearing sunglasses at night?
11	Who is your teacher?
12	When are you going to the beach?
13	I had cake, ice cream, and hot dogs at the party.
14	My mother gave me a dollar, two dimes, and a penny.
15	This summer I plan to go to the park, the beach, and the movies.
16	You have to clean the kitchen, bathroom, and your bedroom today.

Sample Sentences for Punctuation Marks
2nd Grade

Quotation mark (" ") Colon (:) Underline (___)

1	My mother told me "Never talk to strangers," without her permission!
2	"What are you having for lunch today?", Kelly asked
3	"Does your dog bite?', asked the little boy as he reached out his hand.
4	"I don't want to play this game anymore!" yelled Sara as she walked away.
5	Today is going to be a busy day: cooking, cleaning, shopping, and a party.
6	The grocery shopping list is not too long: bread, milk, sugar, and oranges.
7	I have two sisters and two brothers: Sara, Diane, David and Ralph.
8	I'm studying four subjects in school: math, English, science, and history.
9	I have baseball practice today from 4:30 to 6:00.
10	School begins at 8:00 am sharp.
11	Make sure you count your change from the store.
12	Please do not write in the text books.
13	The money is hidden on the top shelf in the kitchen.
14	Always look both ways before crossing the street to make sure it is clear.
15	Do you like to read Time for Kids?
16	My Dad reads The Los Angeles Times Newspaper every morning.
17	Lassie was my mother's favorite TV show when she was my age.
18	I enjoyed the movie The Lost Treasure.

Sample Sentences for Punctuation Marks
3rd Grade

Parenthesis ( ) Hyphen (-)

1	When I went to the zoo (yesterday) I saw all kinds of animals.
2	I had a great lunch (pizza and chicken) at the park.
3	We live in the white house (trimmed in yellow) on Minor St.
4	My best friends (Kevin and Gina) are going to the fair with me.
5	While we were at the zoo, I saw several mon-keys, lions, giraffes and other animals.
6	My friend and I made cup-cakes and brownies for the party.
7	Today is Wednesday and to-morrow will be Thursday.
8	We had fruit punch and hot-dogs after the game.
9	You have to be self-confident to sing in front of everyone on stage.
10	Marvin has two great-uncles.
11	Your mother-in-law is a nice lady.
12	My great-grandmother is ninety-two years old.

Sample Sentences for Punctuation Marks
4th & 5th Grade

Semi colon (;)

1	Most girls don't like to play football; you can get hurt playing football.
2	Junk food may taste good, but it is not good for you; it has a lot of fat and calories.
3	My best friend goes everywhere with me; I never go anywhere alone.
4	Talking about other people is not a nice thing to do; it can hurt their feelings.

The Elements & Styles of Writing
Activity Title: <u>The Writing Process</u>

There are five basic steps in the writing process and the first one doesn't even involve writing. This activity will focus on all five steps of the writing process and creative ways of getting the students involved. All good writers draw from many sources when writing. One such source is their own personal experience. Many young writers may not have many experiences to draw from or may not quite know how to put their thoughts into words. The activities in this section will help students focus on a topic, put their thoughts into words, and finally put their thoughts on paper in an organized manner. Keep in mind that the development of good writers is an ongoing process and improvements can only be made through practice. This activity is not meant to produce excellent writers after the first practice, but to set students on the path to achieve excellence.

Time Frame: **45 - 75 Minutes (per activity)**
- 5 - 10 Activity introduction and explanation.
- 10 - 15 Chart information on the board.
- 5 - 10 Whole group discussion.
- 15 - 20 Independent student activity.
- 5 - 10 Activity assessment.
- 5 - 10 Reflection on the activity.

Lesson Objective: To enhance student writing skills through the steps in the writing process.

Materials & Resources: Paper and pencil.

Instruction Procedure: Explain the lesson and lesson objective to the students.

Whole Group Activity:

Each step in the writing process has a different set of Whole Group Activities which are separated by the student's level of understanding rather than by grade level. Writing inspirations follow the writing process example and are divided by level of ease and topic.

The Elements & Styles of Writing
Activity Title: <u>The Writing Process</u>
Whole Group Instructions:
All Grades

Step 1 – Brainstorming

Have students sit in a group setting (area rug) to allow idea sharing. Tell the students that they are going to perform the first step of the writing process - brainstorming! An easy topic for most students is something they are good at. Work with the students to narrow the topic to something very specific such as "I'm very good at kickball". Allow other students to share one specific thing they are good at and the reasons why. Draw a Web Organizer on the board, select one student's idea to use as an example, and chart their information on the board using a web organizer. In the center circle write the topic: I am very good at kickball. Explain that the outer circles are used for containing the supporting details of why. In the outer circles write the details that would answer the why question: Kick far. Run fast. Catch easy. Roll straight. The preceding thoughts are the details that support why they are very good at kickball. Explain to the students that they now have the information for their topic sentence and supporting details; they are now ready to begin their draft.

Step 2 - Draft

Have the students begin with the topic listed in the center circle and write a sentence that lets their readers know what they are about to tell them (Do not allow students to use the statement: "I'm am about to tell you why I am so good at kickball" - this is a common mistake in writing). Once the students choose a topic sentence for this paragraph, have them turn their supporting details (in the outer circles) into sentences, and develop a closing sentence. The closing sentence basically sums everything up and reiterates (not restate) the topic sentence. At this point punctuation, word usage, and spelling are not an issue. Since this is the draft copy, **students should double space their writing to allow for later corrections.**

The Elements & Styles of Writing
Activity Title: <u>The Writing Process</u>
Whole Group Instructions:
All Grades

Step 3 – Revise

Inform the students that they are going to read over their paper to see what they can do to make it better. Here, one's knowledge of synonyms become important. Students should check to make sure that they are not constantly using the same word over and over again, if so, use synonyms. Also, make sure that the paper makes sense, gets the point across and flows smoothly (if not, now is the time to change some words, add additional sentences and/or change the sentence order. Next, have the students peer edit each others papers by passing their paper to another student to have them read and ask them the following questions:
1. Can you understand my paper?
2. Do you have any questions about my paper?
3. Should I add or delete any information in my paper?
4. What is my paper saying? (If the second student gets a different meaning from the writing, the first student should identify the word or words that caused the confusion and make the necessary corrections.) If all is well, move on to step 4.

Step 4 - Edit and Proof Read

Now is the time to pay special attention to punctuation, word usage, and spelling. Have the students cross out mistakes, rather than use an eraser, and write their corrections on the blank line above. Have them re-read their paper with the corrections to make sure it has the proper punctuation, word usage, and spelling.

Step 5 – Publish

Finally, have the students re-write their paper with the corrections in their best writing. This is the final copy so it must be neat and clean. Students should not skip any lines on their final copy. Students may want to include a picture to go along with their paragraph.

The Elements & Styles of Writing
Activity Title: <u>The Writing Process</u>
All Grades

LEVELS	INDEPENDENT ACTIVITIES
BEGINNING	Select another topic for the whole class to work on and have them complete steps 1 through 3 as a group. Have the students complete steps 4 and 5 independently. For most students, the hardest parts of the writing process is identifying a topic sentence and the supporting details. In this case, the students are being walked through the process, leaving only the revision, editing, proofing, and publishing as an independent work assignment. With enough guidance and practice, the students will soon be able to complete the entire writing process on their own.
INTERMEDIATE	Select another topic for the whole class to work on and have them complete step 1 as a group. Have the students complete steps 2 through 5 independently. For most students, the hardest part of the writing process is identifying a topic sentence and the supporting details in a streamlined and focused manner. In this case, the students are given the topic and supporting details as a guideline and starting point. The students must complete the drafting, revising, editing, proofing, and publishing as an independent work assignment. With enough guidance and practice, the students will soon be able to produce a focused topic with supporting details independently and be able to complete the entire writing process on their own.
ADVANCED	Have the students supply their own topic and supporting details, complete a web organizer, and complete the entire writing process independently.
Assessment Options:	Have the students share their completed work with the class. Have the students explain the steps in the writing process. Have the students lead a lesson in the writing process.

The Elements & Styles of Writing
Activity Title: <u>The Writing Process</u>
All Grades

Reflection: The Writing Process

It is important for students to understand why they are learning this process and how they can apply it to their daily lives. Explain that writing is very important to our method of communication. Being able to think, organize, and document information in a manner in which others understand is crucial.

In this reflection, ask the students these questions in an open discussion:

1. What did they learn?
2. How can they use what they learned in their daily activity?
3. Can they teach what they have learned to someone else?
4. What did they like most about the activity?
5. What did they like least about the activity?

The Elements & Styles of Writing
Visual Step-by-Step Example - The Writing Process

Step 1 - Brainstorming

    Brainstorming is the first step in writing, but it doesn't really involved any writing. The brainstorming process is all about thinking, talking, and gathering information on which to write about. After brainstorming and developing a focus topic, fill in the web organizer. (The web organizer is meant to assist in charting and organizing information).

A- Select A Topic	**B- Develop Supporting Details**
Topic: Something I am very good at - kickball.	Decide on details to support your claim.
Topic Kickball	**Supporting Details:** 1. Kick far. 2. Run fast. 3. Good catcher. 4. Roll straight.

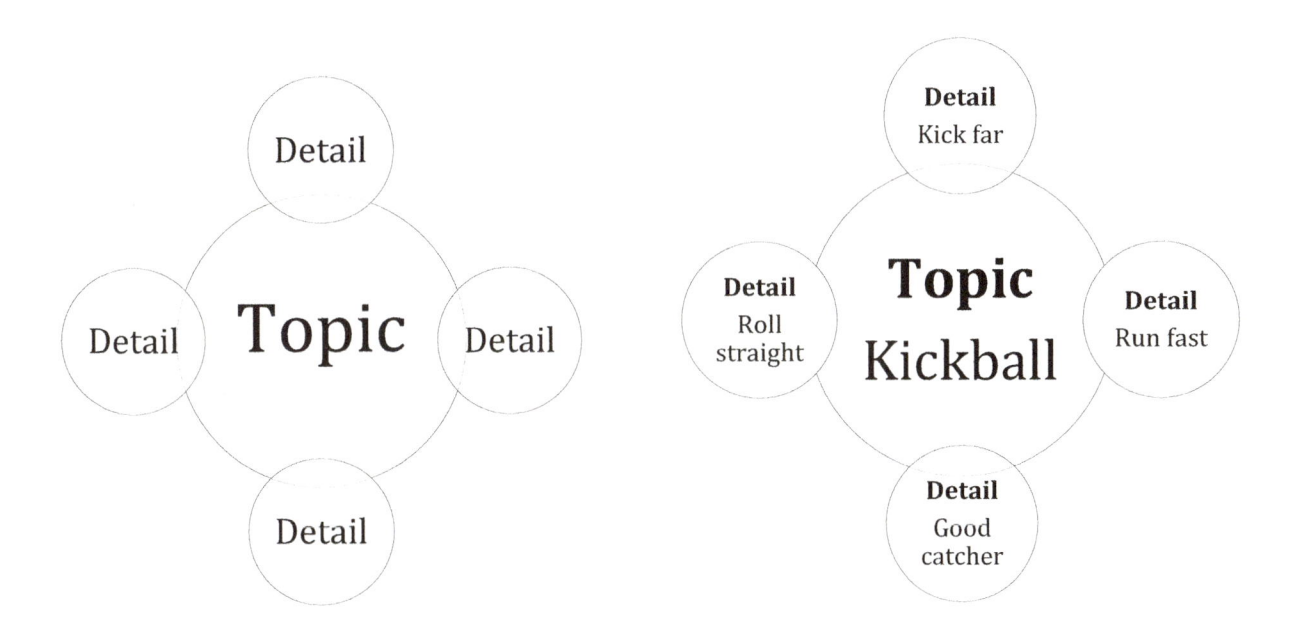

(Left web diagram: Topic in center with four Detail circles around it)

(Right web diagram: Topic "Kickball" in center with four Detail circles — "Kick far", "Run fast", "Good catcher", "Roll straight")

The Elements & Styles of Writing
Visual Step-by-Step Example - The Writing Process

Step 2 - Draft

Using the topic and each of the supporting details in a sentence.

    Topic: *Something I am very good at - kickball.*

    I am a very good kickball player.
    I can kick the ball really far.
    I can run really fast.
    I am a good catcher.
    I can roll ball straight.
    I am a good kickball player for all these reasons.

The Elements & Styles of Writing
Visual Step-by-Step Example - The Writing Process

Step 3 - Revise

The preceding sentences are good starts to a well-developed paragraph; however, some changes must be made. Notice the repetition of the words *I, can,* and *am*. The wording of these sentences must be changed in order to eliminate repetition and add interest. Also, the topic sentence makes a statement, but it is very short. Students may want to add a 'because' ending to this sentence, or indicate the standard of what is good by using a comparison. In this case, the topic sentence may read:

According to my friends, I am a very good kickball player. **Notice how this sentence changed to reveal a source.**

I am a very good kickball player because I know how to play all of the positions really well. **Notice how this sentence now includes the word *'because'* and gives an example.**

When I kick the ball I know how to aim and kick it really hard so that it goes very far. **Notice how this sentence now includes the word *'because'* and gives an example.**

After I kick the ball, I run the bases and no one can catch me because I am so quick. **Notice how this sentence includes the words *'after'* and *'because'*. This gives sequence of the sentence and gives an example of how fast he/she is.**

When my team is in the field, they always count on me to catch the ball because I never drop it. **Notice how this sentence now includes the word *'because'* and gives an example.**

I can roll the ball really fast and make it hard for the other team to kick it, that's why my team always lets me roll the ball. **Notice how this sentence now includes a reason why it is good to be able to roll the ball fast.**

Being good at kickball requires many skills, and I have all the skills necessary to be a good kickball player. **Every paragraph should have a closing sentence to sum up and reiterate the topic.**

In order to help students reach the point of adding the above type of information, you must ask the question words: *who, what, when, where, why,* and *how*. They will not be able to answer all of the question words about each of their sentences; but they will be able to answer some of the questions, and as a result, compose a better sentence. Encourage the students to familiarize themselves with asking the question words in their own work when writing. This will help them become better writers.

The Elements & Styles of Writing
Visual Step-by-Step Example - The Writing Process

Step 4 - Proofread and Edit

This is the time to check for errors. It is very helpful for writers of all levels to use a check list to make sure they do not miss anything and have done their best work. The checklist below is an example of a general checklist.

1	Each sentence begins with a capital letter.	✓
2	Each sentence is complete and not a fragment or run-on.	✓
3	All proper nouns are capitalized.	✓
4	All sentences have an agreeing subject and verb.	✓
5	Each sentence has an end mark.	✓
6	I used synonyms to eliminate repetition.	✓
7	I wrote the entire story in the same person (Note: all in the 1st or 3rd person.).	✓
8	All words are spelled correctly.	✓
9	My topic sentence is clear.	✓
10	My closing sentence sums up all of my paragraphs.	✓
11	My paragraphs read easily and are understandable.	✓
12	I checked my work.	✓
13	I had a friend re-check my work.	✓
14	I prepared a clean copy of my work for the publish copy.	✓
15	I included a title, my name, and the date on my paper.	✓

The Elements & Styles of Writing
Visual Step-by-Step Example - The Writing Process

Step 5 - Publish

Once steps 1 through 4 are complete and the check list is completely checked off, the students are ready to prepare their publish copy. The publish copy must be neat, clean, and single spaced. (The purpose of double spacing in previous copies was to allow room for corrections. By this point, all corrections should be complete.)

    According to my friends, I am a very good kickball player because I know how to play all of the positions really well. When I kick the ball, I know how to aim and kick it really hard so that it goes very far. After I kick the ball, I run the bases and no one can catch me because I am so quick. When my team is in the field, they always count on me to catch the ball because I never drop it. I always get to roll the ball because I can roll the ball really fast and make it hard for the other team to kick it. Being good at kickball requires a lot of practice and many skills, and I have all the necessary skills to be a good kickball player.

The Elements & Styles of Writing
Graphic Organizers - The Writing Process

A graphic organizer helps writers plot the visual picture of their plans for writing. There are many types of graphic organizers available for writers to use, however, for the purpose of this activity, we will focus on six basic graphic organizers.

1. **The Web** - the most basic and most commonly used is called a Web Graphic Organizer, quite possibly, because of its similarity in appearance. It has a circle in the center for the focus topic, and a second tier of circles around the outside for supporting details. This organizer can be expanded to encompass a third (and even more) layer of circles for supporting details of the details and/or examples.

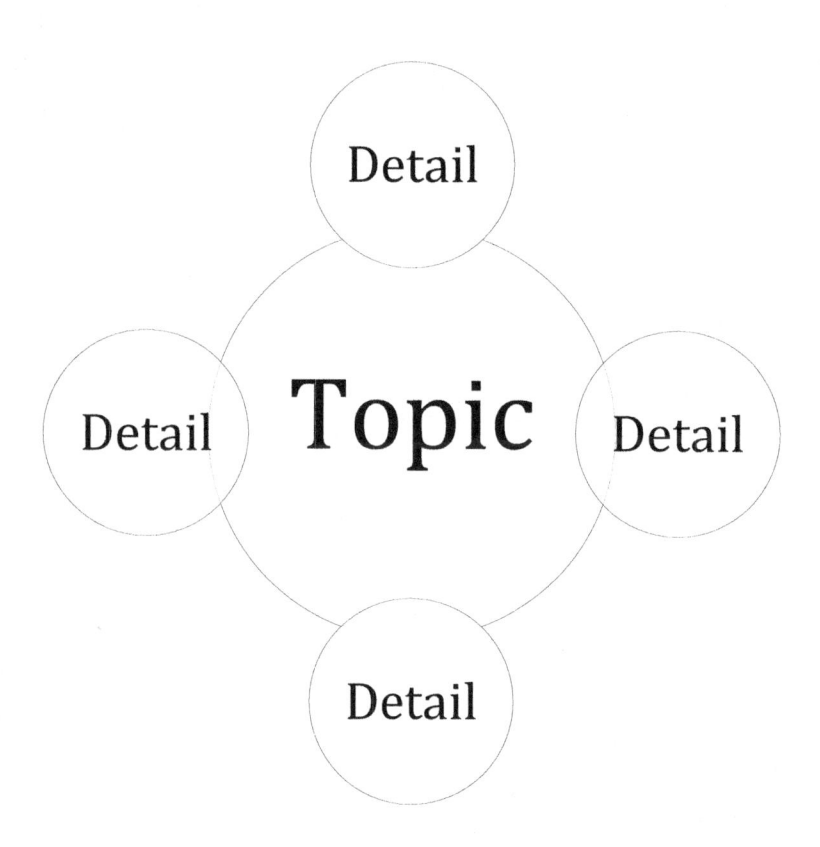

The Elements & Styles of Writing
Graphic Organizers - The Writing Process

2. **The Comparison & Contrast Graphic Organizer** - is used to chart information that is unique to each individual focus topic while identifying the information that each share. The Comparison and Contrast Graphic Organizer is made up of two overlapping circles that reveal three separate spaces. One side holds information that is unique to one focus, the center holds information that is shared, and the third circle holds information unique to the other focus of the comparison.

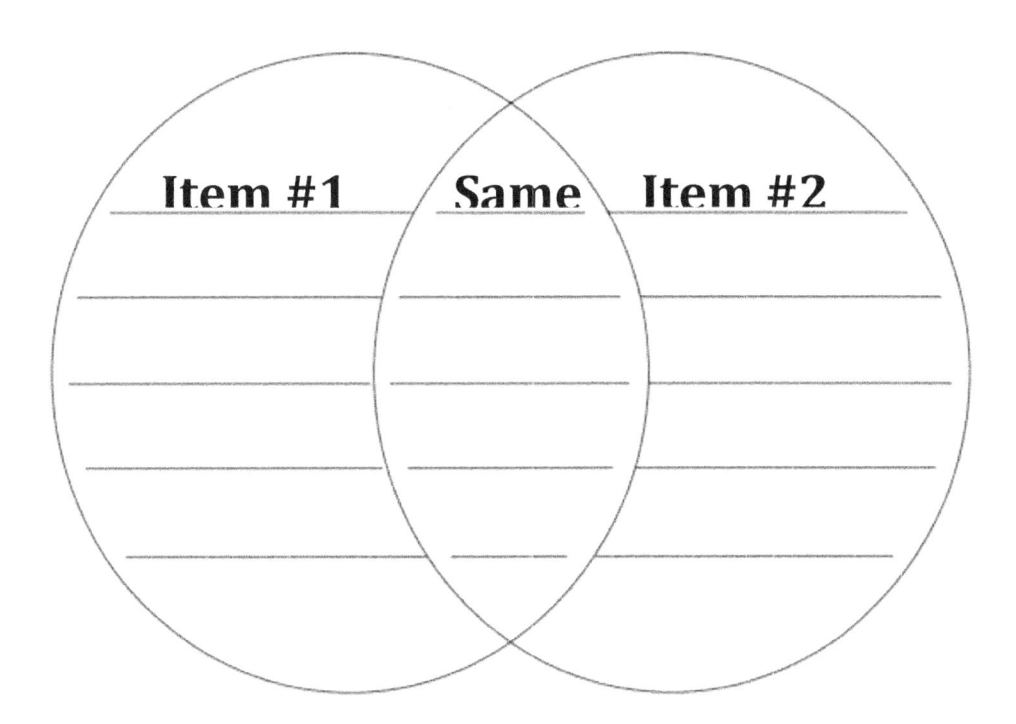

Item #1   Same   Item #2

Graphic Organizers - The Writing Process

3. **The Cause-and-Effect Graphic Organizer** - is used to show what happens as a result of other factors. The Cause and Effect Graphic Organizer can take on a variety of forms, however, the most common is boxes and arrows.

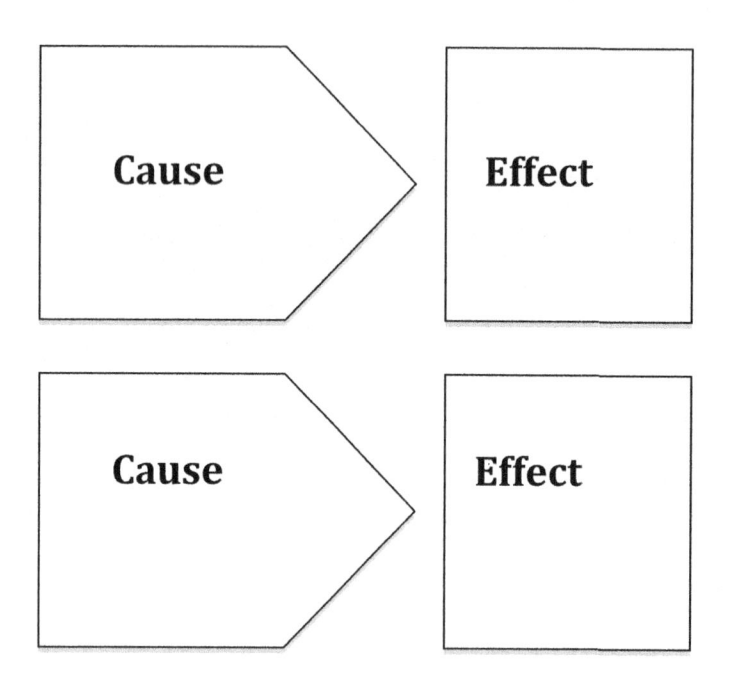

Cause → Effect

Cause → Effect

The Elements & Styles of Writing
Graphic Organizers - The Writing Process

4. **The Sequence Graphic Organizer** - is used to help keep track of the order in which things occur. Although there are many graphic organizers to serve this purpose, the stair-step seems most interesting. Simply insert the information into the correct box in the order in which it is to occur in the story.

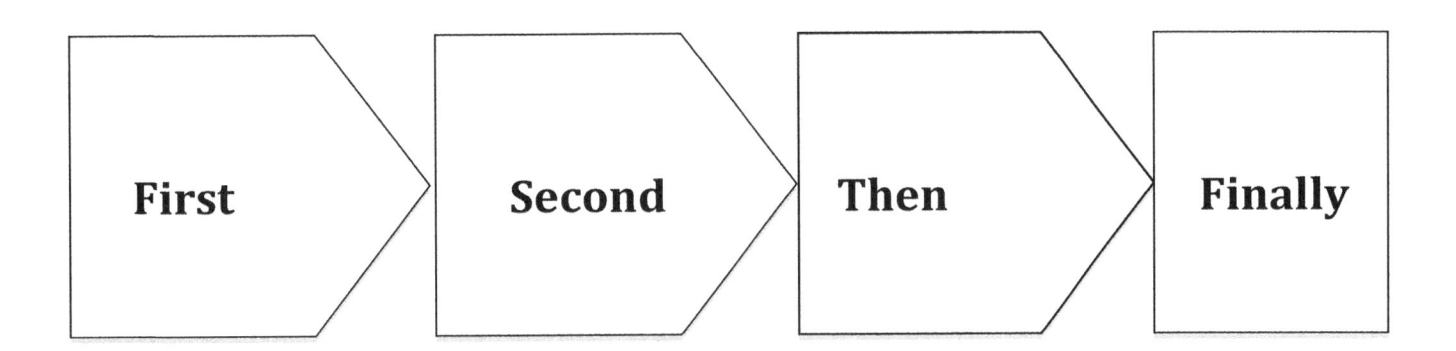

| First | Second | Then | Finally |

The Elements & Styles of Writing
Graphic Organizers - The Writing Process

5. **The Time-line Graphic Organizer** - is very helpful for recording information in chronological order. This is especially useful in tracking the events of a persons life, or even tracking daily activities. The time-line can be set-up with columns for entering pertinent information (dates, years, periods, age, time, etc.) and then add the relevant information.

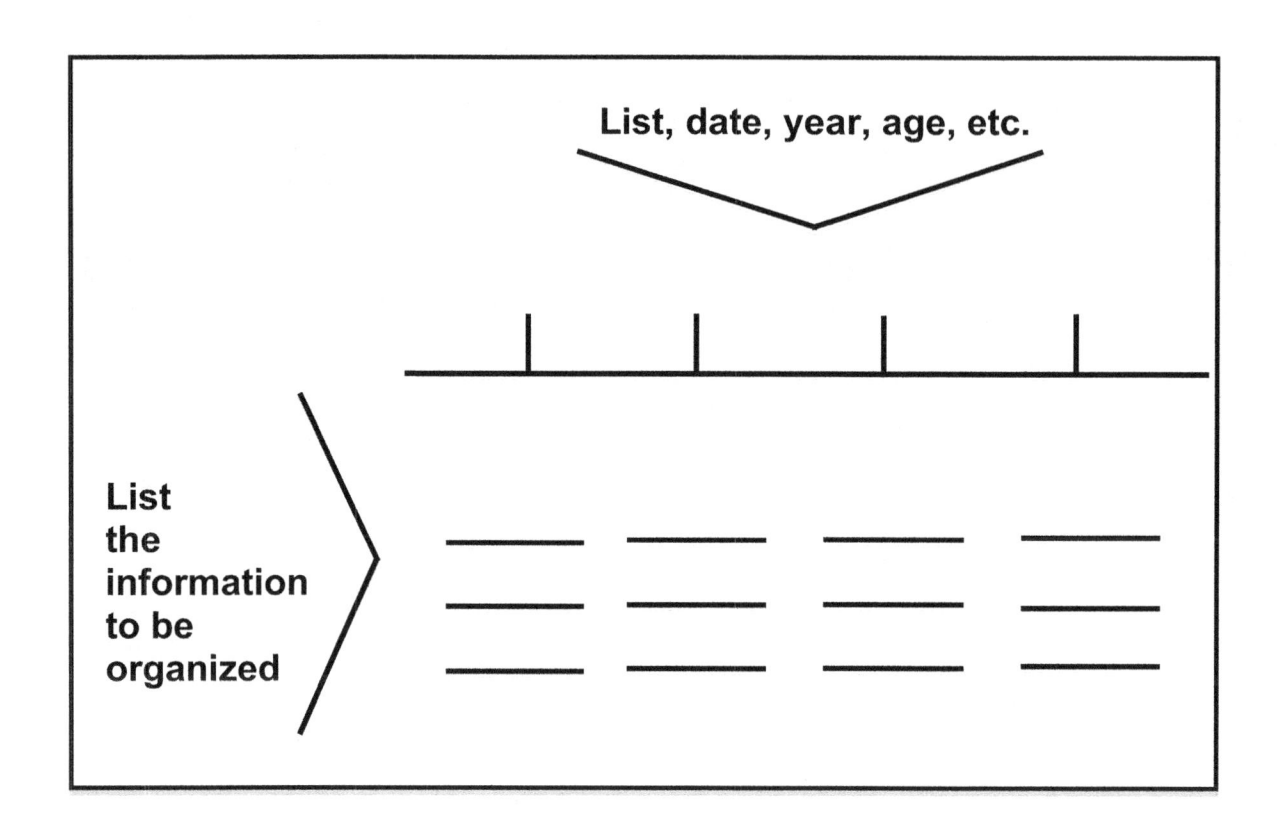

List, date, year, age, etc.

List the information to be organized

The Elements & Styles of Writing
Graphic Organizers - The Writing Process

6. **The Story Map** - is used to organize all of the details of a story. A story contains several elements and a great story is well thought-out and planned. Keeping track of all the important details you want to include in the story would be almost impossible without some type of organization. As with other graphic organizers, story maps come in a wide variety of formats. For the purpose of this activity we will keep it simple and use a basic story map. Keep in mind that this graphic organizer (as well as the others) can be expanded upon, or altered, to suit the writer's needs.

Title
Events

Plot	Character(s)	Setting

Problem	Solution

The Elements & Styles of Writing
Activity Title: <u>**Writing Prompts**</u>

Writing prompts are subject ideas used to give the practicing writer a focused topic. The beginning activities are short and simple: great for beginners or to gauge a student's writing abilities.

Time Frame: **35 - 65 Minutes (per activity)**
- 5 - 10 Activity introduction and explanation.
- 5 - 10 Chart information on the board.
- 5 - 10 Whole group discussion.
- 10 - 15 Independent student activity.
- 5 - 10 Activity assessment.
- 5 - 10 Reflection on the activity.

Lesson Objective: To enhance student writing skills through the steps in the wiring process.

Materials & Resources: Paper and pencil.

Instruction Procedure: Explain the lesson and lesson objective to the students.

Whole Group Activity:

Select a graphic organizer (the web usually works best for this type of general writing) and a topic. You may make-up your own topic, have the students make up their own, or use a topic listed on the following pages. Once the graphic organizer and topic has been selected, allow the students a few minutes of discussion time. Then move on to the appropriate independent activities on the following pages.

The Elements & Styles of Writing
Activity Title: <u>Writing Prompts</u>

LEVELS	INDEPENDENT ACTIVITY
BEGINNING	Select another topic for the whole class to work on and complete steps 1 through 3 as a whole group. Have the students complete steps 4 and 5 on their own. For most students, the hardest part of the writing process is deciding on a topic sentence and developing the supporting details. In this case, the students are being walked through the process; leaving only the revision, editing, proofing, and publishing as an independent work assignment. With enough guidance and practice, the students will soon be able to complete the entire writing process on their own.
INTERMEDIATE	Select another topic for the whole class to work on and complete step 1 as a whole group. Have the students complete steps 2 through 5 on their own. For most students, the hardest part of the writing process is deciding on a topic sentence and developing the supporting details. In this case, the students are given the topic and supporting details as a guideline and starting point. The students must complete the drafting, revising, editing, proofing, and publishing as an independent work assignment. With enough guidance and practice, the students will soon be able to complete the entire writing process on their own.
ADVANCED	Have the students choose their own topic, develop supporting details, complete a web organizer, and complete the entire writing process on their own.
Assessment Options:	Have the students share their completed work with the class. Have the students explain the steps in the writing process. Have the students lead a lesson in the writing process.

Reflection: The Writing Process – Using Writing Prompts

It is important for students to understand why they are learning this process and how they can apply it to their daily lives. Explain that knowing how to write is important for communicating with others.

In this reflection, ask the students these questions in an open discussion:

1. What did they learn?
2. How can they use what they learned in their daily activity?
3. Can they teach what they have learned to someone else?
4. What did they like most about the activity?
5. What did they like least about the activity?

The Elements & Styles of Writing
Writing Prompts

All about me

I am very good at …

I am not so good at …

I would like to learn how to …

I can teach others …

My mother/father taught me …

My sister/brother taught me …

My aunt/uncle taught me …

My friend taught me …

My best friend and I like to …

My family and I like to …

When I grow up I want to …

I'm really brave when it comes to

I get scared when …

When I am at home …

What I like most about myself …

What makes me feel safe ..

What makes me feel proud …

What embarrasses me …

What makes me sad …

What makes me happy …

The day before my birthday …

On my birthday …

On the first day of school I feel …

My favorite …

television show

television star

book

movie

movie star

musician

musical group

pet

action hero

food

sport

after school activity

activity in school

thing to do on the weekend

thing to do during summer

thing to do during winter

thing to do with my family

thing to do with my friend(s)

place to go …

toy …

relative …

outfit…

hiding place …

The Elements & Styles of Writing
Activity Title: <u>Story Starters</u>

Sometimes the hardest part of writing is generating ideas to write about. In this activity students are given ideas for stories. This helps promote the writing process and gives the students assistance in generating ideas.

Time Frame: **45 - 75 Minutes (per activity)**
    5 - 10 Activity introduction and explanation.
    10 - 15 Chart information on the board.
    5 - 10 Whole group discussion.
    15 - 20 Independent student activity.
    5 - 10 Activity assessment.
    5 - 10 Reflection on the activity.

Lesson Objective: To enhance student writing skills.

Materials & Resources: Paper and pencil.

Instruction Procedure: Explain the lesson and lesson objective to the students.

Whole Group Activity:

Copy the Story Map Graphic Organizer on the board and have the students copy it on their paper. Next, select a story starter from the list on the following pages (or make up one of your own), write it on the board, and read it to the students. Demonstrate the writing process beginning with filling in the graphic organizer based on the information from the story starter. Continue on with the writing process through the publish copy stage which can be found on pages later in this lesson.

Now the students are ready to work independently according to their level. Select an independent activity level from the following pages based on student abilities and follow that set of directions.

The Elements & Styles of Writing
Activity Title: <u>Story Starters</u>

LEVELS	INDEPENDENT ACTIVITY
Beginning	Select a story starter and graphic organizer from the following pages. Work with the students to complete the story map with the information from the story starter. Allow the students some time to discuss details for the story as a group and record the information on the board. Using the information from the Story Map on the board, have the students write their story.
Assessment Option:	Have the students share their work with the class.
Intermediate	Complete the story map with the information from the story starter and have the students copy it onto their paper. Allow the students a few minutes to come up with a story on their own (individually) using the basic information compiled on the story map. Have them chart the details of the story on their story map and begin writing.
Assessment Option:	Have the students share their work with the class.
Advanced	Have the students listen to the story starter and individually chart the information on their own story map. Allow the students a few minutes to come up with a story on their own (individually). Have the students chart the details of the story on their story map and begin writing.
Assessment Option:	Have the students share their work with the class.

Reflection: The Writing Process Using Story Starters

It is important for students to understand why they are learning this process and how they can apply it to their daily lives. Explain that knowing how to write is important for communicating with others. The art of story telling through the written word can be entertaining and rewarding.

In this reflection, ask the students these questions in an open discussion:

1. What did they learn?
2. How can they use what they learned in their daily activity?
3. Can they teach what they have learned to someone else?
4. What did they like most about the activity?
5. What did they like least about the activity?

The Elements & Styles of Writing
Story Starters
All Levels

1   **Characters -**   Kimberly, a 12 year old smart-aleck who thinks she knows everything. John - an 11 year old cry baby who's afraid of his own shadow. Martin - a 10 year old practical joker who thinks everything is funny.

       Plot -   Food and supplies keep disappearing in the middle of the night.

       Setting -   The lake and campgrounds of Good Night Camping Resort.

       Main Events -   John is confronted by the food and supply thieves, now he's so afraid that he hasn't spoken for two days.

       Problem -   The children only have enough supplies and food to last them one more day, but they have no way to get back home until the end of the week - seven days away.

Directions: Give the story a title. Using the details provided, write a story and create a solution to the problem describing how the children survive.

2   **Characters -**   Racquel - the bookworm who just loves to read. Ronald - the adventurer who's always looking for a thrill. Tony - greedy, pushy, bossy, and always wants to be in charge.

       Plot -   There is a secret trap door in the tree house that give the children special powers when they enter.

       Setting -   An abandoned tree house in the backyard of a vacant house.

       Main Events -   The children go through the trap door of the tree house and find themselves deep in a forest in the middle of the night.

       Problem -   The children go into the tree house and enter a trap door. They cannot find their way out. The biggest problem is that their parents have told them to stay out of the tree house. Now, no one knows were they are.

Directions: Give the story a title. Using the details provided, write a story and create a solution to the problem describing how the children find their way back through the trap door in the tree house.

The Elements & Styles of Writing
Story Starters
All Levels

3   **Character -**   Robert - a fanatic of computer games.

       Plot -   Every time Robert tries to stop playing the video game his room gets smaller and another panel is added, boarding up his doors and windows

       Setting -   Roberts computer room and the inside of the computer game.

       Main Events -   Robert notices the curse of the video game. Every time he looses a round of the game, something strange happens in his room.

       Problem -   If Robert doesn't finish and win the game soon, his room will cave in on him and the exits will be all boarded up - he'll be trapped!

Directions: *Give the story a title. Using the details provided, write a story and create a solution to the problem that describes whether or not Robert wins the computer game and what effects it causes.*

4   **Characters -**   Joshua - the non believer, his cousin Tony, and their friend Bruce.

       Plot -   The children try to find someone they can trust to swim down to the cave and bring back the treasure. The hardest part is finding someone they can trust, who can also swim.

       Setting -   The swimming pool with a secret tunnel that leads to a cave underground that is filled with treasures.

       Problem-   Neither child can swim good enough to get to the cave and back except for Joshua who doesn't believe that there's a cave or any treasure to be found.

       Main Event-   Playing in the pool while trying to keep untrustworthy people from finding out about the treasure. They also have the adventure of a lifetime when they find a way to retrieve the treasure.

Directions: *Give the story a title. Using the details provided, write a story and create a solution to the problem that describes if and how the children retrieve the treasure.*

The Elements & Styles of Writing
Story Starters
All Levels

5   **Characters -**   Grandma Nellie. Bobby and his 50 pound Collie named Bruiser. Kate and her 6-month old pet Siamese kitten named Mittens.

       Plot -   Grandma Nellie is expecting her grandson from California and her granddaughter from New York. The grandchildren are going to spend two beautiful summer weeks with her - but she doesn't know that they are bringing their pets.

       Setting -   Grandma's home in the country. A small 3-bedroom farmhouse with lots of land surrounding it.

       Main Events -   Bobby and Bruiser are already at grandma's when Kate and Mittens arrive. Bruiser goes berserk at the smell of the cat. Kate grabs Mittens and runs for cover as Bruiser rages out of control.

       Problem -   The grandchildren and pets are trapped at grandma's house for 2 weeks and the animals appear to hate each other.

Directions: Give the story a title. Using the details provided, write a story describing how they resolve their pet problems and tell how the vacation turns out?

6   **Characters -**   Joey, a curious teenager and his parents, Bob and Ada.

       Plot -   Joey is with his family on Safari in Africa. He has been warned repeatedly to stay close to his family.

       Setting -   Deep jungle area of Africa .

       Main Events -   Joey could not resist the temptation to hop onto the back of a giraffe as the giraffe passed under a tree he had climbed into. He did it the first time and thought it was fun, so he continued to hop from the backs of different giraffes into different trees.

       Problem -   Joey is in another tree far away from the family campsite and there are no lower limbs for Joey to climb down and no giraffes around to carry him down.

Directions: Give the story a title. Using the details provided, write a story describing how Joey solves his problem.

The Elements & Styles of Writing
Story Starters
All Levels

7 **Characters -** Jennifer, an 11-year old spoiled brat, and a crowd of elevator riders of all ages and sizes.

  Plot - Jennifer has always insisted on being 'first' in everything.

  Setting - An elevator car.

  Main Events - Jennifer pushed and shoved her way to the front of the crowd so she could be the first one to get into the elevator car.

  Problem - The more people that entered the elevator car, the farther Jennifer had to go toward the back. So many people got on the car that Jennifer found herself all the way in the back and as much as she pushed and shoved, she could not make her way to the front.

  Directions: *Give the story a title. Using the details provided, write a story describing how Jennifer handled the situation of being in the back of the elevator.*

8 **Characters -** Liza and Lisa, 10-year old twins.

  Plot - Liza and Lisa have always insisted on having the exact same toys and clothes, or else they fight over everything. But this year, things have changed.

  Setting - On the carpeted floor near the Christmas tree.

  Main Events - All of the gifts have been opened and every relative and friend has given the twins identical gifts again. Liza could scream! She's desperate to have something - anything - different from what Lisa has.

  Problem - Liza no longer wants the same gifts as her sister, but Lisa prefers to keep it the way it is. She's afraid that Liza may get better gifts than her.

  Directions: *Give the story a title. Using the details provided, write a story describing how they resolve their identical problem.*

The Elements & Styles of Writing
Story Starters
All Levels

9   **Characters -**   Winnie, a 13-year old girl and her dog Signal.

     Plot -   Winnie has this nagging feeling that her dog has been trying to tell her something important for a very long time.

     Setting -   Winnie's bedroom as she is waking up from a deep sleep.

     Main Events -   Before going to bed last night, Winnie wished upon a star... and her wish was to be able to talk with her dog Signal for just one day.

     Problem -   Winnie wakes up to someone softly calling her name, but it is not her father. In fact, she does not recognize the voice at all- and there's no one in the room...that is, no one but Signal.

Directions: *Give the story a title. Using the details provided, write a story describing who was calling Winnie's name, and what happened from there.*

10   **Characters -**   Willie, a 13-year old boy who was/is mechanically inclined.

     Plot -   When Willie arrives at his grandpa's farm and sees his first motorized riding lawnmower, he wants to put a motor and a chair on every piece of equipment or tool on the farm...and in the house too.

     Setting -   Grandpa Joe's tool shed on his country farm in Iowa.

     Main Events -   Willie had built himself a motorized go-cart at his home in the city. His parents wouldn't let him drive it when, where, and as fast as he wanted because it was too dangerous and probably illegal. However, they did permit him to take his go-cart with him when he went to visit his grandpa who had a big corn farm in Iowa.

     Problem -   Willie has motorized everything on the farm, both inside and outside the house. He has even motorized grandma's wheelchair and broom. His problem is convincing the grown-ups that these motorized items can be useful.

Directions: *Give the story a title. Using the details provided, write a story describing how Willie resolved his problem and tell how the everything turns out?*

The Elements & Styles of Writing
Activity Title: <u>Finishing the Story</u>

    In this activity students will hear the beginning of a story and be asked to create, and write an ending to the story. This activity helps students develop good writing skills. By hearing part of the story, most of the writing process is done for them. They simply need to write an ending. The key is to write an ending that remains on track with the beginning of the story.

Time Frame: 45 - 75 Minutes (per activity)
- 5 - 10 Activity introduction and explanation.
- 10 - 15 Chart information on the board.
- 5 - 10 Whole group discussion.
- 15 - 20 Independent student activity.
- 5 - 10 Activity assessment.
- 5 - 10 Reflection on the activity.

Lesson Objective: To enhance student writing skills through the steps in the wiring process.

Materials & Resources: Paper and pencil.

Instruction Procedure: Explain the lesson and lesson objective to the students.

Whole Group Activity:

    Copy the Story Map Graphic Organizer on the board and have the students copy it on their paper. Instruct the students to fill it out with the information they hear in the story. Next, select a story starter from the list on the following pages (or make up one of your own) and read it to the students. Once the students have completed their story maps, they are ready to begin writing their stories.

The Elements & Styles of Writing
Activity Title: **Finishing the Story**

LEVELS	INDEPENDENT ACTIVITY
BEGINNING	Complete the story map with the information from the story starter and have the students copy it onto their paper. Allow the students to discuss an ending for the story as a whole group and complete the story map using the information. Then, using the information from the story map on the board, have the students complete the story.
Assessment Option:	Have the students share their work with the class.
INTERMEDIATE	Complete the story map with the information from the story starter and have the students copy it onto their paper. Allow the students a few minutes to come up with a story ending on their own (individually). Have them chart the details of the story ending on their story map and begin writing.
Assessment Option:	Have the students share their work with the class.
ADVANCED	Have the students listen to the story starter and individually chart the information on their own story map. Allow the students a few minutes to come up with a story ending on their own (individually). Have them chart the details of the story ending on their story map and begin writing.
Assessment Option:	Have the students share their work with the class.

Reflection: The Writing Process - Finishing the Story

It is important for students to understand why they are learning this process and how they can apply it to their daily lives. Explain that knowing how to write is important for communicating with others. The art of story telling through the written word can be entertaining and rewarding.

In this reflection, ask the students these questions in an open discussion:

1. What did they learn?
2. How can they use what they learned in their daily activity?
3. Can they teach what they have learned to someone else?
4. What did they like most about the activity?
5. What did they like least about the activity?

The Elements & Styles of Writing
Finishing the Story
All Levels

1. You wake up one morning and find yourself in a house full of people that you resemble but don't' know. They tell you that they are your family and that you have just awaken from a three day sleep after being sick. As you look around the room, you notice that the people are wearing old fashion clothing; and the house, its contents and surroundings are old like antiques. Then you find out that the year is 1902. You feel fine, so you get out of bed and …

Directions: *Give the story a title and write an ending to the story that tells what you would do and how you would do it.*

2. You're walking home from school with a group of your friends; laughing, talking, and having a good time. Not paying attention, you trip on a crack in the sidewalk and fall down. Your friends start laughing at you; but continue walking as they laugh. As you begin to get up, you notice something next to the curb. It's a wallet. You reach over to pick it up when you notice that it is stuffed with money; not change, but bills. You forget about your scraped knee and open the wallet. You look up to tell your friends; but they are still laughing, and are almost at the end of the next block. Still sitting on the ground, you open the wallet and realize …

Directions: *Give the story a title and write an ending to the story that tells what you would do and what happens next.*

3. You and some friends are at the beach one day just hanging out and having a good time when all of a sudden you see something protruding from the sand. You walk over to take a closer look and see that it is a bottle with a note inside. You call your friends over to take a look; and, together, you all decide to remove the cork and read the note. You unfold the piece of paper to find that it isn't a note at all. Instead, it is a map. The map shows the beach, and cave, and a treasure box. The treasure box is inside of the cave, but the cave can only be accessed by swimming out to a small island about 100 yards away and climbing down into the cave. You and your friends decide to …

Directions: *Give the story a title and write an ending to the story that tells what you and your friends decide to do and the outcome of your decision.*

The Elements & Styles of Writing
Finishing the Story
All Levels

4.   This year for Halloween I decided to dress up as a fairy princess for the costume party. I found a beautiful old-fashioned dress that would make a perfect fairy princess outfit, and some shoes that were a perfect match. My costume was great, but something was missing and I did not know what it was until I passed by the magic shop downtown and saw the perfect finishing touch for my costume - a magic wand. At first, the man in the store did not want to sell it to me. He said that it possessed real powers (like granting wishes) and that it was not a toy. I told him that I was willing to pay full price for it and really wanted it; and after a few minutes of begging and pleading, he wrapped it up, put it into a bag, and sent me on my way. Now my costume was complete. It was very hot and I was extremely tired walking home from the magic shop. "I wish we were at the beach instead of out here in this hot sun" I jokingly said to my friend Sara. The next thing I knew, a big wave of salt water splashed in my face and knocked me down - I was at the beach in water up to my chest. "What's happened" screamed Sara, as she stood beside me dripping wet. "I don't know", I yelled back, "I simply said I wish we were at the beach instead of out here in this hot sun and now we are". That's it," replied Sara, "the magic wand granted your wish." "Now all you have to do is wish us back home," Sara said excitedly. I looked inside the bag searching for my magic wand, but it wasn't there. Maybe the wave washed it away. "Sara the wand is gone, help me find it so that we can get home" I said frantically. Sara and I began looking all around and finally saw the wand far out in the ocean. I took a chance and wished the wand was back in my hand… it worked. Now I may only have one wish left, what should I wish for?

Directions: *Give the story a title and write an ending to the story that tells what happens next, what happened to the third wish, and how the girls get back home.*

The Elements & Styles of Writing
Finishing the Story
All Levels

5.   While walking through the woods one day I noticed a set of railroad tracks. I thought it was strange to see railroad tracks in the middle of nowhere, so I followed them until they came to an end. Strangely, they ended right at the base of a giant tree, so I decided to follow the tracks in the other directions to see where they began. After about 100 feet, the tracks ended. Stranger still, they ended at the end of a giant tree. I wondered why the train tracks ran from one tree to another; and what they were doing in the middle of the woods. Then all of a sudden I saw white smoke and heard a loud train whistle. I looked up and …

Directions: *Give the story a title and write an ending to the story that tells what he/she saw when they looked up. Be sure that what they saw explains why the tracks were in the middle of the woods.*

6.   Your favorite television show is about to come on, but some of your friends have just invited you to go to the new amusement park for its grand opening. Your parents said that you can go and stay as long as you like, and will even give you spending money. You really want to go to the amusement park because your favorite music group is going to be there, as well as a few of your favorite movie stars. The television show isn't scheduled to replay anytime soon, and it isn't on video. You only have a few minutes to decide what to do because your friends are leaving soon.

Directions: *Give the story a title and write an ending that reveals your decision and why.*

7.   On Monday your teacher announced that he was going to have a contest to see who could earn the most points and win the grand prize. Points could be earned by: good behavior, completing assignments, and being courteous to others. The person with the most points at the end of the week would be the winner. On Friday afternoon, the teacher counted all the points and announced that you were the winner and had won the grand prize. He also announce that the grand prize winner would be the teacher for a day. As teacher for a day, you must teach a lesson in math, language arts, and science. Your teacher informed you that you would need to be ready to teach the lesson Monday morning.

Directions: *Describe the exact lessons you plan to teach, how you prepared yourself, and what you did to gather information on preparing and teaching the lessons.*

The Elements & Styles of Writing
Finishing the Story
All Levels

8.   You wake up late one morning, but still in time for school; so you hurry to get ready. You take a quick shower, brush your teeth, wash your face and eat breakfast. Now all you need to do is get dressed for school. You go to your closet and take out your favorite sweater and jeans; but when you put them on, they don't fit. You turn around to look in the mirror, you see the problem; but instead of seeing yourself, you see…

Directions: *Give the story a title and write an ending to the story that tells what you find when you look in the mirror.*

9.   Today is the day of the great magic show. You've had your tickets for months. Your are so excited because, to you, magic is intriguing and you want to learn how to perform the tricks. During the show, the magician asks for audience participation in the next trick. You eagerly volunteer and are picked to go up on stage. The magician tells you and the audience that he is going to make you disappear by placing you in the black box and you're not afraid. You get into the black box thinking it's just the inside of a large box; but once inside, you find yourself in…

Directions: *Give the story a title and write an ending to the story that tells where you find yourself and what happens while you're in there.*

The Elements & Styles of Writing
Activity Title: <u>Descriptive Writing</u>

Descriptive writing uses many sensory details to paint a picture for the reader. When the readers read the story, they are able to clearly see the unfolding events through your descriptions. The use of sensory words, adjectives, and synonyms in descriptive writing is essential and will provide vivid entertainment for the audience.

Time Frame: **35 - 65 Minutes (per activity)**
                                   5 - 10 Activity introduction and explanation.
                                   5 - 10 Chart information on the board.
                                   5 - 10 Whole group discussion.
                                   10 - 15 Independent student activity.
                                   5 - 10 Activity assessment.
                                   5 - 10 Reflection on the activity.

Lesson Objectives: To provide students with guided practice in the writing process and enhance their writing skills using sensory details.

Materials & Resources: Paper, pencil, and crayons.

Instruction Procedure: Explain the lesson and lesson objectives to the students.

Whole Group Activity:

    Select a graphic organizer (the web usually works best for this type of general writing) and a topic. You may make up your own topic, have the students make up their own, or use a topic listed on the following pages. Once the graphic organizer and topic have been selected, allow the students a few minutes of discussion time. Discussions should focus on an adjective that will help the reader get a picture of what the writer is trying to describe. Once the students have had some time for discussion, call on students and begin charting the supporting details/adjectives on the board. Follow the writing process through to completion to allow the students to see how it develops. Once this whole group activity is complete, move on to the level-appropriate independent activities on the following pages.

The Elements & Styles of Writing
Activity Title: <u>Descriptive Writing</u>

LEVELS	INDEPENDENT ACTIVITY
BEGINNING	Have the students write a one paragraph descriptive story. Select a topic and chart it on their web organizer. List all of the words that they can think of to describes their topic. Using the writing process, turn their topic and supporting details into sentences. Have them continue on through all of the steps in the writing process until they have a publishable copy. Students may draw a picture to accompany their story.
Assessment Option:	Have the students share their work with the class.
INTERMEDIATE	Have the students write a three paragraph descriptive story. Select a topic and chart it on their web organizer. List all of the words that they can think of that describes their topic. Using the writing process, turn their topic and supporting details into sentences. Have them continue on through all of the steps in the writing process until they have a publishable copy. Students may draw a picture to accompany their story.
Assessment Option:	Have the students share their work with the class.
ADVANCED	Have the students write a five paragraph descriptive story. Select a topic and chart it on their web organizer. List all of the words that they can think of that describes their topic. Using the writing process, turn their topic and supporting details into sentences. Have them continue on through all of the steps in the writing process until they have a publishable copy. Students may draw a picture to accompany their story.
Assessment Option:	Have the students share their work with the class.

Reflection: Descriptive Writing

It is important for students to understand why they are learning this process and how they can apply it to their daily lives. Explain that knowing how to write is important for communicating with others. Knowing how to write in a descriptive style enables the audience to visualize and experience the written communication or story as if they were there.

In this reflection, ask the students these questions in an open discussion:

1. What did they learn?
2. How can they use what they learned in their daily activity?
3. Can they teach what they have learned to someone else?
4. What did they like most about the activity?
5. What did they like least about the activity?

The Elements & Styles of Writing
Descriptive Writing Using The Five Senses
All Levels

Hearing	Tasting
1. Describe the sounds that you would hear as you walk through a wooded forest during fall. *(animals, dried leaves, fallen branches, bugs, water, wind, etc.)*	1. Describe the taste or effect of a lemon. *(bitter, sour, eye-squinting, tear-jerking, jaw-squeezing, etc.)*
2. Describe the sounds that you would hear on a cold, windy, rainy day. *(rain dropping, wind blowing, water splashing, thunder, etc.)*	2. Describe the taste of an ice cold popsicle on a hot summer day. *(soothing, refreshing, cold, icy, etc.)*
3. Describe the sounds that you would hear at the beach. *(talking, laughing, waves, suds, birds, etc.)*	3. Describe the taste of your favorite food. *(scrumptious, yummy, delicious, etc.)*
4. Describe the sounds you would hear in the city during the day. *(automobiles, horns, people, airplanes, helicopters, etc.)*	4. Describe the taste of food with too much salt or too much sugar. *(salty, grainy, sweet, sugary, syrupy, etc.)*
5. Describe the sounds you would hear in the country at night *(crickets, wind, trees, etc.)*	5. Describe the taste of your least favorite food. *(awful, terrible, appalling, etc.)*
Seeing	**Feeling**
1. Describe what the forest looks like. *(trees, plants, animals, etc.)*	1. Describe how you would feel if you jumped into an ice cold lake in the middle of winter. *(freezing, cold, numb, etc.)*
2. Describe what snow falling looks like. *(cotton or white clouds falling from the sky, hazy, wind blowing, trees swaying, etc.)*	2. Describe how you would feel if you didn't have any friends. *(lonely, abandoned, deserted, alone, etc.)*
3. Describe what your shadow looks like during the middle of the day. *(giant, huge, tall, dark, black, a copycat, etc.)*	3. Describe how you would feel if you won the lottery. *(proud, lucky, excited, etc.)*
4. Describe a lake and its surroundings. *(water, ducks, bank, trees, grass, dirt, sand, mud, etc.)*	4. Describe the best feeling you every had. *(excited, elated, happy, proud, etc.)*
5. Describe the desert. *(hot, dry, cactus, sand, dust, dirt, flat, etc.)*	5. Describe how you feel when you're embarrassed. *(sad, mad, upset, ashamed, etc.)*

The Elements & Styles of Writing
Descriptive Writing
All Levels

Smelling	Assorted
1. Describe the smell of a bouquet of flowers. *(sweet, perfume, fragrance, etc.)*	1. Describe the *smell* of a walk on the beach/forest/mountains/desert. *(Answers will vary.)*
2. Describe the smell of a chocolate cake. *(sweet, chocolaty, delicious, sugary, etc.)*	2. Describe what lightning *looks* like. *(Answers will vary.)*
3. Describe the smell of the air just after a rain. *(fresh, clean, cool, refreshing, etc.)*	3. Describe the *sound* of thunder. *(Answers will vary.)*
4. Describe the smell of clothes after they have just been washed. *(Answers will vary.)*	4. Describe the setting of the sun. *(Answers will vary.)*
5. Describe the smell of your classroom. *(Answers will vary.)*	5. Describe the taste of hot chocolate on a cold day. *(Answers will vary.)*

Descriptive Writing Using Multiple Senses
All Levels

1. Describe the sights, sounds, smells, and feelings of being at the circus.	6. Describe the sights, sounds, and feelings of being on a space ship.
2. Describe the feelings, sights, tastes, and smell of swimming in the ocean.	7. Describe the tastes, smells, and feelings of being in a chocolate factory.
3. Describe the smell, sight, and sound of being in a movie theatre.	8. Describe the smells, sounds, and feelings of being home during the holiday season.
4. Describe the taste, smell, sight, and feeling of playing in a pool of mud.	9. Describe the sights, sounds, and feelings of a long family road trip.
5. Describe the sounds, sights, and feelings one gets, after scoring big points for the team in a game.	10. Describe the sounds, sights, and feelings of riding a giant rollercoaster.

The Elements & Styles of Writing
Descriptive Writing
All Levels

Describe your…
First day of school.
Summer vacation.
Winter vacation.
Trip to the dentist.
Visit to the doctor.
Worst day at school.
Worst day ever.
Best day at school.
Best day ever.
Most memorable birthday.
Describe the following:
Camping in the woods.
A boat ride on the river.
A horseback riding experience.
Learning how to swim.
Learning how to play a difficult game.
Playing a computer game.
Your walk/ride to and from school.
How you feel when someone does something nice for you.
How you feel when someone hurts your feelings.
How you feel when the teacher asks a question and you *know* the answer.
How you feel with the teachers asks a questions and you *don't* know the answer.

The Elements & Styles of Writing
Activity Title: <u>Comparison & Contrast Prompts</u>

The ability to compare and contrast helps to identify similarities and differences between two things. **(Example:** What is the difference between a frog and a toad?) They look about the same, they live in the same type of environment, they are both amphibians, and they both lay eggs. So what are the differences? A frog has long back legs while the toad's back legs are short. This is just one of the differences between the two that otherwise look the same. The best tool to use when doing a comparison and contrast is the Comparison and Contrast Web. This web will help to sort out features that are unique and those that are shared by the two items being compared and contrasted.

Time Frame: **35 - 65 Minutes (per activity)**
- 5 - 10 Activity introduction and explanation.
- 5 - 10 Chart information on the board.
- 5 - 10 Whole group discussion.
- 10 - 15 Independent student activity.
- 5 - 10 Activity assessment.
- 5 - 10 Reflection on the activity.

Lesson Objectives: To enhance student writing skills by elevating their awareness, enhancing their ability to effectively compare and contrast them.

Materials & Resources: Paper and pencil.

Instruction Procedure: Explain the lesson and lesson objectives to the students.

Whole Group Activity:

Select a topic set to compare and contrast (using the list on the following pages or make up your own) and write it on the board. Draw the Comparison and Contrast Web on the board and insert your selected topic set. Have the students contribute information that is both unique and shared by the two items. List the information on the board in the appropriate spaces on the web. Instruct the students on the format to be used in writing a two-to-three paragraph comparison and contrast paper. You may elect to model the paragraph construction on the board using the example below, or make up your own example.

The Elements & Styles of Writing
Activity Title: <u>Comparison & Contrast Prompts</u>

When writing a comparison and contrast paper, there are a few different formats to choose from. There are two that we will use in this activity: alternating and mixed. With either choice the first paragraph must contain the topic sentence and mention both subjects being discussed. The alternating format discusses only one item per paragraph, while the mixed format discusses the similarities in one paragraph and the differences in the other. If the paper is to be more than two paragraphs, simply continue the pattern of either format. (See the examples of both formats.)

The Elements & Styles of Writing
Comparison & Contrast Writing
Explanation & Example

```
        Mouse          Common            Rat
   Weight ¼ to 2 oz.  Visual appearance  Weight 5 oz. to 15lb.
   Length 3 to 14 in. Nocturnal          Length 6 to 223 in.
   Long scaly tail    Rodent             Long tail with little hair
```

Block Format - Paragraph one contains the topic sentence, naming both items and indicating that they are either very different or very similar. The balance of paragraph one must focus on the first item without further mention of the other item. Paragraph two should discuss the second item, comparing and contrasting it to the first item on each point. Students should include a closing sentence that sums up what was discussed, gives their opinion, and asks a question or answers an obvious question. (See example one on the following page.)

Mixed Format - Paragraph one contains the topic sentence, naming both items and indicating that they are either very different or very similar. The balance of paragraph one should focus on the differences or the similarities of both. Paragraph two should only focus on the differences or the similarities of both (whichever was not the focus of paragraph one). You should include a closing sentence that sums up what was discussed, gives your opinion, asks a question, or answers an obvious question. (See example one on the following page.)

Key Words - are important in directing your readers attention to differences and similarities, they also allow a smooth transition.
Key words for describing differences are; whereas, unlike, differ, and on the other hand.
Kew words for describing similarities are: similar, like, and such as.

The Elements & Styles of Writing
Comparison & Contrast Writing
Explanation & Example

Example One: Block Format

Are Mice and Rats One in the Same?

Although these nocturnal rodents may share some features and look alike at first glace, they are not the same. The mouse has a long scaly tail and ranges in length anywhere from 3 to 14 inches. Mice weigh less that a pound, ranging anywhere from ¼ to 2 oz.

Unlike the mouse, the rat has hair on its tail instead of scaly skin. A mouse's length ranges from 3 to 14 inches, which on average is more than twice the length of a mouse. The rat, on the other hand, ranges in weight from 5 oz to 15 lbs, more than 2 ½ times the weight of a small mouse and about he size of a chiwawa (dog). Maybe this contrast alone will help to identiy whether it's a mouse or a rat.

Example Two: Mixed Format
Comparison & Contrast Writing

Explanation & Example

Are mice and Rats One in the Same?

Altough mice and rats look alike at first glance, a cloer look at details can help identify which is which. Mice are much smaller weighing only ¼ to 2 oz, unlike the rat that can weight from 5 oz to 15lb, which is about the size of a small dog. Other differences between the two include the length and the tail. A mouse's tail can measure up to 14 inches, whereas the rat's tail can strentch up to 23 inches. Also, a rats tail apears scaly while the mouse's tail has hair.

Dispite their suttle differences, the mouse and rat share some commonalities. They are both nocturnal rodents that crawl about at night and scare most people. They also share a simular body structure having a pointy nose, tail, and beady little eyes. Maybe this information will help to identify which is which.

LEVELS	INDEPENDENT ACTIVITY – Comparison & Contrast
BEGINNING	Have the students (as a whole group) select a topic that they are familiar with and chart the similarities and differences on the comparison and contrast web. Next, allow the students to work in pairs (or small groups) to develop a topic sentence and create a sentence for the other items listed on the web. Finally, have the groups continue to work until their two-paragraph comparison and contrast (using either format) is complete.
INTERMEDIATE	Have the students work as a whole group to select a topic set that they are familiar with and chart the similarities and differences on the comparison and contrast web. Continue working as a group to develop a topic sentence and write it on the board. All students should use the same topic sentence. *(This will help the focus of the paper.)* Students should work independently to compose the sentences for, and construct their two-paragraph comparison and contrast (using either format).
ADVANCED	Allow the students to independently select their own topic set and chart the similarities and differences on the comparison and contrast web. Students should work independently to compose their topic sentence and construct their two-paragraph comparison and contrast (using either format).
Assessment Options:	Have the students share their completed work with the class. Have the students explain the steps in this writing process. Have the students lead a lesson in the comparison and contrast writing process.

Reflection: Comparison & Contrast

It is important for students to understand why they are learning this process and how they can apply it to their daily lives. Explain that the ability to compare and contrast is invaluable
in everyday life. The ability to compare and contrast is valuable in all aspects of life, especially when it comes to shopping. If you see two similar products for about the same price, how do you decide which one to buy? The method of comparing and contrasting can help you determine which product is right for you.

In this reflection, ask the students these questions in an open discussion:

1. What did they learn?
2. How can they use what they learned in their daily activity?
3. Can they teach what they have learned to someone else?
4. What did they like most about the activity?
5. What did they like least about the activity?

The Elements & Styles of Writing
Comparison & Contrast

Writing Prompts

dogs/cats	two cars
junk food /health food	two music groups
toads/frogs	two people
hamster/mouse	two different foods
boat/jet ski	two different hairstyles
snow ski/water ski	two different books
horse/zebra	two different subjects in school
house/apartment	two different forms of transportation
school rules/home rules	two different cultures
fork/spoon	two different rooms in your house
cup/glass	two sports
pot/pan	two board games
tree/plant	two video games
television show/theatre movie	two cartoons
rain/snow	two cartoon characters
lake/ocean	two television shows
river/ocean	two movies
ocean/pond	two different streets in your neighborhood
forest/wood	two different types of stores
desert/mountain	two different amusement parks
mountain/valley	two different classrooms at your school
pen/pencil	two different pictures in your classroom
book/magazine	two different comic books

The Elements & Styles of Writing
Activity Title: <u>**Persuasive Writing**</u>

Persuasion means to convince someone to change their way of thinking or doing something. Persuasion is much more effective when presented along with factual evidence to support the opposing position and/or some type of benefit to the person or persons being persuaded.

Time Frame: **45 - 75 Minutes (per activity)**
        5 - 10 Activity introduction and explanation.
      10 - 15 Chart information on the board.
        5 - 10 Whole group discussion.
      15 - 20 Independent student activity.
        5 - 10 Activity assessment.
        5 - 10 Reflection on the activity.

Lesson Objective: To enhance student writing skills.

Materials & Resources: Paper and pencil.

Instruction Procedure: Explain the lesson and lesson objective to the students.

Whole Group Activity:

Explain the definition of "persuade" to the students and ask for examples of things they have persuaded others to do, such as: help them with their homework or play a certain game. Select a persuasion topic from the list on the following pages. Have the students suggest a topic (or make up one of your own) and write it on the board. This activity requires the use of the web graphic organizer. Draw the web on the board and chart the topic in the center. Ask the students for details that will help in the persuasion of others, and for benefits that the person would enjoy if they are persuaded. As the students provide the information, chart it on the board. Once the web is complete, have them write sentences for each of the details and benefits. Continue with the steps in the writing process until you have a complete persuasion.

The Elements & Styles of Writing
Activity Title: <u>**Persuasive Writing**</u>

LEVELS	INDEPENDENT ACTIVITY
BEGINNING	Select a topic from the following pages and walk through each step of the writing process with the students. Have the students supply the information as you write it on the board and they copy it onto their paper. Even though this activity is for beginners, try to get the students to do as much of the work as possible in order to build their confidence and skills.
Assessment Option:	Have the students share their work with the class.
INTERMEDIATE	Select a topic from the following pages and write it, along with the web graphic organizer, on the board. Complete the web on the board with the assistance of the students and have them copy it onto their papers. Once the web is complete, have the students complete the balance of the assignment on their own. They should go through each step of the writing process until they have a complete paper.
Assessment Option:	Have the students share their work with the class.
ADVANCED	Select a topic from the following pages and write it, along with the web graphic organizer, on the board. Have the students complete the web organizer on their own. They should go through each step of the writing process until they have a complete paper.
Assessment Option:	Have the students share their work with the class.

Reflection: Persuasive Writing

It is important for students to understand why they are learning this process and how they can apply it to their daily lives. Explain that knowing how to write persuasively has its advantages. People who master the art of persuasion can find gainful employment in many lucrative fields - including advertising. Persuasive writing can also be helpful in many other aspects of life - it can help you get what you want.

In this reflection, ask the students these questions in an open discussion:

1. What did they learn?
2. How can they use what they learned in their daily activity?
3. Can they teach what they have learned to someone else?
4. What did they like most about the activity?
5. What did they like least about the activity?

The Elements & Styles of Writing
Persuasive Writing
All Levels

Persuade someone to
be your friend
share with you
be courteous
recycle
clean up the school
read a book you like
see a movie you think is great
play with you
plant a garden
attend your birthday party
help you with your homework
exercise with you
buy your favorite cereal
help you with a fundraiser
buy candy from you
to be a good student
let you be in the school play
let you be in the school talent show

The Elements & Styles of Writing
Activity Title: Lists & Journals

Lists and Journals are forms of writing that are generally created by the reader for the reader - they are not generally created for an audience or others to read. Keeping this in mind, lists and journals are simply notes that serve as reminders.

List - a group of items that are related and can be included in one category. Lists are used for a variety of reasons but the most common reason is for keeping track of something. (**Example:** a shopping list.) Lists can be organized by the order of importance or a sequence. (**Example:** first, second, third…)

Journals - a place to keep track of information. It's always a good idea to practice good writing skills, however, when you write in a journal it's really not important because it's for your eyes only. No one else should read your journal. It's like a diary. Journals are usually organized by date. And instead of telling a story, it simply includes the important details.

Time Frame: **45 - 75 Minutes (per activity)**
 5 - 10 Activity introduction and explanation.
 10 - 15 Chart information on the board.
 5 - 10 Whole group discussion.
 15 - 20 Independent student activity.
 5 - 10 Activity assessment.
 5 - 10 Reflection on the activity.

Lesson Objective: To enhance student writing skills.

Materials & Resources: Paper and pencil.

Instruction Procedure: Explain the lesson and lesson objective to the students.

Whole Group Activity:

Select a topic for a list or a journal using the list on the following pages, suggestions from the students, or make up your own and write it on the board. Allow the students to give suggestions for what should be included on the list. Once the students have had some time to practice making lists and making journal entries, move on to the level appropriate activities on the following pages.

The Elements & Styles of Writing
Activity Title: **Lists & Journals**

LEVELS	INDEPENDENT ACTIVITY
BEGINNING	Select a topic for a list and have the students suggest or identify ten items as fast as they can for that list. Select a topic for a journal and have the students make at least five entries. Make sure that the entries are in chronological order and the information follows the time order sequence.
Assessment Option:	Have the students share their work with the class.
INTERMEDIATE	Select a topic for a list and have the students suggest or identify twenty items as fast as they can for that list. Select a topic for a journal, and have the students make at least ten entries. Make sure that the entries are in chronological order and the information follows the time order sequence.
Assessment Option:	Have the students share their work with the class.
ADVANCED	Select a topic for a list and have the students suggest or identify twenty-five items as fast as they can for that list. Select a topic for a journal and have the students make at least fifteen entries. Make sure that the entries are in chronological order and the information follows the time order sequence.
Assessment Option:	Have the students share their work with the class.

Reflection: Lists and Journals

It is important for students to understand why they are learning this process and how they can apply it to their daily lives. Explain that knowing how to create a list or write a journal is important for our own personal organization as well as career and business skills.

In this reflection, ask the students these questions in an open discussion:

1. What did they learn?
2. How can they use what they learned in their daily activity?
3. Can they teach what they have learned to someone else?
4. What did they like most about the activity?
5. What did they like least about the activity?

The Elements & Styles of Writing
List & Journal Example
All Levels

List

Things to do today
1. Wash clothes
2. Clean the car
3. Back to school shopping
4. Walk Rover

Journal

Personal Daily Journal
August 16, 2005 – Today was very exciting, I went to my best friends birthday party and we had a lot of fun. She received some really nice gifts but she liked my gift the most. She promised to come to my birthday party next month.
September 2, 2005 – I have been so busy getting ready for my party tomorrow that I almost forgot to make this entry in my journal. I just want to write down how much I love my parents for this great party they have planned for my birthday. I know it is going to be a blast!

The Elements & Styles of Writing
List & Journal Topics
All Levels

Journal Topics	List Topics
The thing you experience each day (a diary).	Things to do today/tomorrow/next week.
Your daily meals	All the books you own.
Your daily exercise.	All the video games you have.
Homework assignments.	All the toys you have.
Things you see on the way to school, or on the way home from school.	Things you would need to give a Halloween party.
Things that you learned in school.	Birthday gift wish list.
What you do with your friends.	Friends you would like to invite to a party.
What you do on the weekends.	Family members.
The changes in the weather.	Foods that are good for you.
The changes in the landscaping of your neighborhood.	Books you want to read.
Your pets activities and habits.	Music you like.
What a fly does.	Television shows you like.
How a plant grows in different settings.	Places you have visited.
Things that make you happy.	Places you would like to go.
Things that make your sad.	Family and friends' birthdays.
How you feel when you are with certain friends.	Thing you want to learn, or learn how to do.
Places that you have read about and would like to travel to someday.	Movies you like, want to see, or have seen.

The Elements & Styles of Writing
Activity Title: <u>Writing Letters</u>

There are two basic forms of letter writing, business (formal) and personal. Business letters are written for three main reason: to complain, to request, or to express concern. The tone of the business letter should be professional and to the point. The personal letter is simply written communication between friends, relatives or acquaintances, and can be written for any purpose. Business and personal letters have their own specific formats that should be followed whenever writing a letter; and of course, remember to use correct grammar, punctuation, word usage, and spelling.

Time Frame: **45 - 75 Minutes (per activity)**
    5 - 10 Activity introduction and explanation.
    10 - 15 Chart information on the board.
    5 - 10 Whole group discussion.
    15 - 20 Independent student activity.
    5 - 10 Activity assessment.
    5 - 10 Reflection on the activity.

Lesson Objectives: To enhance student's letter writing skills.

Materials & Resources: Paper and pencil.

Instruction Procedure: Explain the lesson and lesson objective to the students.

Whole Group Activity:

Decide which letter format to use for the whole group and independent activities. Draw a blank piece of paper on the board to use as a letter. Help the students identify the names of each part of a letter and where each part should be written. Decide on a topic (use the list on the following pages, ask the students for suggestions, or make up one of your own). Next, draw a web graphic organizer on the board and remind students that, even when writing a letter, graphic organizers help organize their thoughts. Place your topic in the center of the organizer and have the students provide input for the supporting details and examples. Once the web is complete, move on to the level-appropriate independent activities on the following pages.

The Elements & Styles of Writing
Activity Title: <u>Writing Letters</u>

LEVELS	INDEPENDENT ACTIVITY
BEGINNING	Continuing from the whole group activity, list the student's supporting details and examples in the web organizer on the board. Once complete, have the students begin writing sentences for all of their information beginning with the main topic, and continue through the writing process until the letter is complete.
Assessment Option:	Have the students share their work with the class.
INTERMEDIATE	Continuing from the whole group activity, list the student's supporting details and examples in the web organizer on the board and have the students copy the information onto their own paper. Once complete, have the students begin writing sentences for all of their information beginning with the main topic, and continue through the writing process until the letter is complete.
Assessment Option:	Have the students share their work with the class.
ADVANCED	Continuing from the whole group activity, have the students list their own supporting details and examples in the web organizer on their paper. Once complete, have the students begin writing sentences for all of their information beginning with the main topic, and continue through the writing process until the letter is complete.
Assessment Option:	Have the students share their work with the class.

Reflection: Writing Letters

It is important for students to understand why they are learning this process and how they can apply it to their daily lives. Explain that letter writing is important for written communications and proper formatting is critical in any professional communication.

In this reflection, ask the students these questions in an open discussion:

1. What did they learn?
2. How can they use what they learned in their daily activity?
3. Can they teach what they have learned to someone else?
4. What did they like most about the activity?
5. What did they like least about the activity?

The Elements & Styles of Writing
Activity Title: <u>Writing Letters</u>
Personal Letter Format

Personal letters have a specific five-part format.
1. **Your Address** – Your mailing address. This is a two line address.
2. **Date** - The current date is directly below your address.
3. **Salutation** - located next to the left margin, the greeting addresses the letters recipient and is preceded by "Dear", and followed by a comma.
4. **Body** - located just two lines below the salutation (the message of the letter) indent the first line of each paragraph five spaces.
5. **Closing** - located two lines below the body of the letter (the ending of the letter). The most common closing is "Sincerely"; however, there are many others. The closing is followed by a comma.
6. **Signature** - located just below the closing, your signed name. (Usually two spaces.)

Sample Personal Letter Format

Your address	My address
	My City, State, and Zip Code
Date	Today's Date
Salutation	Dear Christy,
Body	Thank you so much for coming out to my birthday party. It was really wonderful to spend time with the people I love so dearly. You are one of my best friends and I am so glad you were there.
	I absolutely adore the handbag you gave me as a gift and have already started using it to carry all of my things with me everywhere I go. It is beautiful and matches every outfit I wear. I hope you invite me to your birthday party next month so I can give you a fantastic gift as well.
	Please keep in touch and write back soon. I really miss you not being here but we can keep in through letter writing. I hope to hear from you really soon!
	Sincerely,
	Kelly

The Elements & Styles of Writing
Activity Title: <u>Writing Letters</u>
Business Letter Format

Business letters have a specific format.

1. **Date** - Three to five spaces below the letterhead or margin line; three spaces for a long letter and five spaces for a short letter.

2. **Addressee/Title** - Three to five spaces below the date; three spaces for a long letter and five spaces for a short letter.

3. **Company Name** - The name of the company you are sending the letter to.

4. **Company Address** - The address of the company you are sending the letter to.

5. **Salutation** - Two spaces below the inside address. This is the greeting used to address the recipient of the letter. This usually begins with "Dear," and the recipient's name.

6. **Letter Body** - Two spaces below the salutation and contains the actual letter. Make sure to indent the first line of each paragraph and allow two spaces between each paragraph.

7. **Closing** - located two lines below the body (the ending of your letter). The most common closing is "Sincerely"; however, there are many others. The closing is followed by a comma.

8. **Signature** - located three lines below the closing, this leaves enough room for your signature. Print your full name (and title) below your signature.

9. **Printed Name** - Print your full name underneath your signature.

10. **Your Address** - Your mailing address.

The Elements & Styles of Writing
Activity Title: <u>Writing Letters</u>
Business Letter Format

Sample Business Letter

Date	Current date	
Address/Title	Mrs. Barbara Tucker, CEO	
Company Name	Autos Unlimited	
Company Address	1234 Auto Drive	
	Auto, CA 90259	
Salutation	Dear Mrs. Tucker:	
Body	I recently purchased a car from Autos Unlimited and I am very	
	pleased with both your product and your service. Your sales	
	personnel were so helpful, friendly and professional. This is some-	
	thing I consider to be very important. They really helped me to	
	make the best decision about the car I wanted to purchase. It's also	
	important to note that they were not at all pushy like most sales	
	people. This really made me feel comfortable in my decision to	
	purchase a car from your company.	
	In the future I plan to make more purchases fro your company was.	
	and tell everyone I know how great the experience with your company	
	was.	
Closing	Kindest regards,	
Signature	*Karen Thomas*	
Printed Name	Karen Thomas	
Your Address	1234 Customer Lane	
	Customer, CA 90259	

The Elements & Styles of Writing
Activity Title: <u>Writing Letters</u>
Letter Writing Prompts
All Levels

Personal	Business in the form of request, concern, or complaint.
Write a personal letter to …	**Write a business letter to …**
Your parents to thank them for something nice they did for you.	Your local zoo asking if you can volunteer to work with the animals so that you may learn more about them.
A friend that has moved to another state.	The factory across the street from your school to voice your concern about the pollution it is causing.
A friend to apologize for your bad behavior.	The local police department to voice your concern about the growing problem of graffiti.
Your 1st grade teacher telling her/him how you're doing in your current grade.	Your local politicians to voice your concern about the problems in your neighborhood.
Your grandparents telling them about your new friends.	Your local community service members to ask them to attend your school's Career Day Program.
Your new friend telling him/her why you like them and want to be their best friend.	Your local businesses asking them to donate their recyclable materials to you for a fundraiser.
Your pen pal telling him/her about your new pet.	Your local libraries asking them to donate old book to your newly created book club.
Your friends asking them to come to your birthday party.	A recycling company asking them to allow you to recycle as a form of fund-raising.
Your friends thanking them for attending your birthday party and bringing a gift.	Your local fire department asking them to come to your school and give a demonstration on fire safety.

The Elements & Styles of Writing
Activity Title: <u>Writing Letters</u>
Letter Writing Prompts
All Levels

Your friends' parents asking if you can spend the weekend with your friend.	Your local police department asking them to come to your school and give a demonstration on safety.
Your dentist thanking him/her for repairing your teeth without hurting you.	Multiple community businesses asking them if they will sponsor you in a fund-raiser.
Your neighbors asking them to return your ball that accidentally went over the fence into their yard last week.	Your local newspaper asking them to run a free 'ad' asking residents to observe the speed limit especially in the school zone during school hours.
The new student at your school asking if you can be friends.	Your local movie theatre complaining about the lack of age-appropriate movies they offer.
A friend apologizing for not attending his/her party.	Your local restaurant complaining about the overflowing garbage in the alley behind their business.

The Elements & Styles of Writing
Activity Title: <u>Directions & Instructions</u>

Believe it or not, there is a difference between giving <u>directions</u> and giving <u>instructions</u>. When giving **directions** there may be more than one way of achieving the same goal - this is not true when giving instructions. Giving directions requires the use of prepositions: between, under, around, near, etc. Giving **instructions** is not as easy as it may seem. Instructions must follow a sequence and include every detail. Giving instructions is a step-by-step, detailed process.

Time Frame: **45 - 75 Minutes (per activity)**
- 5 - 10 Activity introduction and explanation.
- 10 - 15 Chart information on the board.
- 5 - 10 Whole group discussion.
- 15 - 20 Independent student activity.
- 5 - 10 Activity assessment.
- 5 - 10 Reflection on the activity.

Lesson Objective: To enhance student's writing skills.

Materials & Resources: Paper and pencil.

Instruction Procedure: Explain the lesson and lesson objective to the students.

Whole Group Activity:

Select one of each (directions and instructions) to study as a whole group activity. For the <u>instruction</u> portion of the activity, you may want to use the sequence graphic organizer in your demonstration. This will help students see why the order is important and how to use the organizer in their independent activity. There is no need to use an organizer for the <u>direction</u> activity.

The Elements & Styles of Writing
Activity Title: <u>Directions & Instructions</u>

LEVELS	INDEPENDENT ACTIVITY
BEGINNING	**Directions:** Have the students draw a map of their school. Select one activity from the list on the following page, and have the students write <u>directions</u> on 'how to get from one place to another'.
	Instructions: Select a topic from the following page and have the students give written <u>instructions</u> on the process.
Assessment Option:	Have the students share their work with the class.
INTERMEDIATE	**Directions:** Have the students draw a map of their school. Select two activities from the list on the following page and have the students write <u>directions</u> on 'how to get from one place to another in order'.
	Instructions: Select a topic from the list on the following page and have the students give written <u>instructions</u> on the process..
Assessment Option:	Have the students share their work with the class.
ADVANCED	**Directions:** Have the students draw a map of their school. Select three activities from the list on the following page and have the students write <u>directions</u> on 'how to get from one place to another in order'.
	Instructions: Select a topic from the list on the following page and have the students give written <u>instructions</u> on the process.
Assessment Option:	Have the students share their work with the class.

Reflection: Directions and Instructions

It is important for students to understand why they are learning this process and how they can apply it to their daily lives. Explain that the ability to properly give directions and instructions is essential for competently co-existing with others, both personally and professionally.

In this reflection, ask the students these questions in an open discussion:

1. What did they learn?
2. How can they use what they learned in their daily activity?
3. Can they teach what they have learned to someone else?
4. What did they like most about the activity?
5. What did they like least about the activity?

The Elements & Styles of Writing
Activity Title: <u>Directions & Instructions</u>
Instructions
All Levels

Give Step-by-Step Instructions
How to make a peanut-butter and jelly sandwich.
How to do an addition (math) problem when you have to carry over a number.
How to tie your shoe laces.
How to brush your teeth.
How to put on a pair of pants.
How to button up a shirt.
How to make lemonade.
How to open a door.
How to swim.
How to jump rope.
How to play a sport.
How to write any letter of the alphabet.
How to draw a picture.
How to catch a ball.
How to format a personal letter.
How to format a (formal) business letter.
How to take a picture.
How to perform a popular dance.

The Elements & Styles of Writing
Activity Title: <u>Directions & Instructions</u>

Directions

Give Directions
How to get from the classroom to the office.
How to get from the office to the auditorium.
How to get from the auditorium to the cafeteria.
How to get from the cafeteria to the playground.
How to get from the playground to the front of the school.
How to get from the front of the school to the bathroom.
How to get from the bathroom to the computer lab.
How to get from the computer lab to the library.
How to get from the library to the learning center.
How to get from the learning center to the classroom.
How to get from the classroom to any other classroom.

The Elements & Styles of Writing
Activity Title: <u>Writing a Personal Narrative</u>

A personal narrative is a true story about the writer with the writer as the narrator. A personal narrative can be just about any length; however, it is generally written in story form, which takes several paragraphs.

Time Frame: **45 - 75 Minutes (per activity)**
                                       5 - 10 Activity introduction and explanation.
                                       10 - 15 Chart information on the board.
                                       5 - 10 Whole group discussion.
                                       15 - 20 Independent student activity.
                                       5 - 10 Activity assessment.
                                       5 - 10 Reflection on the activity.

Lesson Objective: To enhance the student's writing skills.

Materials & Resources: Paper and pencil.

Instruction Procedure: Explain the lesson and lesson objective to the students.

Whole Group Activity:

    Select a topic from the list on the following pages, ask students for their suggestions, or make up your own, and write it on the board. Select a graphic organizer (the web will serve the general purpose for this activity) and draw it on the board placing the topic in the center. Since personal narratives are true stories about individuals, by these individuals; you may want to use a make-believe person for this activity since all of the students will be involved.

Also, since this is a personal narrative, students will not be able to contribute to the supporting details and examples; therefore, instruct the students to make them up and chart them on the board in the web. The students can assist in turning the supporting details and examples into sentences and continuing on through the writing process until all steps have been completed.

The Elements & Styles of Writing
Activity Title: <u>Writing a Personal Narrative</u>

LEVELS	INDEPENDENT ACTIVITY
	Since this is a personal narrative, allow the students to select their own unique topic. If they are having trouble choosing a topic, use the list on the following pages.
BEGINNING	Create a personal narrative that is at least one paragraph. Use sensory details to help paint a picture for the audience/reader. Eliminate repetition of words by using synonyms. Ensure that the story has the correct grammar, punctuation, use of words, and spelling.
Assessment Option:	Have the students share their work with the class.
INTERMEDIATE	Create a personal narrative that is at least three paragraphs. Use sensory details to help paint a picture for the audience/reader. Eliminate repetition of words by using synonyms. Ensure that the story has the correct grammar, punctuation, use of words, and spelling.
Assessment Option:	Have the students share their work with the class.
ADVANCED	Create a personal narrative that is at least five paragraphs. Use sensory details to help paint a picture for the audience/reader. Eliminate repetition of words by using synonyms. Ensure that the story has the correct grammar, punctuation, use of words, and spelling.
Assessment Option:	Have the students share their work with the class.

Reflection: Personal Narrative

It is important for students to understand why they are learning this process and how they can apply it to their daily lives. Explain that knowing how to write is important for communicating with others. The ability to write a personal narrative is important for telling others about yourself and your experiences.

In this reflection, ask the students these questions in an open discussion:

1. What did they learn?
2. How can they use what they learned in their daily activity?
3. Can they teach what they have learned to someone else?
4. What did they like most about the activity?
5. What did they like least about the activity?

The Elements & Styles of Writing
Activity Title: <u>Writing a Personal Narrative</u>
Personal Narrative Writing Topics
All Levels

Choose from the following personal narrative topics.

A time when I was	My First
happy	pet
sad	friend
scared	bicycle
excited	boating experience
proud	horseback riding experience
embarrassed	camping experience
shocked	snow experience
lonely	rain experience
popular	contest or competition
sick	Haircut/hair style
My best memory of	**Other**
a birthday	A time I wish had never happened.
summer camp	A place I like to go to.
playing in the snow	When I did something I shouldn't have.
swimming in a lake	When someone hurt my feelings.
summer vacation	A place that scares me.
any vacation	A special person that influenced my life.
a holiday	A life changing experience.
hanging out with your friends	An important lesson I learned.
a family get together	When I didn't do what I was supposed to do and something bad happened.
school	When I learned how to do something important.

242

The Elements & Styles of Writing
Activity Title: <u>Writing a Fantasy Story</u>

Fantasies are made up of wild ideas based on make believe places, things, people or events. Fantasies include things that are not real and could never exits in real life. Having a good imagination is key to writing a great fantasy story. When developing a fantasy story, consider the setting, plot, and characters. Some of the aspect of a fantasy can be real, such as including yourself or other people; however, in order to qualify as a fantasy, at least one of the aspects of the story must be make-believe.

Time Frame: **45 - 75 Minutes (per activity)**
  5 - 10 Activity introduction and explanation.
  10 - 15 Chart information on the board.
  5 - 10 Whole group discussion.
  15 - 20 Independent student activity.
  5 - 10 Activity assessment.
  5 - 10 Reflection on the activity.

Lesson Objective: To enhance student writing skills through the steps in the writing process using their imagination.

Materials & Resources: Paper and pencil.

Instruction Procedure: Explain the lesson and lesson objective to the students.

Whole Group Activity:

Allow students to talk with one another to generate ideas, or use a beginning sentence or ending sentence from the following pages. Next, draw a blank story map on the board and have the students copy it to their papers. Again, allow the student time to talk with one another to generate information to complete their story maps. Now, cover each element of a fantasy story again, one sections at a time. This time, after each element, allow students time to complete that specific sections on their story maps. Repeat this process with each element until all topics of the story map are complete. Once the students have completed their story maps, they are ready to begin writing their fantasy story.

The Elements & Styles of Writing
Activity Title: <u>Writing a Fantasy Story</u>

LEVELS	INDEPENDENT ACTIVITY
BEGINNING	Create a story that is at least three paragraphs and includes some elements of a fantasy with each element well developed. Use adjectives to describe the setting, character(s), and plot. Eliminate repetition of words by using synonyms. Make sure that the story includes elements of action and suspense with a clear beginning, middle, and ending.
Assessment Option:	Have the students share their work with the class.
INTERMEDIATE	Create a story that is at least five paragraphs and includes all of the elements of a fantasy with each element well developed. Use sensory details to paint a picture for the audience. Eliminate repetition of words by using synonyms. Make sure that the story includes elements of action and suspense with a clear beginning, middle, and ending.
Assessment Option:	Have the students share their work with the class.
ADVANCED	Create a story that is at least eight paragraphs and includes all of the elements of a fantasy with each element well developed. Use sensory details to paint a picture for the audience. Eliminate repetition of words by using synonyms. Include various types of figurative language to make the story more interesting. Make sure that the story includes elements of action and suspense with a clear beginning, middle, and ending.
Assessment Option:	Have the students share their work with the class.

Reflection: Writing a Fantasy Story

It is important for students to understand why they are learning this process and how they can apply it to their daily lives. Explain that knowing how to write is important for communicating with others. Knowing how to write a fantasy story is not only entertaining and fun, but can also become a profitable career.

In this reflection, ask the students these questions in an open discussion:

1. What did they learn?
2. How can they use what they learned in their daily activity?
3. Can they teach what they have learned to someone else?
4. What did they like most about the activity?
5. What did they like least about the activity?

The Elements & Styles of Writing
Fantasy Writing
Beginnings & Endings
All Levels

Below are some beginnings and ending that can be developed into a fantasy story.

Beginning Lines	Ending Lines
When the spaceship landed, we all shook with fear.	From now on I promise to do as my parents tell me.
I was only trying to help clean up the attic when I discovered…	If I ever make it back, I'll never touch that broom again.
I don't usually poke around in other peoples houses, but the door was open and when I peaked in I couldn't believe my eyes.	Each night when I look out past the stars I can see them winking at me and hear them saying hello.
Every time I rub my chin someone disappears.	I learned to never fool with mother nature.
I discovered a door behind the fireplace and that's when…	I woke up in an outer space suit, but I have no idea where it came from.
There's an old game "Don't' step on the crack" that the kids like to play on the sidewalk. I never did until yesterday, and now…	When I checked my pockets, the magic rocks were still there.
The old man said the house was haunted, but I didn't believe him until…	No one will ever believe me, but I'm going to tell them anyway.
The kid seemed normal to me, but when he flapped his arms and started to…	When the sun rose and the gates opened, I ran all the way home.
I woke up this morning to find myself in the kennel with a bunch of stray dogs.	I'm going to bury this wand so deep in the earth that no one will ever find it.
I thought I was alone until I heard…	When I returned, it was as if I had never left the room.
The movie was great, but when it ended I was in the theatre all alone and…	I waved goodbye to my furry friends and promised to keep in touch.
I thought it was a cat, but it walked upright on two legs and spoke to me…	Sometimes things are just not what they seem to be.

Mathematics Made Fun
Activity Title: Count, Read, & Write Whole Numbers

Rule for writing numbers: Numbers zero through nine should be spelled out and numbers 10 and higher should be written it its numeric form. The exception is when you begin a sentence with a number. It is also important to remain consistent.

Numbers are fun when the student knows how they work and how to manipulate them. In this set of activities, students will practice a variety of methods that teach how to read, write, and count numbers.

Time Frame: **35 - 65 Minutes**
                             5 - 10 Activity introduction and explanation.
                             5 - 10 Chart information on the board.
                             5 - 10 Whole group discussion.
                             10 - 15 Independent student activity.
                             5 - 10 Activity assessment.
                             5 - 10 Reflection on the activity.

Lesson Objectives: To increase student knowledge of counting, reading, and writing whole numbers.

Materials & Resources: Paper, pencil, and crayon.

Instruction Procedure: Explain the lesson and lesson objectives to the students.

Whole Group Activity:

Draw a chart with three columns and ten rows. Title the columns: Count, Read, and Write. Then number the rows from one to ten under the *Write* column. Fill-in some of the information in each column and each row. (See example on the following pages.) We elected to use a domino piece under the *Count* column, however, you may use any figure that is easy for the students to draw; and for upper grades and advanced students, use tally marks to indicate larger numbers.

Mathematics Made Fun
Count, Read, & Write Chart

Have the students complete one or all of the following activities according to grade level from the next page.

1. Complete the chart.
2. Identify all even numbers, and then all odd numbers.
3. Identify numbers when counting by 5's, or by 10's
4. Select one of the numbers from the chart and draw a picture; either <u>using</u> the number, or <u>indicating</u> the number. Then write a sentence using the written form of the number.
5. Extend the chart as far as possible.

Count	Read	Write
▪	one	1
	two	
⋰		
		4
	five	
		6
	seven	
⁛ ⁛		
		9
✕ ✕		

248

Mathematics Made Fun
Count, Read, & Write Chart

GRADE LEVELS	INDEPENDENT ACTIVITY
Kindergarten	When setting up the chart and assigning activities, keep in mind the following: Kindergarteners should be able to count, identify, name, and write numbers up to 30, and practice reading numbers in their written form to 10. Select any of the five activities on the first page of this lesson for the students to complete.
Assessment Option:	Select any answer on the chart, cover it with a piece of paper and ask a student for that answer. Ask other students if they agree.
1st Grade	When setting up the chart and assigning activities, keep in mind the following: 1st Graders should be able to count, identify, name, and write numbers up to 100, and practice reading numbers in their written form to 25. Select any of the five activities on first page of this lesson for the students to complete.
Assessment Option:	Select any answer on the chart, cover it with a piece of paper and ask a student for that answer. Ask other students if they agree.
2nd Grade	When setting up the chart and assigning activities, keep in mind the following: 2nd Graders should be able to count, identify, name, and write numbers up to 1000, and practice reading numbers in their written form to 50. Select any of the five activities on the first page of this lesson for the students to complete.
Assessment Option:	Select any answer on the chart, cover it with a piece of paper and ask a student for that answer. Ask other students if they agree.
3rd Grade	When setting up the chart and assigning activities, keep in mind the following: 3rd Graders should be able to count, identify, name, and write numbers up to 10,000, and practice reading numbers in their written form to 100. Select any of the five activities on the first page of this lesson for the students to complete.

Mathematics Made Fun
Count, Read, & Write Chart

Assessment Option: Select any answer on the chart, cover it with a piece of paper and ask a student for that answer. Ask other students if they agree.

4th Grade When setting up the chart and assigning activities, keep in mind the following: 4th Graders should be able to count, identify, name, and write numbers up to the millions, and practice reading numbers in their written form up to the millions.
Select any of the five activities on the first page of this lesson for the students to complete.

Assessment Option: Select any answer on the chart, cover it with a piece of paper and ask a student for that answer. Ask other students if they agree.

5th Grade When setting up the chart and assigning activities, keep in mind the following: 5th Graders should be able to count, identify, name, and write numbers up to the millions, and practice reading numbers in their written form up to the millions.
Select any of the five activities on the first page of this lesson for the students to complete.

Assessment Option: Select any answer on the chart, cover it with a piece of paper and ask a student for that answer. Ask other students if they agree.

Reflection:

It is important for students to understand why they are learning this process and how they can apply it to their daily lives. Explain that the ability to identify and express numbers in any form is an important life skill both academically and personally.

In this reflection, ask the students these questions in an open discussion:

1. What did they learn?
2. How can they use what they learned in their daily activity?
3. Can they teach what they have learned to someone else?
4. What did they like most about the activity?
5. What did they like least about the activity?

Mathematics Made Fun
Activity Title: <u>Compare & Order Numbers</u>

Numbers are fun when the user knows how they work and how to manipulate them. In this set of activities, students will practice a variety of ways and methods to compare and order numbers.

Time Frame: **35 - 65 Minutes**
                                5 - 10 Activity introduction and explanation.
                                5 - 10 Chart information on the board.
                                5 - 10 Whole group discussion.
                               10 - 15 Independent student activity.
                                5 - 10 Activity assessment.
                                5 - 10 Reflection on the activity.

Lesson Objectives: To increase student knowledge of comparing and ordering numbers.

Materials & Resources: Paper, pencil, and crayon.

Instruction Procedure: Explain the lesson and lesson objectives to the students.

Whole Group Activity:

Set up the board using the chart on the following page. Point to each square and have the students identify what number is correct for that square. This will ensure that the students know the numbers. Complete a few of the activities listed with the students to make sure that they know what to do, and then have them complete the balance of the assignments independently.

Mathematics Made Fun
Compare & Order Numbers
Independent Activities

Kindergarten

1. Identify the largest and smallest number in each column, row, and overall.
2. Put the numbers in each column and row in order from largest to smallest and smallest to largest.
3. Identify equal numbers.
4. As a challenge, put all of the numbers on the chart in order from smallest to largest.

	A.	B.	C.	D.	E.
1.	3	6	7	2	1
2.	0	9	4	8	5
3.	7	10	1	9	2
4.	28	16	30	17	12

1st Grade

1. Identify the largest and smallest number in each column, row, and overall.
2. Put the numbers in each column and row in order from largest to smallest and smallest to largest.
3. Identify equal numbers.
4. As a challenge, put all of the numbers on the chart in order from smallest to largest.

	A.	B.	C.	D.	E.
1.	89	23	41	38	26
2.	29	19	0	30	81
3.	63	42	99	92	75
4.	77	50	43	37	82

Mathematics Made Fun
Compare & Order Numbers
Independent Activities

2nd Grade

1. Identify the largest and smallest number in each column, row, and overall.
2. Put the numbers in each column and row in order from largest to smallest and smallest to largest.
3. Identify equal numbers.
4. As a challenge, put all of the numbers on the chart in order from smallest to largest.

	A.	B.	C.	D.	E.
1.	982	516	999	897	422
2.	765	561	696	978	631
3.	389	384	459	689	546
4.	421	291	789	989	454

3rd Grade

1. Identify the largest and smallest number in each column, row, and overall.
2. Put the numbers in each column and row in order from largest to smallest and smallest to largest.
3. Identify equal numbers.
4. As a challenge, put all of the numbers on the chart in order from smallest to largest.

	A.	B.	C.	D.	E.
1.	2,354	5,654	7,012	9,054	10,000
2.	2,543	5,467	7,201	9,045	9,999
3.	2,568	5,896	2,701	9,504	9,898
4.	2,647	5,784	7,210	9,904	8,999

Mathematics Made Fun
Compare & Order Numbers
Independent Activities

4th Grade

1. Identify the largest and smallest number in each column, row, and overall.
2. Put the numbers in each column and row in order from largest to smallest and smallest to largest.
3. Identify equal numbers.
4. As a challenge, put all of the numbers on the chart in order from smallest to largest.

	A.	B.	C.	D.	E.
1.	5.43	99.24	65.36	98.99	75.21
2.	4.99	92.34	69.35	99.10	74.56
3.	5.99	97.21	67.59	98.87	71.20
4.	4.89	94.25	65.66	91.23	70.99

5th Grade

1. Identify the largest and smallest number in each column, row, and overall.
2. Put the numbers in each column and row in order from largest to smallest and smallest to largest.
3. Identify equal numbers.
4. As a challenge, put all of the numbers on the chart in order from smallest to largest.

	A.	B.	C.	D.	E.
1.	1/5	1/5	1/10	1/2	1/16
2.	3/5	1/8	4/10	1/4	1/2
3.	2/5	3/5	6/10	2/7	1/8
4.	5/5	4/5	9/10	3/4	2/3

*If the students have difficulty with the answer, they can draw a figure to express each amount, and then decide which is larger and which is smaller.

Mathematics Made Fun
Compare & Order Numbers

Assessment Option: Have the students share their work with the class.

Reflection:

It is important for students to understand why they are learning this process and how they can apply it to their daily lives. Explain that knowing how to compare and order numbers in any form is an important life skill both academically and personally.

In this reflection, ask the students these questions in an open discussion:

1. What did they learn?
2. How can they use what they learned in their daily activity?
3. Can they teach what they have learned to someone else?
4. What did they like most about the activity?
5. What did they like least about the activity?

Mathematics Made Fun
Activity Title: Place Value

Place value is the value of a number in a specific place. Our numerical system is on a base ten scale, which means that we count from 0 to 9 in the ones place. When we add one more number, the 9 changes to a 0 (zero) and the beginning number of 1 (one) is entered in the tens place, making the new number 10 (ten). Students must understand this concept in order to perform any numerical operation. The activities in this section are focused on providing students practice materials with the place value concept.

Time Frame: 35 - 65 Minutes
- 5 - 10 Activity introduction and explanation.
- 5 - 10 Chart information on the board.
- 5 - 10 Whole group discussion.
- 10 - 15 Independent student activity.
- 5 - 10 Activity assessment.
- 5 - 10 Reflection on the activity.

Lesson Objective: To increase student knowledge of numeric place values.

Materials & Resources: Paper, pencil, and crayon.

Instruction Procedure: Explain the lesson and lesson objective to the students.

Whole Group Activity:

Copy the chart for the grade level you are working with, making sure to leave the blank cells blank. Begin by calling on students to help fill-in the blanks on the chart. Then, allow the students to complete the chart on their own.

Mathematics Made Fun
Place Value Chart

Kindergarten

1. Copy the chart.
2. Fill in the missing values.

	tens	ones	number
1.		9	19
2.	2		23
3.		0	30
4.	0		04
5.	2		26

1st Grade

1. Copy the chart.
2. Fill in the missing values.
3. Write a number sentence for the value of each row.

	hundreds	tens	ones	number
1.		0		901
2.	5			520
3.		5		455
4.	8			876
5.		8		789

Mathematics Made Fun
Place Value Chart

2nd Grade

1. Copy the chart.
2. Fill in the missing values.
3. Write a number sentence for the value of each row.

	thousands	hundreds	tens	ones	number
1.		9		9	2,909
2.	8			1	8,741
3.				9	7,589
4.		0			4,077
5.	0				361

3rd Grade

1. Copy the chart.
2. Fill in the missing values.
3. Write a number sentence for the value of each row.

	ten thousands	thousands	hundreds	tens	ones	number
1.	2		5			20,505
2.		1		1		91,021
3.	8					89,450
4.			0			57,079
5.					1	3,931

Mathematics Made Fun
Place Value Chart

4th Grade

1. Copy the chart.
2. Fill in the missing values.
3. Write a number sentence for the value of each row.

	hundred thousand	ten thousands	thousands	hundreds	tens	ones	number
1.		8			4		986,243
2.	0				0		74,800
3.		0				9	305,919
4.	0		0				20,105
5.			0		0		500,003

5th Grade

1. Copy the chart.
2. Fill in the missing values.
3. Write a number sentence for the value of each row.

	million	hundred thousand	ten thousands	thousands	hundreds	tens	ones	number
1.		0		5		3		5,005,839
2.	8		2		9		4	8,821,914
3.		7		4		1		9,744,510
4.	6		0		7		8	6,507,748
5.	0		0		0		9	9

Assessment Option: Have the students share their work with the class.

Mathematics Made Fun
Place Value Chart

Reflection: Place Value

It is important for students to understand why they are learning this process and how they can apply it to their daily lives. Explain that understanding the concept of <u>place value</u> and <u>base ten</u> is important to performing and understanding all numerical functions.

In this reflection, ask the students these questions in an open discussion:

1. What did they learn?
2. How can they use what they learned in their daily activity?
3. Can they teach what they have learned to someone else?
4. What did they like most about the activity?
5. What did they like least about the activity?

Mathematics Made Fun
Activity Title: Rounding Numbers

The method of rounding numbers is useful in so many ways. It can simplify the process of mentally adding, subtracting, multiplying, and dividing large numbers. Rounding is also useful in making estimations. The activities in this section will focus on rounding numbers.

Time Frame: **35 - 65 Minutes**
                            5 - 10 Activity introduction and explanation.
                            5 - 10 Chart information on the board.
                            5 - 10 Whole group discussion.
                          10 - 15 Independent student activity.
                            5 - 10 Activity assessment.
                            5 - 10 Reflection on the activity.

Lesson Objective: To increase student knowledge of rounding numbers.

Materials & Resources: Paper and pencil.

Instruction Procedure: Explain the lesson and lesson objective to the students.

Whole Group Activity:

Copy the chart for the grade level you are working with, making sure to leave the *Answer* column blank. Begin by calling on students to help fill in the blanks on the chart and allow the students to complete the chart on their own.

Mathematics Made Fun
Rounding Numbers

Kindergarten

1. Copy the chart.
2. Round each number to the nearest (see column heading).

	A.	*Answers* tens	B.	*Answers* tens
1.	17	*20*	26	*30*
2.	11	*10*	8	*30*
3.	13	*10*	14	*10*
4.	19	*20*	9	*10*
5.	16	*20*	7	*10*

1st Grade

1. Copy the chart.
2. Round each number to the nearest (see column heading).

	A.	*Answers* hundreds	B.	*Answers* tens
1.	456	*500*	467	*470*
2.	985	*1000*	876	*880*
3.	364	*400*	654	*650*
4.	201	*200*	236	*240*
5.	98	*100*	125	*130*

Mathematics Made Fun
Rounding Numbers

2nd Grade

1. Copy the chart.
2. Round each number to the nearest (see column heading).

	A.	*Answers* **thousands**	B.	*Answers* **hundreds**	C.	*Answers* **tens**
1.	8,745	*9,000*	4,789	*4,800*	9,001	*9,000*
2.	4,687	*5,000*	9,635	*9,600*	6,152	*6,150*
3.	1,459	*1,000*	5,147	*5,100*	5,140	*5,140*
4.	5,968	*6,000*	9,589	*9,600*	387	*390*
5.	7,236	*7,000*	9,001	*9,000*	999	*1,000*

3rd Grade

1. Copy the chart.
2. Round each number to the nearest (see column heading).

	A.	*Answers* **ten thousands**	B.	*Answers* **thousands**	C.	*Answers* **hundreds**
1.	17,342	*17,000*	10,001	*10,000*	51,999	*52,000*
2.	39,012	*39,000*	9,999	*10,000*	38,499	*38,500*
3.	45,256	*45,000*	38,126	*38,000*	72,501	*72,500*
4.	19,256	*19,000*	49,998	*50,000*	99,199	*99,200*
5.	63,099	*63,000*	71,009	*71,000*	16,509	*16,500*

Mathematics Made Fun
Rounding Numbers

4th Grade

1. Copy the chart.
2. Round each number to the nearest (see column heading).

	A.	*Answers* **hundred thousands**	B.	*Answers* **ten thousands**	C.	*Answers* **thousands**
1.	513,456	*500,000*	639,001	*640,000*	477,708	*478,000*
2.	657,013	*700,000*	154,999	*150,000*	199,099	*199,000*
3.	126,998	*100,000*	901,999	*900,000*	851,269	*851,000*
4.	785,996	*800,000*	978,456	*980,000*	345,759	*346,000*
5.	901,001	*900,000*	364,140	*360,000*	684,751	*685,000*

5th Grade

1. Copy the chart.
2. Round each number to the nearest (see column heading).

	A.	*Answers* **millions**	B.	*Answers* **hundred thousands**	C.	*Answers* **ten thousands**
1.	1,999,001	*2,000,000*	3,256,147	*3,300,000*	3,009,990	*3,010,000*
2.	4,596,458	*5,000,000*	9,456,102	*9,500,000*	4,856,367	*4,860,000*
3.	7,596,366	*8,000,000*	4,125,036	*4,100,000*	7,059,095	*7,060,000*
4.	9,001,001	*9,000,000*	7,458,669	*7,500,000*	6,805,901	*6,810,000*
5.	6,458,369	*6,000,000*	5,099,099	*5,000,000*	1,998,099	*2,000,000*

Assessment Option: Have the students share their work with the class.

Mathematics Made Fun
Rounding Numbers

Reflection: Rounding Numbers

It is important for students to understand why they are learning this process and how they can apply it to their daily lives. Explain that knowing how to round numbers will help them with many numerical functions.

In this reflection, ask the students these questions in an open discussion:

1. What did they learn?
2. How can they use what they learned in their daily activity?
3. Can they teach what they have learned to someone else?
4. What did they like most about the activity?
5. What did they like least about the activity?
6. Ask students to suggest a real-life situation where they might need to round numbers.

Mathematics Made Fun
Activity Title: <u>Money</u>

Knowing the value of money and how to count it is a <u>must</u> in any area of society. The following activities will give students practice with counting, making change, counting back, and making purchases.

Time Frame: **35 - 65 Minutes**
                                5 - 10 Activity introduction and explanation.
                                5 - 10 Chart information on the board.
                                5 - 10 Whole group discussion.
                              10 - 15 Independent student activity.
                                5 - 10 Activity assessment.
                                5 - 10 Reflection on the activity.

Lesson Objective: To increase student knowledge of money.

Materials & Resources: Paper, pencil, and crayon.

Instruction Procedure: Explain the lesson and lesson objective to the students.

Whole Group Activity:

See individual instructions for the appropriate grade level.

Mathematics Made Fun
Money - 1st Grade
Independent Activity

Teacher's Instructions: *Set up chart with row and column headings - do not include answers.*
Have students complete 1 & 2.

1. Complete column A of the chart to indicate how many of each coin or bill it takes to make one dollar.
2. Make up combinations, using more than one coin, to equal one dollar for columns B, C, D, & E. *(Some examples are listed, however, answers will vary.)*

	(Answers)	(T h e s e	a n s w e r s	w i l l	v a r y)
Value	A.	B.	C.	D.	E.
one dollar bill	1				
coin dollar	1				
half dollar	2	1			1
quarter	4	2	2		1
dime	10		5		1
nickel	20			10	2
penny	100			50	5
		$1.00	$1.00	$1.00	$1.00

Mathematics Made Fun
Money - 1st Grade
Independent Activity

Advanced Activity

Teacher's Instructions: Set up chart with row and column headings - do not include answers.
Have students complete 3 through 6.

3. List the amount of change you should receive using one dollar to make each purchase.
4. List the <u>least</u> amount of coins needed, and identify the coins, to purchase each item.
5. List the total quantity of each item you can purchase using one dollar.
6. How many combinations of items can you purchase using one dollar?

			(Answers)	*(Answers)*	
Item	Cost	Change	Least amount of coins needed to purchase this item	How many items can you purchase	Combinations
Ball	$0.25	$0.75	1 quarter =1 coin	4	answers will vary
Doll	$0.50	$0.50	1 half dollar = 1 coin	2	answers will vary
Train	$0.75	$0.25	1 half dollar & 1 quarter = 2 coins	1	answers will vary
Hat	$1.00	$0.00	1 one dollar bill or 1 coin dollar	1	answers will vary

Mathematics Made Fun
INDEPENDENT ACTIVITY
Money
2nd Grade

Teacher's Instructions: *Set up chart with row and column heading - do not include answers.*
Have students complete 1 & 2.

1. Complete column A of the chart to indicate how many of each coin or bill it takes to equal one dollar.
2. Make up combinations, using more than one coin, to equal one dollar for columns B, C, D, & E. *(Some examples are listed however, answers will vary.)*

(These answers will vary)

Value	A.	B.	C.	D.	E.
one dollar bill	1				
coin dollar	1				
half dollar	2	1			1
quarter	4	2	2		1
dime	10		5		1
nickel	20			10	2
penny	100			50	2
		$1.00	$1.00	$1.00	$1.00

Mathematics Made Fun
INDEPENDENT ACTIVITY
Money
2nd Grade

Advanced Activity

Teacher's Instructions: *Set up chart with row and column headings - do not include answers.*
Have students complete 3 through 6.

3. List the amount of change you should receive using one dollar to make each purchase.
4. List the <u>least</u> amount of coins needed to purchase each item, and identify the coins.
5. List the total quantity of each item you can purchase using one dollar.
6. How many combinations of items can you purchase using one dollar?

		(Answers)	(Answers)	(Answers)	
Item	**Cost**	**Change**	**Least amount of coins needed to purchase this item**	**How many items can you purchase**	**Combinations**
Pencil	$0.30	$0.70	1 quarter & 1 nickel = 2 coins	4	answers will vary
Note-book	$0.55	$0.45	1 half dollar & 1 nickel = 2 coins	1	answers will vary
Eraser	$0.70	$0.30	1 half dollar & 2 dimes = 3 coins	1	answers will vary
Back-pack	$.85	$0.15	1 half dollar, 1 quarter, &1 dime = 3 coins	1	answers will vary

Mathematics Made Fun
INDEPENDENT ACTIVITY
Money
3rd Grade

Teacher's Instructions: *Set up chart with row and column headings - do not include answers.*
Have students complete 1 & 2.

1. Complete column A of the chart to indicate how many of each coin or bill it takes to equal five dollars.
2. Make up combinations, using more than one coin or bill, to equal five dollars for columns B, C, D, & E. *(Some examples are listed however, answers will vary.)*

	(Answers)	(These answers will vary)			
Value	A.	B.	C.	D.	E.
five dollar bill	1	1			
one dollar bill	5		5		
coin dollar	5			5	
half dollar	10				3
quarter	20				4
dime	50				5
nickel	100				5
penny	500				25
		$5.00	$5.00	$5.00	$5.00

Mathematics Made Fun
INDEPENDENT ACTIVITY
Money
3rd Grade

Advanced Activity

Teacher's Instructions: *Set up chart with row and column headings - do not include answers.*
Have students complete 3 through 6.

3. List the amount of change you should receive using a five dollar bill to make the purchase.
4. List the <u>least</u> amount of coins and bills needed to purchase each item, and identify the type of currency.
5. List the total quantity of each item you can purchase using a five dollar bill.
6. How many combinations of items can you purchase using a five dollar bill?

Item	Cost	(Answers) Change	(Answers) Least amount of coins and bills needed to purchase this item	(Answers) How many items can you purchase	Combinations
Shirt	$1.25	$3.75	1 dollar & 1 quarter = dollar & 1 coin	3	answers will vary
Hat	$2.50	$2.50	2 dollars & 1 half dollar = 2 dollars & 1 coin	2	answers will vary
Shoes	$3.75	$1.25	3 dollars, 1 half dollar, & 1 quarter = 3 dollars & 2 coins	1	answers will vary
Sun glasses	$4.25	$0.75	4 dollars & 1 quarter 4 dollars & 1 coin	1	answers will vary

Mathematics Made Fun
INDEPENDENT ACTIVITY
Money
4th Grade

Teacher's Instructions: *Set up chart with row and column headings - do not include answers.*
Have students complete 1 & 2.

1. Complete column A of the chart to indicate how many of each coin or bill it takes to make ten dollars.
2. Make up combinations, using more than one coin or bill, to equal ten dollars for columns B, C, D, & E. *(Some examples are listed however, answers will vary.)*

(Answers)   (These answers will vary)

Value	A.	B.	C.	D.	E.
ten dollar bill	1	1			
five dollar bill	2		1		1
one dollar bill	10		5	5	1
coin dollar	1			5	1
half dollar	2				2
quarter	4				4
dime	10				5
nickel	20				5
penny	100				25
		$10.00	$10.00	$10.00	$10.00

Mathematics Made Fun
INDEPENDENT ACTIVITY
Money
4th Grade

Advanced Activity

Teacher's Instructions: *Set up chart with row and column headings - do not include answers.*
Have students complete 3 through 6.

3. List the amount of change you should receive using a ten dollar bill to make the purchase.
4. List the least amount of coins and bills needed to purchase each item, and identify the type of currency.
5. List the total quantity of each item you can purchase using a ten dollar bill.
6. How many combinations of items can you purchase using a ten dollar bill?

Item	Cost *(Answers)*	Change *(Answers)*	Least amount of coins and bills needed to purchase this item *(Answers)*	How many items can you purchase *(Answers)*	Combinations
Ball	$2.80	*$7.20*	*2-$1, 1-.50, 1-.25, 1-.05 = 2 bills & 3 coins*	*3*	*answers will vary*
Doll	$3.62	*$6.38*	*3-$1, 1-.50, 1-.10, & 2-.01 = 3 bills & 4 coins*	*2*	*answers will vary*
Train	$4.41	*$5.59*	*4-$1, 1-.25, 1-.10, 1-.05, & 1-.01 = 4 bills & 4 coins*	*2*	*answers will vary*
Hat	$4.99	*$5.01*	*4-$1, 1-.50, 1-.25, 2-.10, & 4-.01 = 4 bills & 8 coins*	*2*	*answers will vary*

Mathematics Made Fun
INDEPENDENT ACTIVITY
Money
5th Grade

Teacher's Instructions: *Set up chart with row and column headings. Have students complete 1 & 2.*

1. Complete column A of the chart to indicate how many of each coin or bill it takes to equal twenty dollars.
2. Make up combinations, using more than one coin or bill, to equal twenty dollars for columns B, C, D, & E. *(Some examples are listed however, answers will vary.)*

(Answers)   *(These answers will vary)*

Value	A.	B.	C.	D.	E.
twenty dollar bill	1	1			
ten dollar bill	2		2		1
five dollar bill	4			4	1
one dollar bill	20				1
coin dollar	20				1
half dollar	40				2
quarter	80				4
dime	200				5
nickel	400				5
penny	2,000				25
$20.00		$20.00	$20.00	$20.00	$20.00

Mathematics Made Fun
INDEPENDENT ACTIVITY
Money
5th Grade

Advanced Activity

Teacher's Instructions: *Set up chart with row and column headings - do not include answers. Have students complete 3 through 6.*

3. List the amount of change you should receive using a twenty dollar bill to make each purchase.
4. List the least amount of coins and bills needed, and identify the coins and bills, to purchase each item
5. List the total quantity of each item you can purchase using a twenty dollar bill.
6. How many combinations of items can you purchase using a twenty dollar bill?

		(Answers)	*(Answers)*	*(Answers)*	
Item	Cost	Change	Least amount of bills & coins needed to purchase this item	How many items can you purchase	Combinations
CD	$8.90	$11.10	1-$5, 3-$1, 1-.50, 1-.25, 1-.10, & 1-.05. =4 bills & 4 coins	2	answers will vary
DVD	$11.33	$8.67	1-$10, 1-$1, 1-.25, 1-.05, & 3-.01 = 2 bills & 5 coins	1	answers will vary
Show Tickets	$14.97	$5.03	.50, .10, .10 = 3 coins	1	answers will vary
Watch	$16.89	$3.11	1-$10, 1-$5, 1-$1, 1-.50, 1-.25, 1-.10, &4-.04 = 3 bills, & 7 coins	1	answers will vary

Assessment Option: Check Student Work.

Mathematics Made Fun
Money
5th Grade

Reflection: Money

It is important for students to understand why they are learning this process and how they can apply it to their daily lives. Explain that knowing how to identify, count, and convert money is especially important when making purchases.

In this reflection, ask the students these questions in an open discussion:

1. What did they learn?
2. How can they use what they learned in their daily activity?
3. Can they teach what they have learned to someone else?
4. What did they like most about the activity?
5. What did they like least about the activity?

Mathematics Made Fun
Activity Title: <u>**Addition & Subtraction**</u>

The practice of adding and subtracting numbers is simply increasing or decreasing. This skill is used in many ways in all aspects of life, and is the foundation for solving and understanding other mathematical problems. The activities in this section focuses on providing practice with adding and subtracting using word problems and short stories.

Time Frame: **35 - 65 Minutes**
                                     5 - 10 Activity introduction and explanation.
                                       5 - 10 Chart information on the board.
                                       5 - 10 Whole group discussion.
                                    10 - 15 Independent student activity.
                                       5 - 10 Activity assessment.
                                       5 - 10 Reflection on the activity.

Lesson Objective: To increase student knowledge of adding and subtracting in word problems.

Materials & Resources: Paper, pencil, and crayons.

Instruction Procedure: Explain the lesson and lesson objective to the students.

Whole Group Activity:

See individual instructions for the appropriate grade level.

Mathematics Made Fun
INDEPENDENT ACTIVITY
Addition & Subtraction - Kindergarten

Teacher's Instructions: *Read the story to the students and demonstrate the picture on the board.*

Below are several short stories that require adding, subtracting, coloring, and creating. Select one to read aloud to the students. Allow the students time to create an outline for their picture during the reading. Suggest that they color the picture once the story is complete. When the stories and drawings are complete, help the students create an addition or subtraction sentence that corresponds with their drawing. Kindergarteners should be able to add and subtract single digit numbers; however, they may change the quantities in the stories to suit their needs. In addition, you may give the students a number sentence and have them create their own picture and story.

Balloons (Addition)

The children were having a party and decided to use balloons to decorate. The first child blew up two green balloons and the second child blew up three orange balloons. Now the children were finished.

1. How many balloons do they have all together?
   Answer: (2 + 3 = 5 balloons)

Apples (Addition)

Today I helped my father collect the apples that had fallen from our apple tree. I picked up four. I wanted to share my apples in school but there weren't enough, so my father gave me six more to make sure everyone in the class would receive an apple.

1. How many apples did I take to school?
   Answer: (4 + 6 = 10)

Stars (Addition)

I looked straight up to the night sky and saw three shinning stars. I looked to my right and saw one more. I looked to my left and saw two more.

1. How many stars did I see in all?
   Answer: (3 + 1 + 2 = 6 stars)

Mathematics Made Fun
INDEPENDENT ACTIVITY
Addition & Subtraction - Kindergarten

Hearts (Subtraction)

My mother gave me three candy hearts for Valentine's Day. She told me to give one to my teacher and the rest to my good friends.

1. After I gave one candy heart to my teacher, how many candy hearts do I have left to give to my good friends?
    Answer: (3 - 1 = 2)

Flowers (Subtraction)

I picked a daisy for my friend. The daisy was very pretty with a yellow center, green stem, leaves, and seven white petals. Somehow three of the petals fell off when I pulled it from the ground.

1. How many petals were left on the daisy?
    Answer: (7 - 3 = 4 petal.)

Cupcakes (Subtraction)

We had a party at school and I brought a box of ten cupcakes. Five of the cupcakes were strawberry and five of them were lemon. The children ate all of the lemon cupcakes and left all of the strawberry cupcakes, so I took the rest back home.

1. How many cupcakes did I take back home?
    Answer: (10 - 5 = 5 cupcakes)

Mathematics Made Fun
INDEPENDENT ACTIVITY
Addition & Subtraction - 1st Grade

Teacher's Instructions: *Read the story to the students and demonstrate in picture on the board along with a chart to keep track of the numbers to be calculated.*

Below are several short stories that require adding, subtracting, coloring, and creating; and stories that combine adding and subtracting. Select a story to read aloud to the students. Allow the students time to create an outline for their picture during the reading, they may also want to keep track of the numbers on a chart. Tell the students that they can color it in once the story is complete. When the stories and drawings are complete, help the students create an addition or subtraction sentence to go along with their drawing. First grade students should be able to add two digit numbers and subtract a single-digit number from a double digit number. You may change the quantities in the stories to suit the needs of the students. In addition, you may give the students a number sentence and have them create their own picture and story.

Lollipops (Addition)

Everyone in the class brought a box of lollipops to sell at the class fundraiser. Not all of the boxes had the same quantities, some had more and some had less. Karen's box had twelve, Michael's box had fourteen, Ralph's box had nine, and Tiffany's box had twenty-one.

1. How many total lollipops did we have?
   Answer: (12 + 14 + 9 + 21 = 56 lollipops)

Lemons (Addition)

My friends and I are going to sell lemonade to earn some extra money. My mom gave a recipe and my friends and I just need to get the supplies. We need to make a stand, get some lemons, water, ice, a pitcher and some cups. Oh yea! we will also need a big box to hold all of the money we are going to make. My father said that he would get all of the supplies for us and my neighbor said we could pick all the lemons we need from his backyard tree. My friends and I each grabbed a bag and began picking lemons. When we finished, we had more than enough. Carmen had nineteen, Chuck had eight, Robert had fifteen, Sally had twelve, and I had seven.

1. How many lemons did we have all together?
   Answer: (19 + 8 + 15 + 12 + 7 = 61)

Mathematics Made Fun
INDEPENDENT ACTIVITY
Addition & Subtraction - 1st Grade

Ducks in a Pond (Subtraction)

I like to go to the lake with my family during the summer. This is the time of year my father and I spend sailing in our boat. On this one particular day I noticed there were a lot of ducks in the water, so I decided to count them. I counted twenty-seven; but then three flew away, seven swam away, and nine just got out of the water.

1. How many ducks were left in the water?
   Answer: (27 - 3 - 7 - 9 = 8 ducks left in the water)

Candy Canes (Subtraction)

This year we decorated our Christmas Tree with candy canes. On Saturday, we put a total of fifty candy canes on the tree. Over the next day it seemed as though some had disappeared so I decided to count them. I was right, there were only twenty candy canes left on the tree.

1. How many candy canes were missing from the tree?
   Answer: (50 - 20 = 30 candy canes were missing from the tree)

Butterflies (Addition & Subtraction)

Yesterday my friends and I went on a butterfly hunt. We wanted to find out how many butterflies we could catch. We had nets to gently capture them, and screened containers to keep them in. The three of us had a great time, and each caught several butterflies. Kelly caught seven, Clark caught five, and I caught nine. Some of the butterflies flew away when we were putting them in the containers. Kelly caught seven butterflies, but only had five in the container. Clark caught five butterflies, but only had four in his container, and I caught nine butterflies, but I only had three in my container.

1. How many butterflies did we have in all before some flew away?
   Answer: (7 + 5 + 9 = 21 butterflies)

2. How many butterflies did Kelly lose?
   Answer: (7 - 5 = 2 butterflies for Kelly) Kelly lost two butterflies.

3. How many butterflies did Clark lose?
   Answer: (5 - 4 = 1 butterfly for Clark) Clark lost one butterfly.

Mathematics Made Fun
INDEPENDENT ACTIVITY
Addition & Subtraction - 1st Grade

4. How many butterflies did I lose?
   Answer: (9 - 3 = 6 butterflies for me) I lost six butterflies.

5. How many butterflies did we lose all together?
   Answer: (2 + 1 + 6 = 9 butterflies flew way) All together, we lost nine butterflies.

6. How many butterflies did we have left after some flew away?
   Answer: (21 - 9 = 12 butterflies left after some flew away) We had 12 butterflies left after some flew away.

Birds (Addition & Subtraction)

I have a bird-feeder in my backyard and each morning I feed the birds. I put the food out at eight O'clock in the morning, and the first family of ten birds come in to eat. Soon they are joined by another family of birds, this family has twelve birds. There's still plenty of room for more birds, and soon they are joined by a family of five more birds. It doesn't take them long to eat the food and then they begin to leave. First, eight birds flew away and then nine birds flew away. Even though the food was all gone the rest of the birds stayed.

1. How many birds in all came to the feeder to eat?
   Answer: (10 + 12 + 5 = 27 birds)

2. How many birds flew away after eating?
   Answer: (8 + 9 = 17 birds flew away)

3. How many birds remained after the food was all gone?
   Answer: (27 - 17 = 10). Ten birds remained after all the food was gone and some flew away.

Mathematics Made Fun
INDEPENDENT ACTIVITY
Addition & Subtraction - 2nd Grade

Teacher's Instructions: *Read the story to the students and demonstrate the picture on the board.*

Below are several short stories that require adding, subtracting, coloring, and creating. Select one story to read aloud to the students. Allow the students time to create an outline for their picture during the reading. Tell them they can color it in once the story is complete. When the stories and drawings are complete, help the students create an addition or subtraction sentence to go along with their drawing. Second grade students should be able to add and subtract three-digit numbers. You may change the quantities in the stories to suit the needs of the students. In addition, you may give the students a number sentence and have them create their own picture and story.

Rock Collecting (Addition)

This year at summer camp we held a rock-collecting contest to see who could find the most unique rocks, and I won. The rocks I found were black with a clear center; and I found lots of them, but it wasn't easy. I found them in the strangest places. Inside the old barn, I found thirteen under a pile of hay and twenty-six in an empty horse stall. By the river, I found twenty-seven under a bench, and forty-two along the edge of the river. I headed back to the camp to turn in my rocks and found another fifty-eight on the way, now I was sure to win the contest.

1. How many rocks did I find inside the old barn?
   Answer: (13 + 26 = 39 rocks)

2. How many rocks did I find by the river?
   Answer: (27 + 42 = 69 rocks)

3. How many rocks did I find on my way back to the camp?
   Answer: (58 rocks)

4. How many rocks did I find in all?
   Answer: (39 + 69 + 58 = 166 rocks)

Mathematics Made Fun
INDEPENDENT ACTIVITY
Addition & Subtraction - 2nd Grade

Steps At School (Addition)

Mr. March did an awful lot of walking at school and wondered just how many steps he made at school during the day. So one day he decided to count his every step during school. It took sixty-one steps to get from the front gate to the cafeteria, and seventy-three steps to get from there to the classroom. It took him an extra seventeen steps once he got to the classroom because he tried to get in front of the line, but the principal sent him back to the end of the line to wait his turn. Inside of the classroom, it only took him nine steps to get to the closet, and another six steps to his seat. Mr. March met us on the carpet to hear a story and then we returned to our seats. This took him a total of 14 steps. During free time he took twenty-one step between his seat, the classroom library, the listening center and back to his seat. It was finally time for recess. It took him six steps to get to the closet, and nine steps to get in his right place in line. It took seventy-one long steps to get to the playground. He had so much fun during recess that he forgot to count his steps, and just quit counting.

1. How many steps did Mr. March take from the gate to his seat in the classroom?
   Answer: (61+ 73+ 17 = 151 steps)

2. How many steps did Mr. March take inside of the classroom?
   Answer: (9 + 6 + 14 + 21 + 6 + 9 = 65 steps inside the classroom)

3. How many extra steps did Mr. March have to take for trying to cut in line at the classroom door?
   Answer: (17 extra steps)

4. How many steps did Mr. March take outside of the classroom?
   (61 + 73 + 17 + 71 = 222 steps outside of the classroom)

5. How many total steps did Mr. March make before recess?
   Answer: (61 + 73 + 17 + 9 + 6 + 14 + 21 + 6 + 9 + 71= 287 total steps)

Mathematics Made Fun
INDEPENDENT ACTIVITY
Addition & Subtraction - 2nd Grade

Collecting Sea Shells (Subtraction)

My two friends and I spent the day at the beach playing in the water, building sand castles, and collection sea shells. Carol, Clark and I decided to have a contest to see who could collect the most sea shells. We each grabbed a bucket and began the search. After about an hour of searching we sat down and began to count the sea shells we had found. Carol dumped her bucket and counted one hundred and ninety-one shells. Clark poured out his bucket and counted two hundred and twelve sea shells. I emptied my bucket and counted one hundred and ninety-nine sea shells. After looking at the sea shells all spread out, we noticed that some were broken and decided to take out the shells that were damaged. Carol threw out seventeen cracked sea shells. Clark threw out twenty-eight broken sea shells, and I had to throw away twenty-five chipped sea shells.

1. Carol originally collected one hundred and ninety-one sea shells, how many were left once she threw out the cracked shells?
   Answer: (191-17= 174 sea shells)

2. Clark originally collected two hundred and twelve sea shells, how many were left once he threw out the broken sea shells?
   Answer: (212-28=184 sea shells)

3. I originally collected one hundred ninety-nine sea shells, how many did I have left after threw away the chipped sea shells?
   Answer: (199-25=174 sea shells)

Mathematics Made Fun
INDEPENDENT ACTIVITY
Addition & Subtraction - 2nd Grade

Classroom Raffle Tickets (Addition & Subtraction)

Mrs. Talbert gives her students raffle tickets for a variety of reasons like turning in their homework, good behavior, and staying on task. She also takes them away if the students get into trouble, don't do their homework, or don't finish an assignment. The students can use their tickets to buy classroom treats each Friday. Joshua is determined to gain as many raffle tickets as he can to buy treats on Friday. On Monday, he received five tickets for his homework, seven tickets for his good behavior and nine tickets for being a good classroom helper. On Tuesday, he received a total of twenty-one tickets, but lost six because he didn't do his homework. On Wednesday, he received thirty-one tickets and didn't loose any. On Thursday, Joshua didn't have a good day; and for this he didn't receive any tickets. Instead, he lost eight. On Friday, he was determined to catch up; so he turned in his homework, completed his classroom assignments, and was on his best behavior. For this he earned thirty-five tickets.

1. How many raffle tickets did Joshua have by the end of Monday
   Answer: (5+7+9=21 raffle tickets)

2. How many raffle tickets did Joshua have by the end of Tuesday?
   Answer: (21+21=42, 42-6=36 raffle tickets)

3. How many raffle tickets did Joshua have by the end of Wednesday?
   Answer: (36+31=67 raffle tickets)

4. How many raffle tickets did Joshua have by the end of Thursday?
   Answer: (67-8=59 raffle tickets)

5. How many raffle tickets did Joshua have by the end of Friday?
   Answer: (59 + 35 = 94 raffle tickets)

Mathematics Made Fun
INDEPENDENT ACTIVITY
Addition & Subtraction - 2nd Grade

Trading Cards (Addition & Subtraction)

My friends and I like to collect baseball trading cards. I had three hundred forty-seven cards in my collection before I started trading. My goal was to collect all of the cards for the players on my favorite teams, but some of them were kind of hard to get since everyone wanted them. Yesterday, after school, we got together and traded our cards. I knew that I would have to trade several cards to someone just to get one popular card that I wanted badly; but I figured it was worth it. I had twelve cards for one team that I didn't want, so I traded them to Kevin for two cards that I did want. I traded Sandra twenty cards for three, and Billy seventeen cards for one. My last and best trade of the day was to Molly. I traded Molly one hundred and eight cards for twenty-one cards of my favorite team. Although I traded a lot of cards, I now have most of the ones that I really want.

1. How many cards did I have after I traded with Kevin?
   Answer: (347 - 12 = 335, 335 + 2 = 337)

2. How many cards did I have after I traded with Sandra?
   Answer: (337 - 20 = 317, 317 + 3 = 320)

3. How many cards did I have after I traded with Billy?
   Answer: (320 - 17 = 303, 303 + 1 = 304)

4. How many cards did I have after I traded with Molly?
   Answer: (304 - 108 = 196, 196 + 21 = 217)

5. How many cards did I trade away?
   Answer: (12 + 20 + 17 + 108 = 157)

6. How many cards did I gain in trade?
   Answer: (2 + 3 + 1 + 21 = 27)

7. How many cards did I have after all the trading was complete?
   Answer: (217)

Mathematics Made Fun
INDEPENDENT ACTIVITY
Addition & Subtraction - 2nd Grade

Passengers on the Bus (Addition & Subtraction)

This morning, I rode the city but to school with my friend. The ride was boring, so we decided to play a game of counting the number of people who got on and off the bus. The bus made three stops before we got to school, so we had three chances to count the passengers on and off of the bus. There were twenty people already on the bus, so we added those who got on the bus, and subtracted those who exited the bus. At the first stop, twelve passengers entered through the front door and five exited through the back door. At the second stop we picked up fifteen passengers, and eleven got off of the bus. At the third stop, twenty-two passengers got on the bus, and nineteen people, including my friend and I, got off the bus.

1. How many passengers were on the bus after the first stop?
   Answer: (20 + 12 = 32 - 5 = 27 passengers on the bus after the first stop)

2. How many passengers were on the bus after the second stop?
   Answer: (27 + 15 = 42 - 11 = 31 passengers on the bus after the second stop)

3. How many passengers were on the bus after the third stop?
   Answer: (31 + 22 = 53, 53 - 19 = 34 passengers on the bus after the third stop)

Mathematics Made Fun
INDEPENDENT ACTIVITY
Addition & Subtraction - 3rd Grade

Teacher's Instructions: *Read the story to the students and demonstrate the picture on the board.*

Below are several short stories that contain adding, subtracting, coloring, and creating. Select one story to read aloud to the students. Allow the students time to create an outline for their picture during the reading. Tell them they can color it in once the story is complete. When the stories and drawings are complete, help the students create an addition or subtraction sentence to go along with their drawing. Third grade students should be able to add and subtract any digit numbers between 0 and 10,000. You may change the quantities in the stories to suit the needs of the students. In addition, you may give the students a number sentence and have them create their own picture and story.

Birthday Money-Part 1 (Addition)

This year, Kelly turned eighteen years old and had a big party. She received lots of gifts and money from her family and friends. Kelly received a twenty dollar bill from her Aunt Mildred and a twenty dollar bill, from her Uncle Mark. Her cousin Tammy gave her a five dollar bill and she received five ten dollar bills from her parents.

1. How much money did Kelly receive from her aunt and uncle?
   Answer: ($20.00 + $20.00 = $40.00 from her aunt and uncle)

2. How much money did Kelly receive from her cousin Tammy?
   Answer: ($5.00 from her cousin Tammy)

3. How much money did she receive from her parents?
   Answer: ($50.00 from her parents)

4. How much money did Kelly receive in all?
   Answer: ($20.00 + $20.00 + $5.00 + $50.00 = $95.00 total)

Mathematics Made Fun
INDEPENDENT ACTIVITY
Addition & Subtraction - 3rd Grade

Birthday Money-Part 2 (Subtraction)

Kelly received $95.00 in birthday gifts and wanted to go shopping. She decided to buy the following items:

backpack - $7.00	notebook - $4.00	paper - $2.00
clothes - $21.00	pencils - $1.00	pencil box - $1.00
Shoes - $12.00	video game - $9.00	game - $3.00
head phones - $6.00	lunch bag - $2.00	gift - $10.00

1. How much money did Kelly spend on things that can be used for school (not including clothing or shoes)?
   Answer: $7.00 + $4.00 + $2.00 + $1.00 + $1.00 + $2.00 = $17.00

2. How much money did she spend on items to wear?
   Answer: $21.00 + $12.00 = $33.00

3. How much money did she spend altogether?
   Answer: $$7.00 + $4.00 + $2.00 + $21.00 + $1.00 + $1.00 + $12.00 + $9.00 + $3.00 + $6.00 + $2.00 + $10.00 = $78.00

4. How much money did Kelly have left after shopping?
   Answer: *$95.00 - $78.00 = $17.00*

5. How much money would she have if she bought everything except for clothes?
   Answer: $95.00 - $57.00 = $38.00, or $17.00 + $21.00 = $38.00. (The answer is $38.00 however, there are various ways to arrive at the same amount).

Mathematics Made Fun
INDEPENDENT ACTIVITY
Addition & Subtraction - 3rd Grade

Sorting Out the Bad

You are the quality control manager for a plate company. Your job is to remove all of the damaged dishes before they are packed into boxes and sold to the customer. Below is a chart of all the dishes sorted into several damaged categories.

1. Calculate the number of good dishes for each batch.
2. Calculate the total number of broken dishes.
3. Calculate the total number of chipped dishes.
4. Calculate the total number of cracked dishes.
5. Calculate the total number of dishes with bad designs.
6. Calculate the total number of damaged dishes all together.
7. Calculate the total number of good dishes.

Dishes	Quantity	broken	chipped	cracked	Bad Design	Good Dishes
Batch A.	550	-23	-18	-51	-91	
Batch B.	635	-71	-52	-84	-41	
Batch C.	869	-56	-78	-102	221-	
Batch D.	799	-56	-109	-78	-305	
Batch E.	1,250	-67	-75	-112	-340	

Mathematics Made Fun
INDEPENDENT ACTIVITY
Addition & Subtraction - 5th Grade

Teacher's Instructions: *Select an activity for the students and write the base information on the board.* ***Fifth grade*** *students should be able to add and subtract multiple-digit numbers including numbers with decimals. You may change the quantities in the activities to suit the needs of the students.*

You are in charge of taking a department store inventory and must calculate unit totals as well as a grand total, of all the items of merchandise.

1. Calculate the sum of each size.
2. Calculate the sum of each color.
3. Calculate the grand total.
4. What is the most popular color?
5. What is the least popular color?
6. What is the most popular size?
7. What is the least popular size?

Dress Slacks	blue	red	green	purple	black	Size Total
Size 8	375	568	221	47	112	
Size 10	701	422	384	108	98	
Size 12	852	213	405	51	74	
Size 14	224	312	502	36	58	
Size 16	546	240	418	44	96	
Total Per Color						

Mathematics Made Fun
INDEPENDENT ACTIVITY
Addition & Subtraction - 5th Grade

You are in charge of keeping track of the donation of canned-goods being collected by your school for charity. Donation containers were numbered and placed around the school. Complete the chart and answer the following questions.

1. Calculate the total of each days collection.
2. Calculate the total of each containers collections.
3. Which day of had the most donations?
4. Which day had the least donations?
5. Which container held the most donations?
6. Which container held the least donations?

	Mon	Tue	Wed.	Thu	Fri	Total
Container 1	116	216	334	51	84	
Container 2	45	52	75	96	11	
Container 3	213	145	45	64	42	
Container 4	54	155	25	63	88	
Container 5	362	130	63	89	106	
Container 6	112	140	96	78	88	
Container 8	240	150	38	45	91	
Total						

Mathematics Made Fun
INDEPENDENT ACTIVITY
Addition & Subtraction - 5th Grade

Teacher's Instruction*: Read the following story to the students. The focus of this activity is to develop good listening skills and speed. Since fifth grade students should already know addition and subtraction of multiple numbers, they should focus on listening, speed, and accuracy.*

A Scavenger Hunt At Camp (A subtraction story)

During camp this summer, I had a great time and participated in a great scavenger hunt. This scavenger hunt was slightly different than others. In this particular scavenger hunt, we had to hide things instead of find things. Each participant was given a box of 1,000 popsicle sticks to write our names on and later hide in one of the cabins. The object of the game was to hide them and the camp counselors would find them. Whoever had the most amount of popsicle sticks found was declared the winner of the contest. I was determined to be the winner and used a special strategy. I decided to hide my popsicle sticks in bulk - I would be sure to win. I started with 1,000 popsicle sticks and hid large quantities in the following places:

Quantity/hiding place	Balance *(Answer)*
a. 27 behind the chair.	973
b. 32 behind the counter.	941
c. 56 under the sugar bowl.	885
d. 63 under a plate on the table.	822
e. 47 under a pillow.	775
f. 82 on the mantle.	693
g. 91 inside the desk.	602
h. 75 in the bathroom cabinet	527
i. 88 under the living room lamp.	439
j. 67 under the blanket.	372
k. 108 all around the kitchen.	264

By this time, I should have been all out of popsicles sticks; but the quantity in my box just seemed to keep growing. I didn't know how many I should have had left.

Teacher's Instruction: *Ask a student to give you the number of popsicle sticks that should be left in the box - 264. Also, mix and match various combinations that the teacher found and have the student do the math for the balances.*

Assessment Option: Have the students share their best work with the class. Also, students may check each others work on the mixed-and-matched variations.

Mathematics Made Fun
INDEPENDENT ACTIVITY
Addition & Subtraction - 5th Grade

Reflection: Addition & Subtraction

It is important that students understand why they are learning this process and how they can apply it to their daily lives. Explain why knowing how to increase and decrease numbers and understand word problems is important.

In this reflection, ask the students these questions in an open discussion:

1. What did they learn?
2. How can they use what they learned in their daily activity?
3. Can they teach what they have learned to someone else?
4. What did they like most about the activity?
5. What did they like least about the activity?
6. Ask students if they can imagine any real-life situations where they might need to increase or decrease numbers quickly.

Mathematics Made Fun
Activity Title: <u>Multiplication & Division</u>

The process of multiplying and dividing is a basic mathematical skill and the foundation to understanding and solving other mathematical problems. The activities in this sections will focus on providing practice in multiplication and division.

Time Frame: **35 - 65 Minutes**
    5 - 10 Activity introduction and explanation.
    5 - 10 Chart information on the board.
    5 - 10 Whole group discussion.
   10 - 15 Independent student activity.
    5 - 10 Activity assessment.
    5 - 10 Reflection on the activity.

Lesson Objectives: To increase student knowledge of multiplication and division.

Materials & Resources: Paper, pencil, and crayon.

Instruction Procedure: Explain the lesson and lesson objectives to the students. See grade level for specific instructions and procedures.

Whole Group Activity:

See grade level for specific whole group instructions and activities.

Mathematics Made Fun
INDEPENDENT ACTIVITY
Multiplication & Division - 2nd Grade

Teacher's Instructions: Introduce the activity and activity objectives. Demonstrate the steps in solving word problems using the example and explaining the purpose of each step. (To demonstrate and explain division, simply reverse the problem.) First, copy the problem.

> *Step 1:* Identify the clue words.
> *Step 2:* Set-up the problem.
> *Step 3:* Solve the problem.

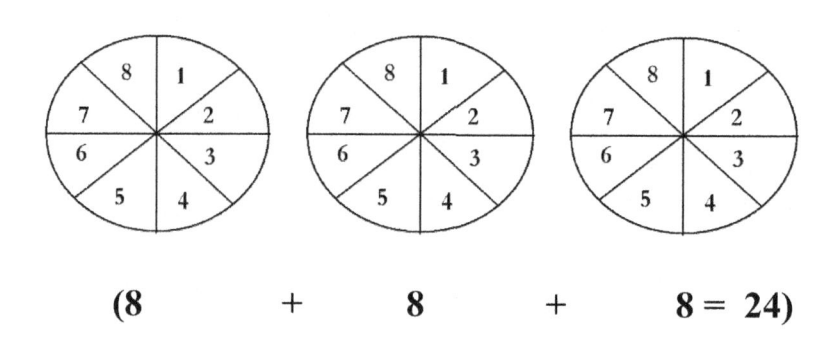

Second grade students should be able to multiply and divide numbers through ten; however, you may adjust the numbers in each problem to suit your student's needs. Write one additional problem (from below) on the board and have the students copy the problem. Complete this problem as a whole group activity generating answers from the students. Make sure to follow the steps in order, this will help the students remember the process of solving word problems. Once the students have completed the whole group activity, write a few more problems (from below) on the board and allow them time to solve the problems on their own. You may want to leave the demonstration example and steps on the board.

Demonstration Example:

Step 1: Identify clue words.   There are **3 pizzas** with **8 slices each**.
                                   How many slices are there **in all**?

Step 2: Set up the problem

(8   +   8   +   8 = 24)

Step 3: Solve the problem.

```
   3    pizzas
  x 8   slices each
 = 24   pieces (in all)
```

Mathematics Made Fun
INDEPENDENT ACTIVITY
Multiplication & Division - 2nd Grade

Teacher's Instructions*: Have the students complete the problem. Additionally, they can name the fact family and create an array to visualize the problem.*

Multiplication

1. There are seven ice cream cones with 3 scoops on each cone. How many scoops of ice cream are there in all?
2. There are 9 dogs with 4 legs each. How many legs are there in all?
3. There are 6 cupcakes with 5 sprinkles each. How many sprinkles are there in all?
4. There are 10 bags with 10 toys in each. How many toys are there in all?
5. There are 9 bags with 3 juice boxes in each. How many juice boxes are there in all?
6. Slice 8 oranges into 7 pieces each. How many total slices do you have?
7. There are 4 busses with 6 passengers each. How many total passengers?
8. There are 6 flowers with 9 petals each. How many petals in all?
9. There are 9 boats on the lake with 3 passengers in each. How many passengers in all?
10. There are 8 letters with 5 stamps each. How many total stamps are there?

Division

1. You can only see under the door of the barn well enough to see the horses legs and you can see 16 horse legs. If each horse has 4 legs, how many horses are in the barn?
2. You have a pizza with 9 slices you want to share with 3 friends. If you divide the pizza evenly, how many slices will each friend receive?
3. There are a total of 21 cupcakes and 7 people? If each person received the same number of cupcakes, how many cupcakes will each person receive.
4. There are 81 tickets for the school carnival and 9 students. If they all receive the same amount of tickets, how many tickets will each student receive?
5. You are reading a book with 108 pages. If you read 9 pages each day how many days will it take you to finish reading the book.
6. There are 18 slices of cake and 6 people. If divided equally, how many slices will each person receive?

Mathematics Made Fun
INDEPENDENT ACTIVITY
Multiplication & Division - 2nd Grade

7. There are 50 playing balls and 10 classrooms. How many playing balls will each classroom receive if the classrooms all receive the same amount?

8. The teacher received a total of 36 flowers from her 6 students. If each student gave her the same amount of flowers, how many flowers did each student give her?

9. There are 54 apples and 9 students. If the apples are divided equally, how many apples will each student receive?

10. You have $20.00 to buy yourself some new shoes and they each cost $10.00 a pair. How many pair can you buy?

Assessment Option: Have the students share their best work.

Mathematics Made Fun
INDEPENDENT ACTIVITY
Multiplication & Division - 3rd Grade

Teacher's Instructions: *Introduce the activity and activity objectives. Demonstrate the steps in solving word-problems, using the example and explaining the purpose of each step. (To demonstrate and explain division, simply reverse the problem.) First, copy the problem.*

> ***Step 1:*** *Identify the clue words.*
> ***Step 2:*** *Set up the problem.*
> ***Step 3:*** *Solve the problem.*

Third grade *students should be able to multiply and divide whole numbers and numbers with decimals. You may adjust the numbers in each problem to suit your student's needs. Write one additional problem (from the following page) on the board and have the students copy the problem. Complete this problem as a whole group activity, generating answers from the students. Make sure to follow the steps in order, this will help the students remember the process of solving word problems. Once the students have completed the whole group activity, write a few more problems (from below) on the board and allow them time to solve the problems on their own. You may want to leave the demonstration example and steps on the board.*

Demonstration Example:

Step 1: Identify clue words.   *There are **4 shelves** with **5 books each**. How many books are there **in all**?*

Step 2: Set up the problem.

1	2	3	4	5
2				
3				
4				20

Step 3: Solve the problem.

```
   4    shelves
 x 5    books each shelf
= 20    books in all
```

Mathematics Made Fun
INDEPENDENT ACTIVITY
Multiplication & Division - 3rd Grade

Teacher's Instructions: Have the students complete the problem. Additionally, they can name the fact family and create an array to visualize the problem.

Multiplication

1. You just walked 7 blocks. Each block had 9 houses. How many houses did you pass?
2. There are 17 houses on our block and each house has a 4 car garage, but contains only 3 cars. How many total cars are there?
3. The train has 8 cars and each car holds 25 passengers. How many passengers are there in all?
4. There were 19 students in a basketball throwing contest. Each student made 9 baskets causing a 19-way tie. How many baskets did the students make all together?
5. I had a party and invited 21 friends. Each friend brought three additional friends. How many people came to my party?
6. During the race, each of the 16 cars made 7 laps around the track. What was the total number of laps made by all the cars?
7. There are 63 cups of sugar cubes and each cup contains 10 cubes. How many sugar cubes are there in all?

Division

1. This year for Teacher Appreciation Day I plan to give the 14 teachers at my school a bouquet of flowers with the same number of flowers in each bouquet. I picked 98 flowers. How many flowers will each teacher have in their bouquet?
2. There are 210 people who need to ride the bus into the shopping center. The bus can only carry 42 people at a time. How many trips will the bus have to make?
3. We are packing all of our books away for the summer, but we only have 56 boxes and 504 books. How many books should we put in each box?
4. There is one train with 38 cars and 154 passengers. If the passengers are distributed equally, how many people are in each car of the train?
5. You need to purchase movie tickets for you and your friends. You have $84.00 and the tickets cost $7.00 each. How many friends can you take to the movie?
6. There are 312 students on the playground which has 8 play areas. How many student will there be per play area if all play areas have the same number of students?
7. You have 399 Easter eggs to hide and want to put 7 in each hiding place. How many different hiding places will you need?

Assessment Option: Have the students share their best work.

Mathematics Made Fun
INDEPENDENT ACTIVITY
Multiplication & Division - 4th Grade

Teacher's Instructions: *Introduce the activity and activity objectives. Demonstrate the steps in solving word-problems using the example below and explaining the purpose of each step. (To demonstrate and explain division, simply reverse the problem.) First, copy the problem.*

*<u>**Step 1:**</u> Identify the clue words.*
*<u>**Step 2:**</u> Set up the problem.*
*<u>**Step 3:**</u> Solve the problem.*

Forth grade *students should be able to multiply and divide multiple digit whole numbers and numbers with decimals. In addition, they should understand the concept of remainders. You may adjust the numbers in each problem to suit your students needs. Write one additional problem (from the list on the following page) on the board and have the students copy the problem. Complete this problem as a whole group activity, generating answers from the students. Make sure to follow the steps in order. This will help the students remember the process of solving word-problems. Once the students have completed the whole group activity, write a few more problems (from the following page) on the board and allow them time to solve the problems on their own. You may want to leave the demonstration example and steps on the board.*

Demonstration Example:

Step 1: Identify clue words.

*There are **<u>16 slices of pie</u>** and **<u>5 people.</u>** How many slices will each person receive, how many slices will be **<u>left over</u>**?*

Step 2: Set up the problem.

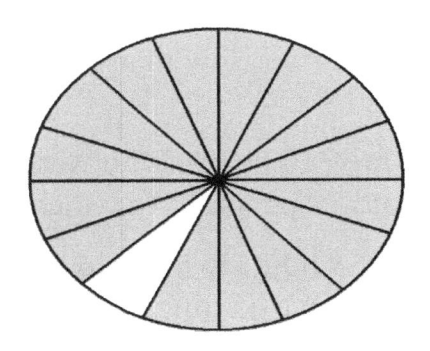

Step 3: Solve the problem.

5 + 5 + 5 = 15
3 slices each for 5 people
1 slice left over

Mathematics Made Fun
INDEPENDENT ACTIVITY
Multiplication & Division - 4th Grade

Teacher's Instructions: *Have the students complete the problem. Additionally, they can name the fact family and create an array to visualize the problem.*

Multiplication

1. There are 400 people from our school going on a field trip. There are 14 busses and each bus hold 30 passengers. Is there enough room for all of the 425 passengers?

2. You have a job making $11.25 an hour and working 12 hours per week. How much money will you make in a week? How much will you earn in 2 weeks? In 6 months? In 1 year?

3. There are 18 red sweaters, 14 orange sweaters, and 12 pair of jeans. Each sweater costs $8.00 How many sweaters are there and what is the total cost of the sweaters?

4. Your family is going on a trip and the airplane tickets cost $125.00 each. There are 7 members in your family including yourself. What is the total cost of all the airplane tickets?

5. Your teacher is grading papers for a total of 30 students (each stack contains 30 papers). It takes him 3 minutes to grades each paper in stack A, 4 minutes to grade each paper in stack B, and 7 minutes to grade the papers in stack C. How much time does it take him to grade stack A, stack B, and stack C. What is the total time needed to grade all three stacks of papers.

6. You have a job earning $10.00 per hour. You work 3 hours for 4 days during the week, and 6 hours on Saturday. How much money do/will you earn for this week?

Division

1. There are 678 same-size books that need to be placed on 32 book shelves in the school library. How many books will each shelf hold, and how many books will be left over?

2. There are 210 people who want to ride the train. The train has 11 cars and each car will hold 19 people. How many people will not be able to ride the train?

3. We have 8 hours to drive to my grandmothers house which is 365 miles away. We can only drive 45 miles per hour. How long will it take us to get to grandma's house, and will we arrive early, late, or on time?

4. There are 21 boats sailing to Catalina, and each boat holds 32 passengers. There are 675 people waiting to board the boats. Will everyone have a seat? Will there be extra seats or will some people have to stay behind?

Mathematics Made Fun
INDEPENDENT ACTIVITY
Multiplication & Division - 4th Grade

5. You are treating 19 of your friends plus yourself to the circus. The tickets cost $12.00 each and you have $250.00. Will you have enough money?

6. You had 732 pieces of candy to hand out on Halloween. You decided to give the trick-or- treaters 8 pieces of candy each. You had a total of 93 trick-or-treaters visit your house. Did you have enough candy for each trick-or-treater, or did someone get tricked?

Assessment Option: Have the students share their best work.

Mathematics Made Fun
INDEPENDENT ACTIVITY
Multiplication & Division - 5th Grade

Teacher's Instructions: *Introduce the activity and activity objectives. Demonstrate the steps in solving word-problems using the example and explaining the purpose of each step. (To demonstrate and explain division, simply reverse the problem.) First, copy the problem.*

> ***Step 1:*** *Identify the clue words.*
> ***Step 2:*** *Set up the problem.*
> ***Step 3:*** *Solve the problem.*
> ***Step 4:*** *Check your work by reversing the problem.*

Fifth grade *students should be able to multiply and divide whole numbers and numbers with decimals. You may adjust the numbers in each problem to suit your student's needs. Write one additional problem (from below) on the board and have the students copy the problem. Complete this problem as a whole group activity generating answers from the students. Make sure to follow the steps in order, this will help the students remember the process of solving word problems. Once the students have completed the whole group activity, write a few more problems (from below) on the board and allow them time to solve the problems on their own. You may want to leave the demonstration example and steps on the board.*

Demonstration Example:

Step 1: Identify clue words.

Kevin Works earns $11.25 per hour, working various hours throughout the week. This week he worked the following hours: Monday - 7, Tuesday - 2, Wednesday - 3, Thursday - 3, Friday - 2, and Saturday - 6. Create a schedule and determine his gross pay per day and for the week (before taxes).

Step 2: Set up the problem.

Day	Sun	Mon	Tue	Wed	Thu	Fri	Sat	Total Pay
Hrs. worked	0	7	2	3	3	2	6	23
Wage per hr.	$11.25	$11.25	$11.25	$11.25	$11.25	$11.25	$11.25	
Total per day	$0.00	$78.75	$22.50	$33.75	$33.75	$22.50	$67.50	**$258.75**

Mathematics Made Fun
INDEPENDENT ACTIVITY
Multiplication & Division - 5th Grade

Step 3: Solve the problem.

    $11.25 hourly pay rate
    <u>x   23 hours worked during the week</u>
    = $258.75 gross pay for the week (Calculate per day separately.)

Step 4: Check the problem.
    23⎴ $258.75 = $11.25

Mathematics Made Fun
INDEPENDENT ACTIVITY
Multiplication & Division - 5th Grade

Teacher's Instructions: Have the students complete the problems.

Multiplication

1. You started your own business of mowing lawns. Because you are in school, you can only mow lawns on the weekend. You have done such a great job that 7 more people want your service. It currently takes you 35 minutes to mow one lawn, and you already have 17 customers. How long does it take you to mow all 17 lawns? Do you have enough time to add 7 more customers; if so, how long will it take you to mow all 24 lawns?
2. You are a great runner and can run 8 blocks in 3 minutes. How long will it take you to run 32 blocks?
3. There are a total of 27 busses leaving for the airport. Each bus can hold 49 passengers. If the busses are at their maximum capacity, how many total passengers are on the busses.
4. There are 12 shelves with 6 slots each. Each slot holds 21 pair of roller skates. How many pair of roller skates will it take to fill all the shelves?
5. There are 34 trucks transporting lemons to the main city for distribution. Each truck contains 84 crates, and each crate contains 205 lemons. What is the total number of lemons on all of the trucks combined?
6. You need to finish reading a certain book for your homework assignment. You know that it takes you 2 ½ minutes to read 1 page. You have 74 pages more to read. How long will it take you to finish reading the book?

Division

1. You have just collected and turned in some old newspapers for a paper-drive fundraiser at your school. You received $5.75 for 98 lbs. of newspaper. How much did you receive per pound?
2. There are 3,944 total students in our school, and we have 17 classrooms with an equal number of students in each. How many students are in each classroom?
3. The cruise ship is at full capacity with a total of 1,692 people on board. If each room hold 4 people, how many rooms are there on the cruise ship?
4. You need to transport the apple harvest to the main city for local distribution. You have 18,000 apples and 350 containers. Determine the number of apples to be placed in each container and how many apples will be left over.
5. You need to stock the new shipment of books on the shelves at the book store. You have a total of 4,500 books to place on 75 shelves. How many books will be on each shelf, and will any books be left over?
6. You just purchased a bag of fruit that cost you $7.41 and weighed 19 lbs. How much did your fruit cost per pound?

Mathematics Made Fun
INDEPENDENT ACTIVITY
Multiplication & Division - 5th Grade

Teacher's Instructions: Have the students complete the problems.

1. You are the new store manager in charge of stocking the shelves. You have the following products and number of shelves to display.
2. Calculate the total units per shelf, left over units, and cost per unit for each.

Do not chart columns A, B, or C, have the students calculate the answers.

Item	Qty.	Shelves	A. Items per Shelf	B. Items left over	Cost per Unit	C. Total Unit Cost
Robots	337	42	8	1	$8.00	$2,696.00
Beach Balls	429	21	20	9	$3.00	$1,287.00
T-Shirts	864	36	24	0	$4.50	$3,880.00
Jeans	986	42	23	20	$12.50	$12,325.00
Sunglasses	391	18	21	13	$3.25	$1,270.75
Handbags	784	54	14	28	$6.75	$5,292.00

3. Sandra worked the following schedule: Sunday - 2 hrs, Monday - 5 hrs, Tuesday - 4 hrs, Wednesday - 6 hrs, Thursday 5 hrs, and Saturday 8 hrs. During the week she earns $14.75 for hours worked, and on the weekend she earns $18.75 with a $50.00 bonus if she works on Sunday. How much money did she earn for the week? On which day did she earn the most money? On which day did she earn the least amount of money?
4. You are in charge of stocking the new shipment of coats. Distribute the total amount of coats among the colors evenly.

Dress Slacks	blue	red	green	purple	black	total
Size 8						190
Size 10						305
Size 12						495
Size 14						155
Size 16						900

Assessment Option: Have the students share their best work.

Mathematics Made Fun
INDEPENDENT ACTIVITY
Multiplication & Division - 5th Grade

Reflection: Multiplication and Division

It is important for students to understand why they are learning this process and how they can apply it to their daily lives. Explain that the ability to multiply and divide numbers is an important life skill both academically and personally.

In this reflection, ask the students these questions in an open discussion:

1. What did they learn?
2. How can they use what they learned in their daily activity?
3. Can they teach what they have learned to someone else?
4. What did they like most about the activity?
5. What did they like least about the activity?

Mathematics Made Fun
Activity Title: <u>Fractions</u>

A fraction is a portion of a whole number. Understanding how to interpret and manipulate fractions is important for determining portions of a whole. The activities in this sections will focus on providing practice in using fractions. *The words piece and parts are interchangeable throughout this lesson. In some cases younger student identify with the word **piece** and older students identify with the word **part**.*

Time Frame:	35 - 65 Minutes
	5 - 10 Activity introduction and explanation.
	5 - 10 Chart information on the board.
	5 - 10 Whole group discussion.
	10 - 15 Independent student activity.
	5 - 10 Activity assessment.
	5 - 10 Reflection on the activity.

Lesson Objectives:	To increase student knowledge and use of fractions.

Materials & Resources:	Paper, pencil, and crayon.

Instruction Procedure:	Explain the lesson and lesson objectives to the students.

Whole Group Activity:

See grade level for specific whole group instructions and activities.

Mathematics Made Fun
INDEPENDENT ACTIVITY
Fractions - 2nd Grade

Teacher's Instructions: *Demonstrate the example below to the students while explaining to them that a fraction represents a certain part of a whole number (or a piece of).* ***Second grade*** *students should be able to write, identify, add and subtract fractions in the simple form. Further, students should understand that fractions and decimals are two different forms of the same concept.*

Demonstrate the steps in solving fraction word-problems, using the example and explaining the purpose of each step. First, copy the problem.

Step 1: *Identify the clue words.*
Step 2: *Set up the problem.*
Step 3: *Solve the problem.*

Make sure to follow the steps in order. This will help the students remember the process of solving word-problems. Once the students have completed the whole group activity, write a few more problems (from the list on the following page) on the board and allow them time to solve the problems on their own. You may want to leave the demonstration example and steps on the board.

Demonstration Example:

Step 1: Identify clue words.   *Karen **divided** her candy bar in **half** and*
      gave
                                    __1 / 2__ to her friend, Carmen. Identify the
      part   *she gave to Carmen by shading it in.*

Step 2: Set up the problem.   Draw the whole candy bar, then
                                                  divide it in 1 / 2, and shade 1 half.

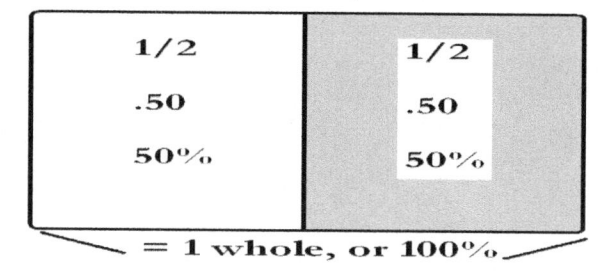

1/2	1/2
.50	.50
50%	50%

= 1 whole, or 100%

Step 3: Solve the problem.

  1 / 2 **candy bar for Karen**
+ <u>1 / 2 **candy bar for Carmen**</u>
= 1 **whole candy bar**

312

Mathematics Made Fun
INDEPENDENT ACTIVITY
Fractions - 2nd Grade

Teacher's Instructions: *Select one or more of the following activities. Write the activity on the board and have the students select one or more items and complete the activity using the item(s).*

1. *Draw a picture to represent the object.*
2. *Divide the object according to the fraction.*
3. *Shade the required part.*

Challenge:

4. *Write the fraction as a percentage and as a decimal.*

Activities - Draw the picture, divide it in the following equal parts:

1. 1/2 and shade 1/2 .
2. 3rds (3 equal pieces) and shade 1/3, and 2/3.
3. 4ths (4 equal pieces) and shade 1/4 , 2/4, and 3/4.

Items to Draw

Ball	Triangle (½ only)	Rectangle	Liquorish stick
Pie	Box	Heart (½ only)	Apple
Cake	Lollipop	Piece of Bread	Orange
Donut	Stack of pancakes	Sandwich	Watermelon
Square	Piece of paper	Plate	Hamburger

Assessment Option: Have the students share their best work.

Mathematics Made Fun
INDEPENDENT ACTIVITY
Fractions - 3rd Grade

Teacher's Instructions: *Demonstrate the example below to the students while explaining to them that a fraction represents a certain part of a whole number (or a piece of).* **Third grade** *students should be able to write, identify, add and subtract fractions in the simple form. Further, students should understand that fractions and decimals are two different forms of the same concept. Select one or more of the following activities. Write the activity on the board and have the students select one or more items and complete the activity using the item(s) to draw below.*

1. *Draw a picture to represent the object.*
2. *Divide the object according to the fraction.*
3. *Shade the required part.*

Challenge:
4. *Write the fraction as a percentage and as a decimal.*

Activities - Draw the picture, divide it in the following equal parts:

1. 1/2 and shade 1/2 .
2. 3rds (3 equal pieces) and shade 1/3, and 2/3.
3. 4ths (4 equal pieces) and shade 1/4 , 2/4, and 3/4.
4. 5ths (5 equal parts) and shade 1/5, 2/5, 3/5, and 4/5.
5. 6ths (6 equal parts) and shade 1/6, 2/6, 3/6, 4/6, and 5/6.
6. 7ths (7 equal parts) and shade 1/7, 2/7, 3/7, 4/7, 5/7, and 6/7.
7. 8ths (8 equal parts) and shade 1/8, 2/8, 3/8, 4/8, 5/8, 6/8, and 7/8.

Items to Draw

Ball	Triangle (½ only)	Rectangle	Liquorish stick
Pie	Box	Heart (½ only)	Apple
Cake	Lollipop	Piece of bread	Orange
Donut	Stack of pancakes	Sandwich	Watermelon
Square	Piece of paper	Plate	Hamburger

Assessment Option: Have the students share their best work.

Mathematics Made Fun
INDEPENDENT ACTIVITY
Fractions - 4th Grade

Teacher's Instructions: Demonstrate the example below to the students while explaining to them that a fraction represents a certain part of a whole number (or a piece of). **Forth grade** students should be able to write, identify, add and subtract fractions in the simple form. Further, students should understand that fractions and decimals are two different forms of the same concept. Select one or more of the following activities. Write the activity on the board and have the students select one or more items and complete the activity using the item(s) to draw below.

1. Draw a picture to represent the object.
2. Divide the object according to the fraction.
3. Shade the required part.
4. Write the fraction as a percentage and as a decimal.

<u>Activities</u> - Draw the picture, divide it in the following equal parts:

1. 1/2 and shade 1/2.
2. 3rds (3 equal pieces) and shade 1/3, and 2/3.
3. 4ths (4 equal pieces) and shade 1/4, 2/4, and 3/4.
4. 5ths (5 equal parts) and shade 1/5, 2/5, 3/5, and 4/5.
5. 6ths (6 equal parts) and shade 1/6, 2/6, 3/6, 4/6, and 5/6.
6. 7ths (7 equal parts) and shade 1/7, 2/7, 3/7, 4/7, 5/7, and 6/7.
7. 8ths (8 equal parts) and shade 1/8, 2/8, 3/8, 4/8, 5/8, 6/8, and 7/8.

<u>Items to Draw</u>

Ball	Triangle (½ only)	Rectangle	Liquorish stick
Pie	Box	Heart (½ only)	Apple
Cake	Lollipop	Piece of bread	Orange
Donut	Stack of pancakes	Sandwich	Watermelon
Square	Piece of paper	Plate	Hamburger

Assessment Option: Have the students share their best work.

Mathematics Made Fun
INDEPENDENT ACTIVITY
Fractions - 5th Grade

Teacher's Instructions: *Demonstrate the example below to the students while explaining to them that a fraction represents a certain part of a whole number (or a piece of). Fifth grade students should be able to write, identify, add, subtract, multiply, and divide fractions in the simple form. Further, students should understand that fractions and decimals are two different forms of the same concept. Select one or more of the following activities. Write the activity on the board and have the students select one or more items and complete the activity using the item(s).*

1. *Draw a picture to represent the object.*
2. *Divide the object according to the fraction.*
3. *Shade the required part.*
4. *Write the fraction as a percentage and as a decimal.*

<u>**Activities -**</u> Draw the picture, divide it in the following equal parts:

1. 4ths (4 equal pieces) and shade 1/4, 2/4, and 3/4.
2. 5ths (5 equal parts) and shade 1/5, 2/5, 3/5, and 4/5.
3. 12ths (12 equal parts) and shade 1/12, 2/12, 3/12, 4/12, 5/12, 6/12, 7/12, 8/12, 9/12, 10/12, and 11/12. ***<u>Reduce all fractions to their lowest form.</u>***
4. 15ths (15 equal parts) and shade 1/15, 2/15, 3/15, 4/15, 5/15, 6/15, 7/15, 8/15, 9/15, 10/15, 11/15, 12/15, 13/15, and 14/15. ***<u>Reduce all fractions to their lowest form</u>***.
5.

<u>Items to Draw</u>

Ball	Triangle (½ only)	Rectangle	Liquorish stick
Pie	Box	Heart (½ only)	Apple
Cake	Lollipop	Piece of bread	Orange
Donut	Stack of pancakes	Sandwich	Watermelon
Square	Piece of paper	Plate	Hamburger

Assessment Option: Have the students share their best work.

Mathematics Made Fun
INDEPENDENT ACTIVITY
Fractions - 5th Grade

Reflection: Fractions

It is important for students to understand why they are learning this process and how they can apply it to their daily lives. Explain that knowing how to use fractions is an important part of one's mathematical foundation. Fractions are also used in everyday life with such things as ordering food. "I could only eat ½ of the pizza".

In this reflection, ask the students these questions in an open discussion:

1. What did they learn?
2. How can they use what they learned in their daily activity?
3. Can they teach what they have learned to someone else?
4. What did they like most about the activity?
5. What did they like least about the activity?

Mathematics Made Fun
Activity Title: Measurement - Tools, Length & Width, and Weight

The system of measuring plays an important role in all of our everyday lives. It is important to know which tools are used to measure what; and how to read, write and use those measurements. The activities in this sections focuses on providing practice with identifying and using a variety of measuring tools.

Time Frame: **35 - 65 Minutes**
- 5 - 10 Activity introduction and explanation.
- 5 - 10 Chart information on the board.
- 5 - 10 Whole group discussion.
- 10 - 15 Independent student activity.
- 5 - 10 Activity assessment.
- 5 - 10 Reflection on the activity.

Lesson Objectives: To increase student knowledge of measuring tools and methods of measure.

Materials & Resources: Paper, pencil, crayon, paper clips, ruler, paper cups, other classroom items (and short strips of paper for Kindergarten about 3 to 4 inches long).

Instruction Procedure: Explain the lesson and lesson objective to the students.

Whole Group Activity:

See individual grade level activities for the whole group and individual instructions.

Mathematics Made Fun
Measurement - Tools, Length and Width, Weight, and Capacity
Kindergarten

Teacher's Instructions: *Select an activity below. Explain the lesson and lesson objective to the students while demonstrating the process. Walk the students through the beginning of the activity, allowing them to complete the activity on their own.*

1. **Determining Tools of Measure**

    This activity is designed to help young students determine which type of tools are used for different types of measures. List the four tools of measure on the board, using a picture and the word: ***clock, calendar, ruler, scale, cup. (However, you will not need these physical items for the lesson.)***

    Select one or more items from the list below and have the students identify the best tool (above) to use in order to measure the item(s). Once complete have the students select one item, draw a picture, and write a short sentence (with your assistance) that describes the picture.

    ### Items To Measure

water	doorway	desk	rock	desk top
hours	hand size	milk	minutes	number of days
lemon	shoe size	time	rug	how tall someone is

2. **Measuring Length and Width**

    This activity is designed to help young students distinguish length from width; and practice measuring by comparison, or using a variety of non-standard methods. Explain the meaning of and difference between length (how long an object is, usually the distance from top to bottom) and width (the distance across, usually from side to side). Although length and width are usually measured with such tools as a ruler, tape measure, yard stick etc.., for this activity we will use non-standard units or methods. List one tool of measure and one item to measure. Demonstrate the technique for the students. After the whole group demonstration, have the students select the same tool of measure and a different item (have the whole class use the same second item) to measure. Have the students measure the item, write down their results in words (or in a sentence), and draw a picture to depict their sentence.

Tools for measuring length & width.	Items	
paper clips	book	desk top
pencil	teachers desktop	a persons arm
strip of paper	desk height	a persons hand
crayons	student's height	a persons foot

Mathematics Made Fun
Measurement - Tools, Length and Width, Weight, and Capacity
Kindergarten

3. Measuring Weight

This activity is designed to help young students understand that some items are measured by how much they weight. Although weight is generally measured with a scale, for this activity we will use non-standard units or methods. List one tool of measure and one item to be measured. Demonstrate the technique for the students. After the whole group demonstration, have the students select the same tool of measure and a different item (have the whole class use the same second item) to be measured. Have the students measure the item, write down their results in words (or in a sentence), and draw a picture to depict their sentence.

Tools for measuring Weight	**Items**
student hands	pencil - piece of paper
visual	eraser - piece of chalk
	bottle of glue - glue stick

(Have the students look around their classroom for other pairs of items to compare).

4. Measuring Capacity

This activity is designed to help young students understand that some items are measured by **how much it can hold**. Although capacity is usually measured by a type of container (cup or box), for this activity we will use non-standard units or methods. List one tool of measure and one item to measure. Demonstrate the technique for the students. After the whole group demonstration, have the students select the same tool of measure and a different item (have the whole class use the same second item) to be measured. Have the students measure the item, write down their results in words (or in a sentence), and draw a picture to go along with their results.

Tools for measuring Capacity	**Items**
student hands	pencil
cup	pieces of chalk
	crayon
	pieces of paper
	paper clips

Mathematics Made Fun
Measurement - Length, Weight, & Capacity & Unit Conversion
1st Grade

Teacher's Instructions: Select an activity below. Explain the lesson and lesson objective to the students while demonstrating the process. Walk the students through the beginning of the activity, allowing them to complete the activity on their own.

1. **Determining Tools of Measure**

    This activity is designed to help young students determine which type of tools are used for different types of measurement. List the five tools of measure on the board using a picture and the word: *1) clock, 2) calendar, 3) ruler, 4) scale, and 5) cup.*

    Select one or more items from the list below and have the students identify the best tool (above) to use in order to measure the item(s). Once complete, have the students select one item, draw a picture, and write a short sentence (with your assistance) to depict the picture.

    ### Items To Measure

water	doorway	desk	rock	desk top
hours	hand size	milk	minutes	number of days
lemon	shoe size	time	rug	how tall someone is

2. **Measuring Length and Width**

    This activity is designed to help young students learn to measure <u>length</u> and <u>width</u>. Students will also practice using standard and non-standard methods to measure, and to compare the two. Explain the difference between, and meaning of, <u>length</u> (how long something is, usually the distance from top to bottom) and <u>width</u> (the distance across, usually from side to side). Although length and width are usually measured with such tools as a ruler, tape measure, yard stick, etc..; for this activity, we will use both standard and non-standard units to measure items and compare the two. List one tool of measure and one item to be measured. Demonstrate the technique for the students. After the whole group demonstration, have the students select the same tool of measure and a different item (have the whole class use the same second item) to be measured. Have the students measure the item, write down their results in words (or in a sentence), and draw a picture to depict their sentence.

Tools for measuring length & width.	Items	
paper clips	book	desk top
pencil	teachers desktop	a persons arm
strip of paper	desk height	a persons hand
*ruler	student's height	a persons foot

Mathematics Made Fun
Measurement - Tools, Length and Width, Weight, and Capacity
1st Grade

3. Measuring Weight

This activity is designed to help young students understand that some items are measured by how much they weight. Although weight is generally measured with a scale, for this activity we will use non-standard units or methods. List one tool of measure and one item to be measured. Demonstrate the technique for the students. After the whole group demonstration, have the students select the same tool of measure and a different item (have the whole class use the same second item) to be measured. Have the students measure the item, write down their results in words (or in a sentence), and draw a picture to depict their sentence.

Tools for measuring Weight	**Items**
student hands	pencil - piece of paper
visual	eraser - piece of chalk
	bottle of glue - glue stick

Have the students identify other items in the classroom to compare.

4. Measuring Capacity

This activity is designed to help young students understand that some items are measured by how much it can hold. Although capacity is usually measured by a type of container (cup), for this activity we will use non-standard units or methods. List one tool of measure and one item to be measured. Demonstrate the technique for the students. After the whole group demonstration, have the students select the same tool of measure and a different item (have the whole class use the same second item) to be measured. Have the students measure the item, write down their results in words (or in a sentence), and draw a picture depict their sentence.

Tools for measuring Capacity	**Items**
student hands	pencil
cup	pieces of chalk
	crayon
	pieces of paper
	paper clips

Assessment Option: Have the students share their best work.

Mathematics Made Fun
Measurement - Tools, Length and Width, Weight, and Capacity
1st Grade

Reflection: Measurement - Tools, Length and Width, Weight, and Capacity

It is important for students to understand why they are learning this process and how they can apply it to their daily lives. Explain that knowing which tools are used to measure different items is important. After all, would you use a ruler to measure how much you weigh?

In this reflection, ask the students these questions in an open discussion:

1. What did they learn?
2. How can they use what they learned in their daily activity?
3. Can they teach what they have learned to someone else?
4. What did they like most about the activity?
5. What did they like least about the activity?

Mathematics Made Fun
Activity Title: <u>Measurement - Time, Duration, Concept, & Intervals</u>

Understanding how to tell and measure time is a vitally necessary part of life. We use these skills at school, at home, to cook, and to go places. The activities in this section will focus on providing practice with the concept, duration, and measurement of time.

Numbers are fun when we know how they work and how to manipulate them. In this set of activities, students will practice a variety of methods to read, write, and count numbers.

Time Frame: **35 - 65 Minutes**
- 5 - 10 Activity introduction and explanation.
- 5 - 10 Chart information on the board.
- 5 - 10 Whole group discussion.
- 10 - 15 Independent student activity.
- 5 - 10 Activity assessment.
- 5 - 10 Reflection on the activity.

Lesson Objective: To increase student knowledge of the different aspects of time.

Materials & Resources: Paper, pencil, and crayons.

Instruction Procedure: Explain the lesson and lesson objective to the students.

Whole Group Activity:

See individual grade level activities for the whole group and individual instructions.

Mathematics Made Fun
Time - Duration, Concept, & Intervals
Kindergarten & 1st Grade

Teacher's Instructions: *Select an activity below. Explain the lesson and lesson objective to the students while demonstrating the process. Walk the students through the beginning of the activity, allowing them to complete the activity on their own. (Although the activities for this sections are the same for Kindergarten as for first grade students; first grade students should be able to determine exact times for activities, and be able to distinguish between morning, afternoon, evening, and night.)*

Kindergarten *students should have an understanding of the concept of time and be able to distinguishing time; day from night, today, tomorrow and yesterday, names of the days of the week as well as the number of days in a week, and the months of the year. In addition, they should be able to* estimate *the time of specific daily events. The activities below are focused on, and will provide practice for, the aforementioned activities.*

First grade *students should have a firm understanding of the concept of time and be able to distinguishing time; day from night, today, tomorrow and yesterday, names of the days of the week as well as the number of days in a week, and the months of the year. In addition, they should be able to determine the* accurate *time of specific daily events. The activities below are focused on, and will provide practice for, the aforementioned activities.*

1. **Day and Night**

    This activity is designed to help young students determine which activities take place at certain times of the day or night.

    Below are titles of events that generally take place at a certain time each day or night. Select one or more, read the title to the students and ask the students about what time this event should take place. Have the students draw a picture depicting the event, and have them include a sentence that indicates the time. Assist the students with their sentence if necessary.

Example:

Events and Activities - Time of Day

breakfast	start of school	brush teeth	recess
lunch	end of school	watch television	homework
dinner	wake up	go to bed	play outside

Mathematics Made Fun
Time - Duration, Concept, & Intervals
Kindergarten & 1st Grade

2. Yesterday, Today & Tomorrow

This activity is designed to help young students understand the concept of time when dealing with, and referring to, days. For this activity, you may want to have the students sit on the rug for a brief discussion. Select a topic for the activity discussion from the selection below. After the discussion, send the students back to their desk with a sheet of paper folded into thirds. Explain that each part (3rd) of the paper should depict an item or event for the day in the correct order.

Example:

Events and Items - Yesterday, Today, & Tomorrow

clothing	food for breakfast	snacks	games
shoes	food for lunch	behavior	after school
places	food for dinner	lunch time	during recess

Mathematics Made Fun
Time - Duration, Concept, & Intervals
Kindergarten & 1st Grade

2. Days of the Week

This activity is designed to help young students practice daily use of the number of days in a week and the names of the days of the week in their correct order. For this activity, you may want to have the students sit on the rug for a brief discussion about the days of the week.

Ask the students to tell you something special they do on each day of the week. Begin with Sunday and continue in order through Saturday. Chart this information on the board to allow the students to visualize the activity. After the discussion, send the students back to their seats with 7 quarter cuts of paper (*cut one sheet of blank into 4 equal pieces*). With the students at their desks, work as a whole group to label each piece or cut with a day of the week and a number. The number represents the number day of the week. Once complete, allow students to complete the activity on their own by adding a picture and title, or brief sentence telling something special they do on that day of the week.

Example:

Events - Days of the Week

| swimming | babysitter | painting | music | dance | park |
| church | tennis | museum | movie | visiting | skating |

Mathematics Made Fun
Time - Duration, Concept, & Intervals
Kindergarten & 1st Grade

3. Months of the Year

This activity is designed to help young students familiarize themselves with the number of months in the year, and the names of the months in the correct order. For this activity, you may want to have the students sit on the rug for a brief discussion about the different events that occur during certain months of the year.

Ask the students to tell you something special about a month, beginning with January and continuing through December. Chart this information on the board to allow the students to visualize the activities with the month. After the discussion, send the students back to their seats with 12 quarter cuts or pieces of paper *(cut one sheet of blank paper into four equal pieces)*. With the students at their seats, work as a whole group to label each piece with a month and a number. The number represents the number month of the year. Once complete, allow students to complete the activity on their own by adding a picture and title or a brief sentence telling something special that occurs during that month.

Example:

January 1	February 2	March 3	April 4	May 5	June 6
It rains a lot.	Valentine's Day is in February.	St. Patrick's Day is in March.	April Fool's Day is in April.	Flowers bloom in May.	My birthday is in June.

July 6	August 8	September 9	October 10	November 11	December 12
Independence Day is in June.	Our camping trip.	We go back to school.	We go tricker treating.	Thanksgiving is in November.	Christmas is in December.

Events - Months of the Year

rain	snow	summer	vacation
birthday	April Fool's Day	camping	Easter
Christmas	Independence Day	school begins	Labor Day
Valentine's Day	Halloween	Thanksgiving	New Years Day

Mathematics Made Fun
Time, Duration, Concept, & Intervals
2nd Grade

Teacher's Instructions: *Select an activity below. Explain the lesson and lesson objective to the students while demonstrating the process. Walk the students through the beginning of the activity, allowing them to complete the activity on their own.*

Second grade *students should be able to: determine the approximate hour of daily events such as the start of school, lunch time, or bed time; know that yesterday, today, and tomorrow are each a 24 hour period of time; know the days of the week (in order), and the months of the year (in order). Furthermore, second grade students should be familiar with the duration of intervals of time.*

1. **Day and Night, Duration of Intervals of Time**

    This activity is designed to give students practice with determining which activities take place at certain times of the day or night. The focus here is the hour of the event, rather than the broad range of day and night.

    Select a few activities from below, write them on the board, and have the students complete the work on their own. Each answer should be in the form of a complete sentence, indicating the time and including AM or PM.

    a. If it takes 1 hour to do your homework and you begin at 5:00 PM, what time will it be when you finish? Indicate AM or PM and tell the total amount of time it took.
    b. If it takes 1 hour to mow the lawn and you begin at 3:00 PM, what time will you finish, and how long will it take?
    c. If school begins at 8:00 AM and it is 7:00 AM, how much time before school starts?
    d. If you have dance practice at 3:00 PM for 1 hour, what time does dance practice end?
    e. If your father said he watched your baseball practice for an hour and it is now 7:00 PM, what time did he begin watching your baseball practice?
    f. If your mother is baking a cake which takes 1 hour, and she began baking at 11:00 AM, what time will the cake be ready? How long does it take the cake to bake?

Mathematics Made Fun
Time, Duration, Concept, & Intervals
2nd Grade

Challenge:

Set up a schedule for the following activities to take place during one week. Indicate the duration of time (when the event begins, when it ends, and the time it takes). Make sure to include AM or PM to indicate day or night. *(The students may require some assistance in setting up the table to contain the information.)*

clean your room	eat dinner	homework
get out of school	walk the dog	take a bath
play outside	go to bed	brush your teeth

Mathematics Made Fun
Time, Duration, Concept, & Intervals
2nd Grade

2. Days of the Week - Including Yesterday, Today & Tomorrow

This activity is designed to give students practice with duration of time as it relates to days and weeks. The focus is on the duration of days and weeks, and specific days, rather than simply knowing the days of the week in order.

Select a few activities from below, write them on the board, and have the students complete the work on their own. Each answer should be in the form of a complete sentence specifying a day or number of days.

a. Today is Tuesday and your birthday is 1 week away. How many days away is your birthday, and what day will it fall on?

b. Two days from now will be Monday. What is the day of the week?

c. How many days are in two weeks?

d. How many weekdays are there in one week? How many days make up the weekend?

e. Today is Friday, and in 1 week and two days I will be leaving to go to camp. On what day of the week will I go to camp, and how many days are there from now until then?

f. How many days are there between Friday and Friday (not including the Fridays)?

3. Months of the Year

This activity is designed to give students practice with months of the year and duration of time of months. The focus is on the duration of months and months in a year, rather than knowing the names and order of months.

Select a few activities from below, write them on the board, and have the students complete the work on their own. Each answer should be in the form of a complete sentence specifying a month or number of months.

a. Which month of the year has the fewest days?

b. Today is August 1 and you begin school on September 1. How much time do you have before school begins?

c. How many months are there from January to June, including both January and June?

d. If you go to the dentist each month, how many times during the year do you visit the dentist?

Mathematics Made Fun
Time, Duration, Concept, & Intervals
2nd Grade

If you go to the doctor every other month, how many time during the year do you go to the doctor? (hint - skip count).

e. What month is your birthday? How many months from now until your birthday?

Challenge:

Create a chart to show the amount of time until: your birthday, the last day of school, and Christmas.

Mathematics Made Fun
Time, Duration, Concept, & Intervals
3rd Grade

Teacher's Instructions: *Select an activity below. Explain the lesson and lesson objective to the students while demonstrating the process. Walk the students through the beginning of the activity, allowing them to complete the activity on their own.*

Third grade *students should be able to: determine time to the minute, quarter, half-hour, and hour; and, the duration of the same. In addition, they should be able to calculate and convert time into minutes, hours, days, weeks, months, and years.*

1. **Time Duration and Conversion**

    This activity is designed to give students practice with duration and conversion of time. Select a few activities from below, write them on the board, and have the students complete the work on their own. Each answer should be in the form of a complete sentence.

    a. If it takes you 1 hour and 30 minutes to do your chores at home, and you begin at 3:15 PM, what time will it be when you finish?

    b. If it takes you 45 minutes to walk home, and you begin walking at 2:30 PM, what time will you arrive home?

    c. If school begins at 8:00 AM, and it is now 7:01 AM, how much time do you have to get to school?

    d. Which time is later in the day: 2:15 PM, or a quarter past 2 in the afternoon?

    e. Your basketball practice normally begins at 5:00 PM; but, today they started at a quarter past the hour. What time did your basketball practice begin?

    f. You promised to babysit for 1 hour and 45 minutes, but you stayed 30 minutes longer. How long did you babysit?

    g. It is currently 4:50 and you want to bake a cake that requires 35 minutes baking time. You have to leave at exactly 4:40. What time will the cake be ready, and do you have enough time to bake the cake before you leave the house?

Challenge: How many...

   a. Seconds in a minute?
   b. Minutes in an hour?
   c. Hours in a day?
   d. Days in a week?
   e. Weeks in a year?
   f. Days in a year?
   g. Months in a year?

Mathematics Made Fun
Time, Duration, Concept, & Intervals
3rd Grade

2. Months of the Year

This activity is designed to give students practice with duration of time involving weeks, months, and years. Select a few activities from below, write them on the board, and have the students complete the work on their own. Each answer should be in the form of a complete sentence.

a. Name a special event that happens every 12 months on the same date?

b. How many months are there from November, 2005, to December, 2006?

c. On May 1, your mother told you that you would receive a special gift in exactly 4 months. On what date did you expect to receive your special gift?

d. My puppy will be 3 months old on February 2. In what month was my puppy born?

e. The current month is March. I will be 9 years old on my birthday, which is in November. How many months away is my birthday?

f. It is 7 months before our family vacation in August. What month is it now?

g. I have been going to the dentist every other month to have my braces tightened. My appointments began in April. List the names of the months that I went/must go to the dentist to have my braces tightened.

h. My cat had kittens in July, The veterinarian said to bring the kittens in for a check-up and shots every two months for 6 months. List the names of the months that the kittens must see the veterinarian.

i. My birthday is in September. My sister's birthday is in October. How many months are there between our birthdays?

Assessment Option: Have the students share their work with the class.

Mathematics Made Fun
Time, Duration, Concept, & Intervals
3rd Grade

Reflection: Time, Duration, Concept & Intervals

It is important for students to understand why they are learning this process and how they can apply it to their daily lives. Explain that the ability to compute and convert time is an important life skill - both academically and personally.

In this reflection, ask the students these questions in an open discussion:

1. What did they learn?
2. How can they use what they learned in their daily activity?
3. Can they teach what they have learned to someone else?
4. What did they like most about the activity?
5. What did they like least about the activity?

Mathematics Made Fun
Activity Title: <u>Graphs, Charts, & Tally Marks</u>

    Graphs, charts, and tally marks help us to visualize and explain results, by showing numerical information more clearly. A chart or a graph is simply the picture displaying the story that the numbers tell. This activity will focus on learning to create, analyze, and use charts, graphs, and tally marks.

Time Frame: **35 - 65 Minutes**
- 5 - 10 Activity introduction and explanation.
- 5 - 10 Chart information on the board.
- 5 - 10 Whole group discussion.
- 10 - 15 Independent student activity.
- 5 - 10 Activity assessment.
- 5 - 10 Reflection on the activity.

Lesson Objectives: To increase student knowledge of graphs, charts, and tally marks.

Materials & Resources: Paper, pencil, and crayon.

Instruction Procedure: Explain the lesson and lesson objectives to the students.

Whole Group Activity:

See individual grade level activities for the whole group and individual instructions.

Mathematics Made Fun
Graphs, Charts, & Tally Marks
Kindergarten

Teacher's Instructions: *Select an activity below, Explain the lesson and lesson objective to the students while demonstrating the process. Walk the students through the beginning of the activity, allowing them to complete the activity on their own.*

Kindergarten *students should be familiar with (or need to learn) the concept of using a chart or graph (pictograph) to track information - using tally marks. In addition, they should be able to calculate and explain the results.*

Explanation and Use of Graphs, Charts, and Tally Marks

This activity is designed to help young students gain an understanding of, and practice the use of graphs, charts, and tallies. Select a topic from below and write it on the board. Have the students sit on the rug for a brief discussion about the topic. Ask the students to name their favorite thing within this topic and ask other questions, such as why? Then take a vote to limit the graph items to two choices. The idea is to get the students talking about the topic. Then demonstrate how to set-up the graph using tally marks. Leave the finished graph on the board for the students to use as a reference. Select another topic. This time, have the students work within small groups as you walk around and monitor. Each group should produce a graph for the information in their group.

Example:

Favorite Pet		
pet: Cat	tally mark: |||	total: 3
fish	⦀⦀ |	6

The pictograph shows that the class favors fish to cats because the fish has more tally marks.

Topics for Graphs and Charts - Our Favorite...

food	movie	tv star	clothing item
snack	teacher	toy	game
pet	holiday	tv show	day of the week
cartoon	character	name	subject in school

Mathematics Made Fun
Graphs, Charts, & Tally Marks
1st Grade

Teacher's Instructions: *Select an activity below. Explain the lesson and lesson objective to the students while demonstrating the process. Walk the students through the beginning of the activity, allowing them to complete the activity on their own.*

First grade *students should be able to create charts and graphs, and use tally marks to track information with little assistance. In addition, they should be able to calculate and explain the result, both written and verbally.*

Use of Graphs, Charts, and Tally Marks

This activity is designed to give students practice with creating and reading graphs and charts; and with using tally marks to keep track of information. Select a topic from below and write it on the board. Ask the students to tell you what their favorite type/kind among this topic is. Take a vote after the discussion to narrow the list to three items. Demonstrate how to set-up the graph and use tally marks. Leave the finished graph on the board for the students to use as a reference. Select another topic. This time have the students work within small groups as you walk around and monitor. Upon completion, each student should produce a finished graph and written explanation of the results. Assist the students with their written explanation if necessary.

Example: Food > fruit > banana, apple, grapes.

Our Favorite Fruit		
Banana	|||| ||	7
Apple	|||| |||	8
Grapes	||||	4

The pictograph shows that the class favors apples to grapes and banana's because the apples have the most tally marks.

Topics for Graphs and Charts - Our Favorite…

food	movie	tv star	clothing item
snack	teacher	toy	game
pet	holiday	tv show	day of the week
cartoon	character	name	subject in school
color	chore	book	fruit

Mathematics Made Fun
Graphs, Charts, & Tally Marks
2nd Grade

Teacher's Instructions: *Select an activity below. Explain the lesson and lesson objective to the students while demonstrating the process. Walk the students through the beginning of the activity, allowing them to complete the activity on their own.*

Second grade *students should be able to create charts and graphs, and use tally marks to track complex information. In addition, they should be able to calculate and explain the result - both written and verbally.*

Use of Graphs, Charts, and Tally Marks

This activity is designed to give students practice with creating and reading graphs and charts, and using tally marks to keep track of information. Select a topic from below and write it on the board. Ask the students to tell you what their favorite type/kind among this topic is. Take a vote after the discussion to narrow the list to five items. Ask the students for assistance in setting up the chart on the board and recording the information. Have one student come up to the board and record the votes, and another to chart the tally marks. Erase the completed graph from the board. Select another topic. This time have the students work within small groups as you walk around and monitor. Upon completion, each student should produce a finished graph - complete with a written explanation of the results.

Example: Food > pizza, hot dogs, hamburgers, chicken, spaghetti

Our Favorite Food

Foods	Tally Marks	Total
pizza	ℍℍ ℍℍ I	11
hot dogs	I I	2
hamburgers	I I I	3
chicken	I I I I	4
spaghetti	I I	2

The favorite food of our class is pizza. The pictograph shows that the class favors pizza over hot dogs, hamburgers, chicken, and spaghetti.

Topics for Graphs and Charts - Our Favorite...

food	movie	tv star	book	subject in school
fruit	teacher	movie star	game	video game
pet	holiday	tv show	color	character

Mathematics Made Fun
Graphs, Charts, & Tally Marks
3rd Grade

Teacher's Instructions: *Select an activity below. Explain the lesson and lesson objective to the students while demonstrating the process. Walk the students through the beginning of the activity, allowing them to complete the activity on their own.*

Third grade *students should be able to create and read basic graphs and charts, as well as use tally marks. In addition, they should be able to calculate and explain the result, both written and verbally. The focus for this activity is using the bar and line graphs.*

Bar & Line Graphs

This activity is designed to give students practice with creating and reading bar and line graphs, and analyzing the results.

Example: Marvin received the following scores on his math test in school last year: Sept. - 21, Oct. - 56, Nov. - 68, Feb. - 81, and Jun. - 100. His scores are charted on the graphs below.

Bar Graph

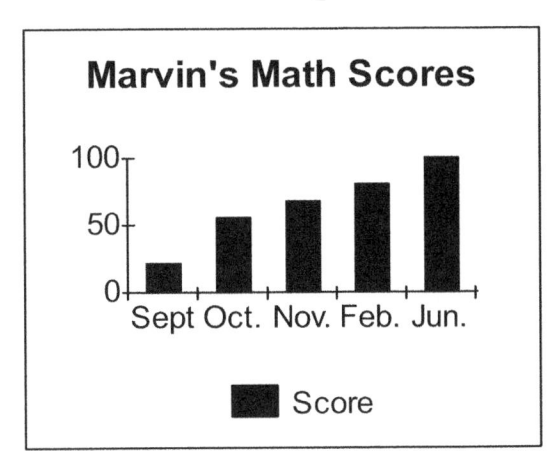

Marvin's Math Scores

Line Graph

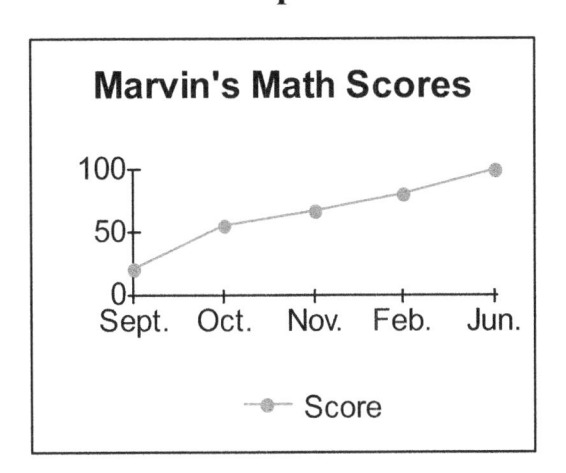

Marvin's Math Scores

Analysis

At the beginning of the school year, Marvin was doing very poorly in math. Beginning in October, his scores began to increase. Marvin now understands the math and is doing very well. By the end of the school year he had reached a perfect score.

Mathematics Made Fun
Graphs, Charts, & Tally Marks
3rd Grade

1. Select one or more items to chart along with the corresponding scores for each day, from below. Have the students create a bar graph and a line graph for each item, and write an analysis explaining their findings.

	Items to Chart	Mon.	Tue.	Wed.	Thu.	Fri.
1	Reading Scores	99	98	31	97	99
2	Math Scores	50	49	51	52	50
3	Running Time	5:01	4:29	3:16	2:59	2:30
4	Baskets in a row	37	35	42	59	60
5	Homeruns	6	3	2	0	0
6	Temperature	85	89	91	94	99
7	Happy Faces	2	4	6	8	10
8	Writing Grades	1	1	2	2	3
9	Laps on the Track	3	3	3	3	3

Mathematics Made Fun
Graphs, Charts, & Tally Marks
4th Grade

Teacher's Instructions: *Select an activity below. Explain the lesson and lesson objective to the students while demonstrating the process. Walk the students through the beginning of the activity, allowing them to complete the activity on their own.*

Forth grade *students should be able to create and read basic graphs and charts, as well as use tally marks. The focus for this activity is using the bar and line graphs to chart information, analyze results, and make predictions about trends and future outcomes.*

Bar & Line Graphs

This activity is designed to give students practice with creating and analyzing information on a graph, and predicting trends and future outcomes.

Example: Marvin received the following scores on his math test in school last year: Sept. - 21, Oct. - 56, Nov. - 68, Feb. - 81, and Jun. - 100. His scores are charted on the graphs below.

Bar Graph

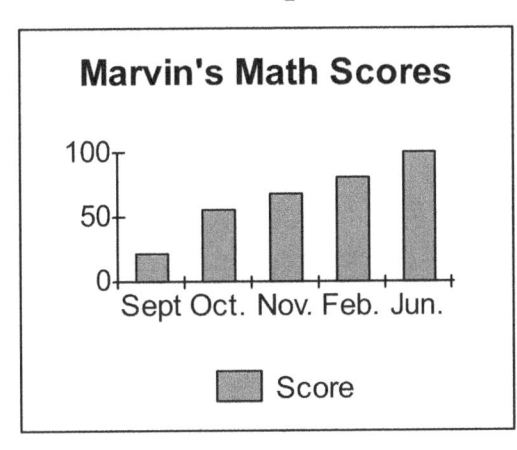

Marvin's Math Scores

Line Graph

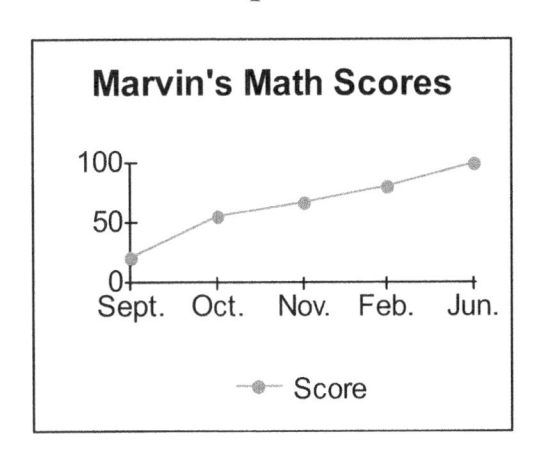

Marvin's Math Scores

Analysis

At the beginning of the school year, Marvin was doing very poorly in math. This could be because he either didn't understand the assignments or didn't do his homework. Either way, his grades were very low. Beginning in October, his scores began to increase. The increased test scores could have resulted from a variety of sources. Marvin now understands the math and is doing very well. By the end of the school year he had reached a perfect score. Marvin should do well in math this year.

Mathematics Made Fun
Graphs, Charts, & Tally Marks
4th Grade

1. Select one or more items to chart, along with the corresponding scores for each day, from below. Have the students create a bar graph and a line graph for each item and write an analysis explaining their findings. The analysis should also include a prediction of performance based on past trends.

	Items to Chart	Mon.	Tue.	Wed.	Thu.	Fri.
1	**Reading Scores**	134	141	146	149	153
2	**Math Scores**	83	83	80	81	82
3	**Running Time**	3:29	3:20	3:04	3:59	3:30
4	**Baskets in a Row**	21	20	16	14	12
5	**Homeruns**	2	2	16	3	1
6	**Temperature**	49	48	45	42	39
7	**Sit ups**	21	10	9	10	11
8	**Writing Grades**	4	4	0	4	4
9	**Laps on the Track**	1	2	3	4	5

2. Select one or more items to chart, along with the corresponding scores for each day, from below. Have the students predict the final outcome based on past performance and fill in the missing score. Students must also explain the basis for their prediction. Next, create a bar graph and a line graph for each item and write an analysis explaining their findings.

	Items to Chart	Mon.	Tue.	Wed.	Thu.	Fri.
1	Temperature	56	59	61	63	
2	Rainfall	1 in.	3 in.	5 in.	7 in.	
3	Snowfall	0 in.	0 in.	1 in.	0 in.	
4	Reading Score	115	116	117	118	
5	Math Score	95	96	97	98	
6	Baskets in a Row	15	20	21	25	
7	Arrival Time	8:00	7:50	7:50	7:55	

Mathematics Made Fun
Graphs, Charts, & Tally Marks
5th Grade

Teacher's Instructions: *Select an activity below. Explain the lesson and lesson objective to the students while demonstrating the process. Walk the students through the beginning of the activity, allowing them to complete the activity on their own.*

Fifth grade *students should be able to create and read basic graphs and charts, as well as use tally marks. The focus for this activity is using graphs to chart, compare, and analyze information, and use that information to make predictions about trends and future outcomes.*

Bar & Line Graphs

This activity is designed to give students practice with creating, comparing, and analyzing information on a graph, and using the information to make prediction about future trends and outcomes.

Example: Sally and Sara received the following scores throughout the school year: Sally: Sept. - 30, Oct. - 54, Nov. - 63, Jan. - 65, and May - 72. Sara: Sept. - 30, Oct. - 49, Nov. - 55, Jan. - 75, and May 90. Chart the scores to show a comparison, analyze the information, and make a predictions about future trends and results based on the analysis.

Comparing Information on a Bar Graph

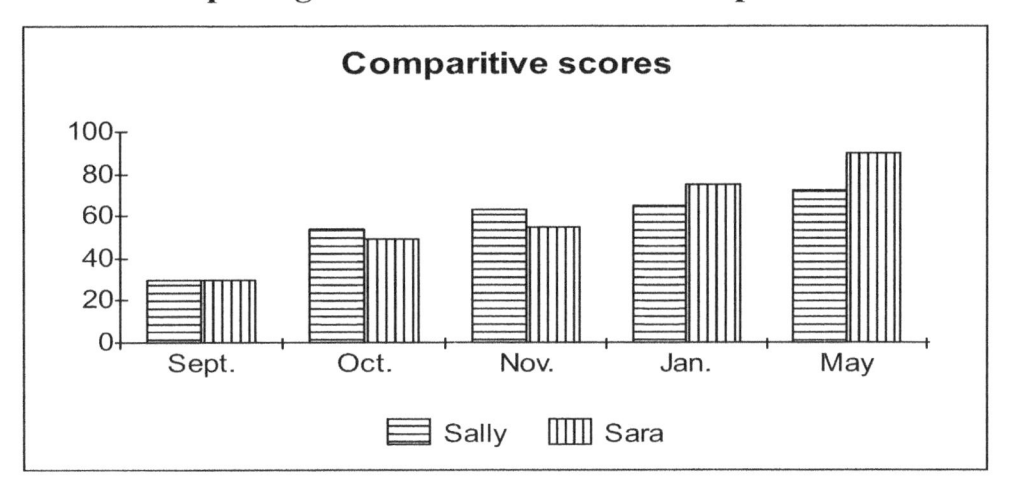

Comparitive scores

Month	Sally	Sara
Sept.	30	30
Oct.	54	49
Nov.	63	55
Jan.	65	75
May	72	90

Analysis

Sally and Sara had equal scores during the month of September. Although they both continued to excel, Sally's scores excelled at a faster rate than Sara's during October and November. A change occurred between November and January, resulting in Sara's scores surpassing Sally's, and continuing through May.

Mathematics Made Fun
Graphs, Charts, & Tally Marks
5th Grade

1. Select one or more item sets (AB) to chart along with the corresponding scores for each day, from below. Have the students create a bar graph and a line graph for each set and write a comparative analysis explaining their findings. The analysis should include a explanation of the comparison and a prediction based on past trends.

	Items to Chart	Mon.	Tue.	Wed.	Thu.	Fri.
1	Reading Score A Reading Score B	99 89	98 97	31 95	97 96	99 98
2	Math Scores A Math Score B	50 50	49 49	51 51	52 52	50 50
3	Running Time A Running Time B	5:01 4:58	4:29 4:58	3:16 4:30	2:59 4:30	2:30 4:00
4	Baskets in a Row A Baskets in a Row B	37 42	35 47	42 51	59 57	60 61
5	Homeruns A Homeruns B	10 5	9 6	8 7	7 8	6 9
6	Temperature A Temperature B	85 102	89 101	91 102	94 105	99 107
8	Writing Grade A Writing Grade B	1 3	1 3	2 3	2 4	3 4
9	Laps on the Track A Laps on the Track B	3 3	3 3	3 4	3 5	3 7

Mathematics Made Fun
Graphs, Charts, & Tally Marks
5th Grade

2. Select one or more item sets (AB) to chart along with the corresponding scores for each day, from below. Have the students predict the final outcome based on past performance and fill in the missing score. Students must explain the correlation between A and B, give a comparative analysis on their similarities and/or differences, and predict the future outcomes based on the information.

	Items to Chart	Mon.	Tue.	Wed.	Thu.	Fri.
1	Temperature A Temperature B	56 92	59 95	61 96	63 98	
2	Rainfall A Rainfall B	1 in. 7 in.	3 in. 5 in.	5 in. 3 in.	7 in. 1 in.	
3	Snowfall A Snowfall B	0 in. 7 in.	0 in. 14 in.	1 in. 21 in.	0 in. 28 in.	
4	Reading Scores A Reading Scores B	115 134	116 130	117 115	118 110	
5	Math Scores A Math Scores B	95 87	96 88	97 89	98 92	
6	Baskets in a Row A Baskets in a Row B	15 34	20 44	21 54	25 64	
7	Arrival Time A Arrival Time B	8:00 8:05	7:50 8:05	7:50 8:00	7:55 7:58	

Assessment Option: Have the students share their best work with the class.

Mathematics Made Fun
Graphs, Charts, & Tally Marks

Reflection: Graphs, Charts, & Tally Marks

It is important for students to understand why they are learning this process and how they can apply it to their daily lives. Explain that the ability to create, analyze, and use graphs, charts, and tally marks is essential for measuring success and predicting outcomes.

In this reflection, ask the students these questions in an open discussion:

1. What did they learn?
2. How can they use what they learned in their daily activity?
3. Can they teach what they have learned to someone else?
4. What did they like most about the activity?
5. What did they like least about the activity?

Mathematics Made Fun
Activity Title: Mode, Mean, Median, Range, & Outliers

Understanding how to distinguish between the different types of averages is important to the end results. Although each heading is a type of average, each type uses a slightly different method; therefore, returns slightly (and sometimes not so slightly) different results. The ability to determine and use the different types of averages is important to the bottom line outcome. The activities in this sections will focus on how to distinguish and use a variety of methods used to determine an average.

Time Frame: **35 - 65 Minutes**
 5 - 10 Activity introduction and explanation.
 5 - 10 Chart information on the board.
 5 - 10 Whole group discussion.
 10 - 15 Independent student activity.
 5 - 10 Activity assessment.
 5 - 10 Reflection on the activity.

Lesson Objectives: To increase student knowledge of distinguishing and using different methods to produce an average.

Materials & Resources: Paper and pencil.

Instruction Procedure: Explain the lesson and lesson objectives to the students.

Whole Group Activity:

See individual grade level activities for the whole group and individual instructions.

Mathematics Made Fun
Mode, Mean, Median, Range, & Outliers
3rd Grade

Teacher's Instructions: *Use the example below to demonstration the activity for the students. Explain the lesson, lesson objective, and steps to the students while demonstrating the process. Once the demonstration is complete, select an activity from below and walk the students through the beginning of the activity, allowing them to complete the activity on their own.*

Third grade *students should have the basic skills (adding multi-digit numbers and dividing a multi-digit number by a single digit number including remainders) necessary for calculating the mean average. The activities in this section will focus on the process of calculating the mean average.*

Example: Find the mean average of the following basketball shot scores: 16, 18, 17, 19, 21

Step 1: Add all the scores. 16 + 18 + 17 + 19 + 21 = 91

Step 2: Divide the total of all the numbers by the number of items being added. 5⌐ 91 = 18.2, or 18 rounded

Step 3: This is you mean average 18.2, or 18 rounded.

Select one or more items along with its number set from below. List them on the board and have the students practice calculating the mean average.

Baseball scores	17	32	51	21	25	36	5	16	21
Basketball scores	102	101	95	96	72	101	107	115	99
Football scores	49	56	77	89	45	75	89	63	24
Feet	7	2	4	9	8	6	3	1	4
Miles	17	32	35	39	45	44	58	68	41
Weight	88	115	89	79	96	94	98	98	90
Age	16	18	14	16	17	15	13	14	11
Math scores	77	79	78	74	75	76	79	73	79

Challenge - These units may need to be converted.

Feet	6 ½	7	8 ½	9	10 ½
Height	5'1"	4'9"	5'5"	5'7"	5'0"
Travel Time	1hr	30 min	2hr, 45 min.	4 hr.	55 min.
Running Time	2:03	2:49	2:15	1:55	3:15

Mathematics Made Fun
Mode, Mean, Median, Range, & Outliers
4th Grade

Teacher's Instructions: *Use the example below as a demonstration. Explain the lesson, lesson objective, and steps to the students while demonstrating the process. Once the demonstration is complete, select an activity from below and walk the students through the beginning of the activity, allowing them to complete the activity on their own.*

Forth & Fifth grade *students should have the basic skills (adding multi-digit numbers and dividing multi-digit numbers by single digit-numbers, including remainders, ordering numbers, and identifying numbers) necessary for calculating the mean average.*

Explanation of Terms

Mean average - a middle number of a group of given numbers.
Mode - the number that occurs most frequently, or the number repeated the most.
Median - the middle point of a group of ordered numbers.
Range - the distance between the lowest and highest value.
Outliers - a single number far away from the other numbers.

Example: Find the **mean** of the following basketball shot scores: 16, 18, 17, 19, 21.

   Step 1: Add all the scores. 16 + 18 + 17 + 19 + 21 = 91
   Step 2: Divide the total of all the numbers by the number 5⌐ 91 = 18.2, or 18 rounded.
   Step 3: This is you mean average **18.2, or 18 rounded**.

Example: Find the **mode** of the following basketball shot scores: 16, 18, 17, 19, 21.

   Step 1: Arrange the scores from lowest to highest 16,17,18,19,21.
   Step 2: Find the middle value. 16,17,**18**,19,21.
   Step 3: This is you mode - Since all numbers are listed only once, there is **no mode**.

Example: Find the **median** of the following basketball shot scores: 16, 18, 17, 19, 21.

   Step 1: Arrange the scores from lowest to highest 16,17,18,19,21.
   Step 2: Find the middle number.   16,17,**18**,19,21.
   Step 3: This is you median - 18.

Example: Find the **range** of the following basketball shot scores: 16, 18, 17, 19, 21.

   Step 1: Add all the scores.
   Step 2: Divide the total of all the scores.
   Step 3: The range of the basketball scores is 5.

Mathematics Made Fun
Mode, Mean, Median, Range, & Outliers
4th Grade

Example: Find the **<u>outliers</u>** of the following basketball shot scores: 16, 18, 17, 19, 21.

Step 1: Add all the scores.

Step 2: Divide the total of all the numbers by the total of numbers used.

Step 3: In this example, there are no outliers because all of the numbers are close in range.

Select one or more sets of numbers from below, list them on the board and have the students practice calculating the following:

A - mean average
B - mode
C - median
D - range
E - Identify the outliers.

Baseball scores	17	32	51	21	25	36	5	16	21
Basketball scores	102	101	95	96	72	101	107	115	99
Football scores	49	56	77	89	45	75	89	63	24
Feet	7	2	4	9	8	6	3	1	4
Miles	17	32	35	39	45	44	58	68	41
Weight	88	115	89	79	96	94	98	98	90
Age	16	18	14	16	17	15	13	14	11
Math Scores	77	79	78	74	75	76	79	73	79

Challenge: These units may need to be converted.

Feet	6 ½	7	8 ½	9	10 ½
Height	5'1"	4'9"	5'5"	5'7"	5'0"
Travel Time	1hr	30 min	2hr, 45 min.	4 hr.	55 min.
Running Time	2:03	2:49	2:15	1:55	3:15

Assessment Option: Have the students share their work with the class.

Mathematics Made Fun
Mode, Mean, Median, Range & Outliers
All Grades

Reflection: Mode, Mean, Median, Range, & Outliers

It is important for students to understand why they are learning this process and how they can apply it to their daily lives. Explain that knowing how to distinguish and use various methods to produce an average is an important life skill both academically, and professionally.

In this reflection, ask the students these questions in an open discussion:

1. What did they learn?
2. How can they use what they learned in their daily activity?
3. Can they teach what they have learned to someone else?
4. What did they like most about the activity?
5. What did they like least about the activity?

No Copies Required – Classroom Activities

Copyright © 2006 by L. Lee
In the United States of America

All rights reserved. No part of this publication may be reproduced or distributed in any form, or by any means, or stored in a database or retrieval system, without the prior written permission of the publisher. For more information contact the author by email: nocopiesrequired@gmail.com

First printing February 2007

Published by L. Lee
Printed in the United States of America

Disclaimer

No Copies Required provides information and activities that are useful to elementary educators throughout the United States of America. No Copies Required does not express or imply inclusion of all areas of subject matter, nor does it express or imply responsibility for errors and/or omissions.

Made in the USA
Las Vegas, NV
02 December 2022